February-June 2024 edition

Original title: Il crollo occidentale (Diario del 2024), ed. Amazon
Translated by Oddid Littlehouse

MIKOS TARSIS

THE WESTERN COLLAPSE

DIARY OF 2024

(February-June)

It's easy to love your friend,
but sometimes the hardest lesson to learn is to love your enemy.

Sun Tzu

Amazon

Born in Milan in 1954, graduated in Philosophy in Bologna in 1977, former teacher of history and philosophy, Mikos Tarsis (aka Enrico Galavotti) has been interested in two main topics all his life:
Secular Humanism and Democratic Socialism, which he covered in homolaicus.com and now in t.me/multipolare.
To contact him:
info@homolaicus.com
His publications on Amazon.it

Premise

Anything can happen in life, even a world war. After all, my grandparents lived through two. My parents, on the other hand, born in the 1930s, endured part of fascism and the Second War.

My generation, on the other hand, born in the mid-1950s, was able to benefit from the economic boom (which, in general, is inevitable after every catastrophe), then allowed itself to be entangled in the years of lead, which goes from the worker-student protest of 1968 until the Moro crime of 1978. After which, reflux, revisionism and the progressive dismantling of the welfare state including many acquired rights dominated the period.

Today we are witnessing the declared colonial subjugation of the entire European Union towards the American empire. This thing had been noticed, but only on a military level, when NATO could calmly go and bomb socialist Yugoslavia. Then, again on a military level, we saw it in the wars against Iraq, Afghanistan, Libya, Syria etc. All wars that served no purpose other than stealing other people's resources (especially energy resources), experimenting with and selling self-made weapons, positioning various military bases in strategic points... For the rest, in fact, all this has left behind only enormous human and natural tragedies.

But with the Russian-Ukrainian war we witnessed an economic and financial colonial subjugation. The breakdown in relations with Russia has made the decline of Europe inevitable, which is no longer able to compete with either the USA or China.

It's not just a problem of "deindustrialization". If it were only this, we could actually rejoice: nature would certainly have to suffer less. The real problem is that there is no real alternative on the horizon. We are so used to an artificial life induced by machinery that we no longer know what it means to live a human and natural life.

p.s. At the beginning of this diary I intended to talk about events that were not as dramatic as the Russian-Ukrainian and Israeli-Palestinian wars, which made me lose sleep. But after a few days I already regretted it. I prefer to be crushed by the weight of world problems.

February

February 1st

Scrapping philosophy

This morning I bought a Panda which cost, turnkey, 13,000 euros, a pittance compared to current standards. As an alternative I had the Dacia Streetway, much more spacious, even with the same price, but since they make it in Romania, it seemed to me to be disrespectful to "patriotism", given that the Panda is produced in Pomigliano d'Arco, where they work a good 4,000 people.

I'm the usual naive one. Stellantis actually doesn't care about Italy, so much so that it will have the electric Panda produced in Serbia in 2026. We must stop thinking that by purchasing "Italian" we are doing our country a favor. If I look at what Italian I have on, it's probably just my white hair.

I asked what would happen to my glorious Renault, Clio Storia (40,000 km since 2008, therefore used very little), which has always loved me, apart from its bodywork. I was told that it will be transformed into a pressed cube for the Savignano sul Rubicone scrap yard. Too bad, an immigrant, like me, would have been more than happy if he could have bought it for 1,000 euros. But that's the way the world is going. If I want to get the 2,000 euros for scrapping, I really have to take it to the scrap yard, even if it works perfectly on both petrol and LPG. And to think that it could certainly have done another 60,000 km.

Of course we talked about color. The employee told me that if I wanted to spend as little as possible, he would give it to me in black. All other colors cost 600 euros more. With the Dacia the basic color was white; with the Clio the horrible orange.

Inevitably I asked him: "Sorry, does white also cost more than black?". "This year Fiat decided like this," he replied. Naturally I thought about the current right-wing government and I adapted...

Then when I read in the contract that it was of the "Nero Cinema" type, I almost had to laugh. Once upon a time we would have said "Seppia Black" or "Ink Black". Even more intriguing would have been "Nero Anima", like that liquorice liqueur which, according to the advertising, has "a unique and decisive personality". With a Panda at most you can just go to the cinema! But where is the "black" in the cinema? When do they turn off the lights?

February 2

The Salis case is worrying

Strange that the two neo-Nazis beaten by Ilaria Salis did not report her. Maybe because they had laughable bruises. I can't imagine a 39-year-old elementary school teacher with a truncheon causing "potentially lethal injuries" (as the prosecution claims) to two beefy males. I bet that when she entered the courtroom smiling, it was to show that she has indomitable courage. Except that by declaring herself innocent and therefore refusing the plea deal of 11 years, she now risks more than 20. If I think that the YouTuber Matteo Di Pietro agreed to a plea deal of 4 years and 4 months and avoided prison, despite having killed a 5 year old boy at 120 hours, it makes me think that our country is a bonanza for criminals. After of course they force you to combine politics with law.

However, in Hungary they are in bad shape. Instead of being happy that someone reacts against the fascists, they put someone in a pillory. I had formed a good opinion of Orbán, given that towards Russia he had gone against the flow of the EU. Appearances be damned…

*

Salis wrote in a memo dated October 2, sent to her lawyers and made public by the journalist and TV presenter, Enrico Mentana, that when they arrested her they had confiscated her shoes and clothes, leaving her in her underwear, bra and socks. Then they forced her to dress in dirty, battered and smelly clothes, not hers, and to wear a pair of stiletto-heeled boots that were not her size. She stayed in these clothes for 5 weeks. For 7 days she had no toilet paper, soap or sanitary products, which was only remedied thanks to a Hungarian inmate. In those weeks she remained without having her sheets changed. For the first 3 months she was tormented by bed bug bites. The corridors were full of cockroaches, while mice often roamed the external corridor just outside the building.

The prison was maximum security, so for 8 months she couldn't talk to anyone. The cell was completely closed: she spent 23 hours a day there with only one hour of fresh air.

The food was scarce and in poor hygienic conditions: for breakfast she usually received a slice of salami in bad state; at lunch very watery soups with very little solid food, but where instead she often found pieces of paper or plastic, hair or fur.

She also said she has a lump in her breast that appears benign, but which several doctors in Italy have recommended she check periodically. In prison in mid-June she was taken to a clinic where she was given an ultrasound and mammogram, but she never received any written report.

She was unable to enroll in Hungarian primary school lessons (the language in which all communications take place), on the grounds that she "does not speak Hungarian".

She had only gone to Budapest to protest against the celebration of the "Day of Honour", in which far-right groups from all over Europe had gathered in the city to commemorate a Nazi battalion which in 1945 had attempted to prevent the entry of the 'Red Army in the city.

It's true that they found her in a taxi with a truncheon, but the attackers were unrecognizable because their faces were covered. But then she could have kept that weapon for personal defense.

The Italian embassy has already participated in at least 4 hearings in which Salis was taken to court, so diplomats are well aware that she reported not having been able to view the images which, according to the prosecution, demonstrate her involvement in the beating. She also said that she had not had the opportunity to read the indictments against her because they had not been translated into either Italian or English.

She pleaded not guilty, rejecting the offer of a plea deal of 11 years in prison. They obviously don't contemplate house arrest. However, in this case she risks up to 24 years in prison.

It seems that such treatment is an exemplary punishment for an unwanted foreigner. In any case, if this is the practice in Hungary for all those accused of something, poor us. Instead of being happy that someone reacts against fascists, do they put someone in a pillory? I had formed a good opinion of Orbán, given that towards Russia he had gone against the flow of the EU. In fact, he was threatened that if he did not approve the 50 billion to be given to Kiev, the Hungarian economy and finance would collapse. But there would be enough here to drive him out of Europe. Or maybe it's his strategy to leave?

February 6

Sgarbi's conflicts of interest

We all know Sgarbi, he is an unbearable conceited man who, when he goes into a rage, utters words of unprecedented vulgarity, which no one would think possible from a man of culture, and one who is also politically involved. To the journalist from Report, who accused him of violating the Frattini law, of having stolen a painting, etc., he even wished he would die in a road accident. The strange thing is that he knew that next to the journalist there was a cameraman who was filming everything.[1] Here we are right at psychiatry levels. Instead of leaving, as Alemanno did when the journalist asked him embarrassing questions about his pro-mafia role as mayor, he sometimes showed his gadget to the camera to interrupt the filming. It really seems that he likes being immortalized so altered and decomposed. This too, ultimately, is a form of narcissism.

Luckily he was only Undersecretary of Culture: just think if they had made him Minister of Education!

*

The 2004 Frattini law on conflict of interest is clear (a law also wanted by the Berlusconi government of which Sgarbi was also part): "Holders of government offices cannot carry out professional activities in matters connected with their office".

He, however, defended himself by saying: "My activities are a legitimate exercise of copyright." In what sense?

Then he added: "I became Undersecretary of Culture because I am a writer, lecturer and art critic. But this cannot be considered a profession like being a doctor." So?

No one can stop him from doing anything in his capacity as Undersecretary of Culture: he just needs to do it free of charge or at most by demanding reimbursement of expenses. In fact, it is obvious that if you charge (even by invoicing and reporting, this is not the problem), the suspicion of a conflict of interest automatically arises. By "interests" we mean something "material". I don't think it's something "ideological".

That is, if he had been Minister of Transport, like the do-nothing Salvini, who would have said anything to him if in private, as an art critic, he held a conference and took 200,000 euros?

February 8

Broken myth of PoltroneSofà

Tonight I saw a documentary on Youtube about the Forlì company

---

1 The video is here:
www.lastampa.it/politica/2024/01/29/video/sgarbi_report_minacce-14029496/

PoltroneSofà. I was quite disconcerted.

The company practically doesn't exist, it mainly exploits under-paid Chinese workers (and other nationalities) and then manages resale, logistics and advertising. It does not respect the standard rules of competition and calmly pays the fines imposed on it, so much so that with all its publicity it has earned the wrath of God.

Officially it appears that the company only has three workers. It is significant that the trade associations refused to say the slightest word.

However, the material of the sofas is poor and poorly assembled, and the service leaves a lot to be desired. And above all there is nothing artisanal about it.

Source: youtube.com/watch?v=X3969qnzErA

February 10

Free words on Sanremo

I wonder who will be able to replace Amadeus, giving Sanremo the same youthful physiognomy that he so strongly wanted, especially someone with the same incredible musical competence as him (as an experienced deejay), able to choose 30 songs, overall of good quality, in in the middle of another 400. And then where to find an incredible sidekick like Fiorello, who even if he mistakenly treated Travolta like a child, gave an incredible performance mixing Modugno with Michael Jackson.

I must say that Cinquetti seemed rather painful to me. One cannot sing a song at the age of 76 (*I'm not old enough*) which was fine when she was 16. If anything she should have sung *I'm no longer old enough* (to do certain things...). She entered the scene looking like she had just emerged from a cemetery manhole. Why didn't she sing any of her other songs? Is it possible that one doesn't understand that everything has its time? Who told you that your song has entered the classics of pop music with the same spirit as when you sang it? Today kids do certain things well before the age of 16 and they throw a song like that in the bin. Which certainly doesn't mean that they've put all the songs from 60 years ago into oblivion. Today's young people love Mogol-Battisti just like we do.

Also an eyesore are the last two survivors of the Ricchi e Poveri, who complain about receiving a pension of only a thousand euros a month. You can act as young as you want, but the more you do it, the more out of tune you are in relation to your venerable age, especially in a singing context in which the youthful element is 90% predominant.

Incomprehensible text, because it is in Neapolitan dialect, by

Geolier. How did he manage to come second? They say he is famous on social media. But, if this is the case, then democracy doesn't work.

However, I really liked the dancer Bolle: he has an exceptional physique. How much time does he spend in the gym? Even with twice the age of the other dancers, he was stratospheric. He looks like a Greek Adonis. Looking at him, I give up on attributing the exclusivity of beauty to women.

Ghali did well in Sanremo to leave the scene with the phrase "Stop the genocide", sending Milan's Jewish community to hell who had contested his song, judging it to be pro-Palestinian. His entire song is an invitation to peace. The text should have been rewarded, but there wasn't enough courage. After all, when do our journalists ever have any (except those of "Fatto Quotidiano", of course).

"Sons of a distant desert" (why Berber? Arab? Islamic origin?).

"Shut up, I can't talk about it" (Western Islamophobia?).

"What will I tell my children? Welcome to the Truman show" (capitalism supported by a *mainstream* hypocritical).

"Don't ask me how I'm doing. I would like to go away. But the road doesn't lead home if you don't know what your home is" (due to colonialism?).

"My home" (African, Islamic). "Your home" (Western, Jewish). "What's the difference? There is not. I miss my area. I miss my neighborhood" (immigration to Europe).

"I don't feel like raising a fuss" (quiet life?). "But how can you say that everything is normal here? To draw a border with imaginary lines, bomb a hospital" (genocide in Gaza). "For a piece of land or a piece of bread there is never peace" (Western capitalism, Jewish colonial settlements).

The video on Raiplay was cut without including either the final thanks or the political message mentioned above. The clip was restored after a few hours. Shame. Then Dargen D'Amico also asked for a ceasefire (subsequently interrupted by Mara Venier when she spoke about immigration, with the phrase: "But this is a party and there is no time needed to address such an important issue").

Amadeus's fall in style when he used the great Sergio Endrigo in an instrumental way to talk about the foibe. In all his lyrics Endrigo spoke about the Dalmatian exodus only in his song "1947", mentioning his hometown Pola. But who remembers this? And in any case a presenter can never take sides in such an explicit way, also because the Italian fascists carried out unspeakable massacres in Yugoslavia. A host must play the role of moderator, which even last year, reading Zelensky's text, was wrong for him to do. At most he should let the singers express themselves.

February 11

But how are we doing in Italy?

On Facebook they were surprised that I watched Sanremo. But how can you not watch an event that involved up to 14 million people in Italy alone and which was broadcast live to 16 other European nations? At least the last episode, for reasons of media and sociological curiosity, is a must. Do you want something strange not to happen? In fact, it was punctual as usual.

I have already said that the Ghali case broke out, with his pro-Palestinian song and his rather embarrassing exit for the Italian *mainstream*: "Stop the genocide", which had even aroused the ire of the Israeli ambassador Alon Bar in Rome, who had expressed himself thus, in the most arrogant and delusional way possible: "I consider it shameful that the stage of the Sanremo Festival has been exploited to spread hatred and provocations in a superficial and irresponsible way. In the massacre of October 7, among the 1,200 victims, there were over 360 young people murdered and raped during the Nova Music Festival. Another 40 of them were kidnapped and are still in the hands of terrorists together with dozens of other Israeli hostages. The Sanremo Festival could have expressed solidarity with them. It's a shame this didn't happen."

Arrogant because an ambassador cannot interfere in the artistic and media decisions of a national festival like Sanremo, also because no country has been explicitly accused in any song context (they would not have allowed it during the pre-selection). *Delirious* because by saying "Stop the genocide" you don't spread "hatred and provocations" but quite the opposite.

Ghali had already responded to the ambassador by saying: "I have always talked about this since I was a child, it hasn't been since October 7th and the Internet can document it. People are increasingly afraid to say 'stop the war and stop the genocide' and the fact that the ambassador says this is not good, this policy of terror continues. People feel that they are losing something if they say 'long live peace', but this must not happen. Italy brings completely opposite values. There are children involved."

Yesterday the servile scene of the *mainstream* happened again.

Mara Venier, live on "Domenica In", felt compelled to read the following statement from RAI CEO Roberto Sergio: "Every day our news and our programs tell and will continue to do so, the tragedy of the hostages in the hands of Hamas as well as remembering the massacre of children, women and men on 7 October. My solidarity with the people of Israel and the Jewish Community is heartfelt and convincing."

She added that "we all share these words". Why did she say "everyone"? Why didn't she just speak for herself? Why didn't she say that only a part of Italians share them, while another part doesn't? Why is someone at 73 still struggling to please her employer? What consequences could she fear for her career? Hasn't she earned enough to be able to speak freely? What was the need to say to the journalists who interviewed her: "don't get me into trouble"? In short, why doesn't she retire and make room for younger and braver people?

But above all, how does the administrator of a public service, paid for with citizens' taxes, allow himself to express a personal opinion passed off as representative and therefore binding for everyone? How dare he force a TV host to read his personal opinion? Why didn't he read it himself? Was it perhaps an official statement from a Board of Directors, approved unanimously? No it was not. And in any case, if it had been, the right to speak of an artist would have had to be defended, and also the autonomy of a public service. How can you not understand that such an ambassador should be expelled from any democratic country? And not understanding that such an administrator and such a presenter should be fired?

The slaughter continues in Gaza

The Israeli army carried out over 50 air, land and sea attacks tonight, targeting at least 20 residential buildings and two mosques across Rafah, resulting in the killing of over 109 Palestinian civilians, mostly children. Over 200 injured.

All in order to free two hostages! Who then involuntarily killed three more! Without considering the two hostages (Louis Har and Fernando Marman) had already been freed, according to the Israeli newspaper "Haaretz", on February 2nd, being on an *ad hoc* list already official. In short, they seem not only murderers but also serial liars.

And we in Italy have an Israeli ambassador who takes issue with the Sanremo festival because it allowed the singer Ghali to say "Stop the genocide" and because the host didn't say anything about the Hamas attack on October 7th.

*

Israeli forces have been besieging the Nasser hospital, west of Khan Yunis, in the Gaza Strip, for days, shooting anyone in sight and terrorizing hundreds of civilians seeking refuge there. In particular, snipers shoot anyone who tries to reach the wounded or recover the bodies at the hospital. If this isn't Nazi behavior, what is it? What term can we use?

*

The Egyptian army is on high alert: around 40 tanks have been deployed in north-eastern Sinai, near the border with Israel and Gaza, ahead of the Israeli army's ground operation in Rafah.

Cairo reiterated to Tel Aviv that any violation of the border by the Israeli army could trigger a war. Not only that, but they also declared that any forced transfer of Palestinians from Gaza would be the end of the peace agreement with Israel.

In Egypt they have not understood that these maneuvers and these declarations are accepted by Israel at face value, as objective no. 1 of the USA is to widen the conflict as much as possible.

February 12

The first words in the universe

What are the words I would like to hear when I live in another dimension? They are very simple and above all consolatory and operational.

"Now that you have completely destroyed the Earth, making it uninhabitable for any living being, I reveal to you some fundamental truths and show you some basic conditions for continuing to live in the universe.

In the entire universe there are no other human beings different from you. The only planet inhabited by humans was yours. There are no beings or entities in the universe that have powers greater than yours.

Now you have understood that death does not exist, as everything is subject to transformation.

Here, based on your skills, you can do whatever you want and wherever you want. The universe is eternal, infinite, unlimited like you are. The human being, as a universal essence, has always existed, was never born and will never die. You can only die inside, when you don't want to be who you are.

The only condition to be respected is freedom of conscience, that is, the fact that no one can be forced or induced to do something they do not want to do.

Respecting freedom of conscience means being aware of freedom. No other value is greater than this. Anyone who thinks they cannot live this value because they feel guilty about something should ask for forgiveness from those who have disrespected them. Just remember that consciousness is unfathomable, just like the universe that contains it.

The task you have is to reconstruct the materiality of life according to your desires and respecting the universal laws of matter, which, in turn, depend on the laws of energy, which is not only material but also immaterial, relating precisely to consciousness .

All the knowledge acquired during the period in which you lived on Earth can be useful to you in this work of reconstruction. Knowledge must only be made compatible with the objective laws of consciousness and matter.

Living according to conscience means living in peace with everyone, in harmony with the nature of things, being masters of one's own destiny, facing common problems together, being transparent and respecting each other with conviction."

*

I don't know how the problem of infinite human languages will be solved. If I want to talk to Sitting Bull, what language will I use? The ideal would be for everyone to continue speaking their own language and for everyone to understand each other. Then if one also wants to speak the Sitting Bull language, he will start studying it by hanging out with the Sioux tribe.

Surely all languages are fascinating and none deserve to disappear. Do you know how many linguistics books could be written? For a lover of beautiful writing it would be a treat.

*

Sometimes I wonder if time and space really make sense in the universe (or afterlife). These are purely earthly conditions. If all of us will be young and beautiful forever, why sleep? why have embarrassing, anxious, incomprehensible dreams? Why stay tied to gravity? Why reproduce? Why have such material needs? Why do things that do not depend on our will?

You retire when you are tired of work, when you feel inadequate, when you no longer have a connection with the new generations. But this should apply to anything. That is, at a certain point the fetus turns upside down and decides it's time to come out. I would like to do it too, without knowing what's out there. We'll open our eyes later.

February 13

Who forces us to war?

A 208-ton Russian RS-28 Sarmat missile carries up to 15 different thermonuclear warheads in the range of 500-1,000 kilotons. It has a range of 18,000 km and an accuracy of 10 meters. How to hit a clay pigeon in clay pigeon shooting with a bullet 200 km away. It travels at 33,000 km/h (mach 26.7). Evades enemy missile defenses.

In 5 minutes it arrives easily in Italy starting from Russian soil. Nuclear submarines armed with such a missile can halve the distance and therefore the flight time.

In half an hour it can reach the other side of the globe.

Just one of these missiles can directly kill something like 20 million people in various forms and ways. The luckiest are those vaporized instantly. Further incalculable deaths follow due to epidemics, famines, economic collapse of society. Nuclear winter limits agriculture for years.

With these means does war make sense? Where does Italy want to go? Is it possible that words such as peace, negotiation, diplomatic agreement disappeared from its vocabulary overnight? Who wants to drive us to suicide?

February 14

We don't stick our noses into sensitive issues

Sensitive issues relating to freedom of conscience should not be interfered with when the exercise of that freedom does not violate the freedom of others. In Italy we are still too far behind to accept such a principle. There are still people who think that if euthanasia is allowed for elderly and/or disabled people, everyone could deduce that every problematic person who does not self-eliminate voluntarily creates improper costs and damage for their family and for society. So if a quadriplegic wants to kill himself, we have to force him to live because we can't make him believe that by leaving he would be doing us a favor on an economic level. The Catholic world is full of this absurdity.

Imagine if today for Valentine's Day I had said to my wife: "Look dear, I wanted to give you a set of stainless steel knives, well sharpened, not like hotel ones, because I saw that ours, by putting them in the dishwasher, they all have damaged handles. But then since we hear of many husbands who slaughter their wives, I was afraid that you would have strange thoughts about me, so I preferred to give you a set of teaspoons. Is that okay with you? Maybe we make Elah pudding more often!"

If anything, it is necessary to establish who should be authorized to apply the exercise to free will when the person concerned is not in the physical conditions to be able to do so. Hence the urgency of signing a living will when you are in possession of your mental faculties, also so as not to embarrass others about what to do when our turn comes. No one can start a dispute if, in signing the aforementioned will, one thinks of doing a favor to the state coffers or thinks of any other motivation. In the Municipality the employee must limit himself to taking note of an irrevocable decision, he cannot start asking "existential" questions.

What's the problem if two Dutch spouses (his name was Dries van Agt, her name Eugene) aged 93, of which 66 were married, chose to leave together? How long does one have to live? It's so obvious that at that age we are full of ailments. Medicine has its pluses and cons. It can't keep you alive like a zombie against your will just because it preaches an abstract right to life. Those were adults capable of deciding (he had even been a prime minister of his country and what's more he was of the Catholic religion).

Even assuming that nature made us live up to 100 years, in fact we live in urban contexts where it is very easy to get sick with something. If anything, we could ask ourselves the reasons why we get sick so often and sometimes in such a serious way that it is unexpected. But it is clear that one must be the master of one's own destiny as much as possible, especially in matters of conscience. A time when we were freer, *Habeas corpus* were the words.

Return the stolen goods

More than 50 years have passed since the Six Day War. Yet Leviticus says that after 49 years the Jews must return the lands to the "historical" owners, prior to those who took over later.

Thus says Yahweh, who represents the collective demand: "The lands cannot be sold forever, because the land is mine and you are with me as strangers and guests. Therefore, in all the land that you possess, you will give the right of redemption for the lands." "Each of you will return to his property, and each of you will return to his family." The ransom was free.

If the lands were purchased illegally, even worse: they must be returned immediately, regardless of the Jubilee, and with 1/5 of compensation relating to their value. Restitution was made to the owner (not to the government or to third parties) and the compensation had to be accompanied by a guilt offering to the Lord.

Not only that, but in the Jubilee "freedom" had to be proclaimed throughout the entire country, so the slaves had to be emancipated.

This is to say that the Palestinians, close relatives of the Jews, as Semites like them, descendants of Ishmael, Isaac's half-brother: must be freed from prison and must regain possession of what they sold to the Jews or gave away for reasons beyond their control .

But Zionists are known to interpret the Bible as they please. We don't talk about the settlers then.

And then they say we are not at war

Naval units armed with OTO Melara 76/62 guns participate in the war operations against Gaza. They are multi-role cannons produced by the Leonardo SpA group company of the same name with headquarters in Rome and factories in La Spezia and Brescia. These weapons of war are characterized by a very high rate of fire, especially in the Super Rapid version (120 shots per minute), for anti-aircraft and anti-missile "defense" and naval and coastal bombardment.

Source: infoaut.org

February 15

Why not resign?

The Interior Ministry has decided to assign personal protection to the CEO of RAI for security reasons. This is the lowest level of protection that preludes personal escort. The measure was taken by the Ministry of the Interior on the basis of threats that were received by Sergio and his family for taking a position in defense of Israel, after the statement read by the presenter Mara Venier of "Domenica In" and followed to the intervention against the bombings on Gaza by the singer Ghali from the Sanremo stage.

Poor thing, this delegate is not from RAI but from the Israeli embassy. A singer managed to catch him with his hands in the cookie jar, while the presenter even had hers in ...

But why don't they resign? You made it big. You have demonstrated that our country is not only a servant of the USA but also of Israel. Are there perhaps others who command us?

Phase 2 of Gaza

In Rafah there are over a million displaced Palestinians, at risk of being involved in the military operation aimed at the south of the Strip. According to Egyptian sources, Israel demands that the costs of the camps - with medical facilities - be borne by the USA and Arab countries.

Meanwhile, Israel has prepared a plan involving the evacuation of civilians along the coast of Gaza and presented it to Egypt. 15 locations have been identified, each with 25,000 tents, ranging from the southern tip of Gaza City to Moassi, north of Rafah city.

The audacity of this behavior is incredible: first they create a disaster of enormous proportions; then they attribute the costs to third parties; finally they appropriate all the assets of over 2 million people who are literally expelled from their territory.

February 16

Better late than never

Amadeus said on the February 13 episode of "Porta a Porta": "I respect everyone's decisions, but I absolutely disagree with the Israeli ambassador. I would never have dreamed, nor the singers, of bringing hatred, in fact we bring exactly the opposite. The singers who come to the competition launch messages and appeals of peace, of freedom, of freedom of ideas, of thought, of equality of skin, of values. I feel like saying that in the history of Sanremo, without sounding presumptuous, in recent years there has been a great sense of inclusion that must be absolutely respected and never changed, otherwise we'll go back."

Finally: "War on any side is to be condemned, there is no war on one side or the other, any war in the world must be stopped."

It took him a while to say these things, but he finally said them, as generic as they are, and without arguing about the meaning of the words used by Ghali.

Fiorello also shared them in part on "Viva Rai2": "Letting those papers read was a mistake, but now let's all calm down. It happened and was stigmatized abundantly. Now calm down, because when violence comes into play it is no longer okay. They even had to assign the escort to the CEO Sergio, in the end they will give it to me too...".

He worries about himself. He worries about violence. Why, what is there in Gaza? From those who should not fear being fired by RAI or no longer receiving contracts from RAI, we would expect more courage.

Young people must always be listened to when they are spontaneous, when they do not use the forked tongue of adults. In Italy, however, they do something completely different: they marginalize themselves, they exploit themselves, they censor themselves, and now, to make them understand better how things are, they beat themselves up, and without much ceremony.

The limit of tolerability

Sanchez and Varadkar, prime ministers of Spain and Ireland respectively, asked Brussels to "urgently verify" Israel's respect for human rights in Gaza.

The International Court of Justice in The Hague is carrying out its own checks on the accusations of genocide made by South Africa, while in Washington they are investigating possible war crimes committed by Tel Aviv in the Strip.

Hearing these things should make you happy, but instead you get very nervous. In fact, we wonder what the limit is beyond which a genocide, a massacre, an ethnic cleansing, an extermination can be qualified with their names.

Macron called Netanyahu directly to tell him that the death toll in Gaza is "intolerable" and that the Tel Aviv operation must "cease".

What does "intolerable" mean? Is there perhaps a mathematical calculation that statesmen must make to avoid being dethroned? As the Nazis did for example, at the Fosse Ardeatine: for every German killed, 10 Italians shot.

Von der Leyen's European Commission was asked to carry out checks on possible human rights violations on Palestinian soil.

"Possible"... Naturally, we do not fail to add that if Hamas had released the hostages immediately, the deaths would have been much fewer. It still hasn't been understood that Israel wants the whole Strip, so the later Hamas returns the hostages the better it is for Netanyahu.

But they understood that something else is better for them: putting their hands forward and washing them like Pilate. In fact, in Rafah, the last refuge city for the millions of displaced Palestinians in the Strip, the feared ground attack is expected which could cause yet another carnage.

The USA is the most hypocritical of all: the State Department wants to investigate the possible use of white phosphorus to attack civilians in Lebanon and also the attack on October 31st on the Jabaliya refugee camp, in which more than 135 people died. It is thought that Israel used bombs weighing over 900 kg, which are used to destroy buildings and underground bunkers, but which, given their great destructive power, are not used in densely populated areas such as cities.

That is, they are thinking that Israel may have used American weapons "improperly". Like when in their country they allow eighteen-year-olds to buy weapons that fire 100 shots per minute, and then are surprised that they use them against their former schools.

We really have great foresight, a special sensitivity to understand the various ways of using the devices that cause death and destruction.

February 17

I was misunderstood

How accurate is the Israeli ambassador in Rome in his arrogant hypocrisy, after having criticized cardinal Pietro Parolin, who allowed himself to say that it made no sense to talk about the "right to defense" when there were 30,000 murdered people in Gaza, half of whom were minors.

The Zionist would have said that there was a quiproquo in the translation. The adjective of the sentence "It is a regrettable declaration" (referring to Parolin's declaration) was to be translated as "unfortunate" or "unhappy" not as "deplorable".

He took it out on the translator. The blame for one's absurdities had to be placed on someone.

It's a shame, however, that the clarification is just an ugly leap of faith. In fact, "regrettable" actually means "deplorable" or, if you prefer, "unpleasant", "deplorable", "unfortunate", "reprehensible", anything but "unfortunate".

By saying "unlucky" he made Parolin seem like someone who doesn't measure his words when he speaks. Just him! A Vatican cardinal who speaks out of turn, out of nonsense! Doesn't this lawyer know that the Catholic Church is a master of diplomacy, having inherited it from the times of the Roman Empire?

With quick steps

In Europe we are already starting to think that if Trump wins in the USA, NATO will come to a bad end. In fact, Trump does not want to spend money on the Europeans, as he believes that the decisive clash will be with China.

Hence the utterances of Macron, who has already gone to his head. Also because European statesmen, in their paranoid delusions, fear that Russia will attack the EU within 5-8 years.

The main objective is only one: to make Europe an area militarily so strong that no one wants to compete with us. All countries will have to have nuclear bunkers and arsenals.

Therefore, even if we take it for granted that NATO's nuclear weapons will remain protected, it still requires a lot of strengthening. And who if not France will take charge of it? The British are outside the EU and then they have nuclear weapons, especially in their submarines.

In short, we are quickly moving towards the complete self-destruction of Europe. There are no alternative forms of peaceful coexistence.

February 18

Being democratic by being on the side of the singers

A Schlein collaborator, Marfo Furfaro, wrote about the censorship scandal of the CEO of Rai, Roberto Sergio, and Mara Venier: "Rai belongs to everyone, it is a public service, it is and must be a free place where artists can say what they think without censorship. Whether we like it or not. Because people are not stupid, they will judge them without the filter of regime propaganda. The disgust that was broadcast, the pressure on artists, the embarrassments, the Rai statement, show a country where the press is not free, artists must be subjected to the control of those who govern, criticism is not accepted. Italy deserves more, freedom deserves more."

Basically he's right, also because in the last five editions Amadeus and Fiorello have revitalized a singing event that had had its day and that young people certainly didn't like at all.

Unfortunately, Venier, in her interviews, continues not to understand how she should have behaved. She continues to defend herself by saying: "Never in my life have I censored anyone, nor have I ever been accused of censorship." And to "Repubblica", which defined her as "the vestal of melonism", she replied: "If I have been on TV for thirty years, it is because I have never embraced a political party. I am addressing the entire public, regardless of everyone's political ideas, and respecting them all."

She still hasn't understood what she should have done with the CEO's personal message, and for someone who has been at Rai for 30 years this is serious. 1) She was not required to read it, because it was not an official statement from the Board of Directors; 2) after reading it, she didn't have to share it; 3) by sharing it, she was completely wrong in saying that Italians had to do it too. Also because the opposite is evident to 99% of Italians, namely that Israel's reaction is enormously disproportionate.

Her attitude betrayed shameful positions, which evidently became second nature to her, such as flattery, opportunism, servility. She didn't understand that Rai is a public service, paid for by citizens' taxes. And the CEO, visibly arrogant and presumptuous, understood it even less.

Unfortunately there are still people who do not understand why it was right to give Ghali and Dargen D'Amico the freedom to express their anti-Israeli position, while the CEO of Rai had to remain silent and Mara Venier refused to read her statement which expressed solidarity with Israel. It's not that freedom of opinion doesn't apply to them. It's that they are in a position of power capable of taking this freedom away from singers, while singers are unable to do the same thing to them.

These regime subjects still haven't understood that if Sanremo has had an incredible success with the public, it is thanks to the singers. It is also to them that the CEO and Venier owe their salary, their career, their power.

For each episode of "Domenica In" Venier takes 19,000 euros. What should a young Italian say? Especially those who, despite having graduated, do absurd jobs or are forced to emigrate? Or do they turn to crime because they have no alternatives? Even the lyrics of their songs denounce an unbearable discomfort. It was enough to read them to offer them all the freedom of opinion they wanted.

*

Next year I want a Sanremo that is also open to foreign singers who live here without citizenship, free to say what they want. In fact, I want one for poetry too, to demonstrate that you can become famous even without putting words to music.

February 19

Dilemmas and fools

Netanyahu is a fascist, we know it. When he then uses biblical verses to justify his genocidal actions, it is even revolting. It is surprising that the International Criminal Court did not issue an arrest warrant against him, given that it had done so with such diligence against Putin, when the Russians had transferred approximately 700,000 Ukrainian children to their country, saving them from a tragic fate. The value of this ridiculous Court can also be understood from this absurdity.

The fact is that now Netanyahu finds himself faced with a Hamlet-like doubt, which he doesn't quite know how to resolve with his usual hasty methods.

Having not achieved the fundamental objectives he had set himself, such as free all the Israeli hostages, eliminate the bulk of the Hamas movement (and above all its leaders), force as many civilians as possible to emigrate to Sinai, now the prime minister is wondering what to do.

If it bombs the south of the Strip as it did the north, it risks losing Western support, without which it would be unable to do anything decisive. But if he doesn't, his government will collapse. He will end up on trial, not only for the charges of corruption, fraud and breach of trust in three different cases that had been brought against him before last October 7, but also for all those of genocide that will rain down on him from all over the world (now also from Lula's Brazil).

Furthermore, despite world opinion, he has no intention of granting the Palestinians the possibility of having their own autonomous state, not only because, in order not to grant this possibility, he had to sacrifice the lives of many of its soldiers, killed by the resistance of Hamas, but also because such a concession would force him to leave Gaza and therefore to give up exploiting the large gas fields discovered off the coast of that Strip.

This is why, whatever happens, at least they want to keep the northern part, even if this would make it impossible for the over two million Palestinians to live in the southern area. Among the dead, missing, wounded and maimed, approximately 100,000 Palestinians have already been directly involved in this massacre. Hundreds of thousands more are affected by the consequences of the indiscriminate bombing of their homes and by the lack of humanitarian aid (and let's leave aside the psychological trauma on the surviving minors here).

We are already in the presence of a catastrophe of immense proportions. Where do you want to go? And thank goodness that the conflict has not expanded as Biden, fresh from a resounding defeat in Ukraine, would have liked. In fact, the Iranians showed cold blood. They know they can attack any city in Israel, but evidently someone (China? Russia?) persuaded them not to do so.

Hezbollah limits itself to skirmishes; the Egyptians (although now supported by Macron) to threats. As for Syria and Iraq, they are currently watching, but pushing the US to dismantle their illegal military bases. So the only ones who are really worrying the Westerners (of course on an economic level) are the Houthis, who however know very well that they cannot do it for long on a military level, without substantial external help.

In short, even in the Middle East, as already in Ukraine, the American-led West is making a terrible impression.

February 20

Months for a useless opinion

The International Court of Justice, the UN's highest court, has begun hearings in a case concerning the legal consequences of Israel's occupation of the West Bank and East Jerusalem, as well as the Golan Heights. There are depositions from over 50 countries, which accuse Israel of strong discrimination.

This case is separate from the genocide case brought by South Africa against Israel in the same Court, as it was born on 31 December 2022, thanks to a resolution passed by the UN General Assembly.

The ridiculous thing is that the Court was not asked to issue a ruling, but only a non-binding opinion.

But what's even more ridiculous is that it will take months to get a verdict. And when it is issued, Israel will calmly not care.

Starting from military non-interference

When you see a government carrying out genocide against a population, it is instinctive to wish them all possible harm. Especially if innocent, unarmed, defenseless populations are exterminated, especially children, their mothers, the elderly, the sick, and in any case, in general, the weakest people.

It is a temptation that we must not fall into, since we put ourselves on the same level as those who commit these horrendous crimes, even if it doesn't take long to understand that, if they are committed with impunity, it is because someone, who plays important roles, justifies them, indeed it makes them materially possible.

Unfortunately, however, in the West we know well how things go:

having to choose who to relate to, between Judaism and Islam, we prefer Judaism. It is not just a cultural question: we consider Judaism as part of the "Christian" nature of the European continent (a nature which, in its Catholic guise, we have transferred with the Spanish-Lusitanians to the South American one, and in its Protestant guise, to the North America, Oceania and many African states).

It is also a psychological issue: towards the Jews, due to the anti-Semitism of past centuries and the more recent Shoah, we feel guilt. The Zionists know this and take advantage of it to show off all their unbearable arrogance.

Furthermore, Muslims scare us because there are too many of them. The impressive migratory flows of the last 30 years have made them neighbors to us. This is not enough time to have respect or friendship for them. We still feel that they are too different from us: they speak an incomprehensible language, the women dress strangely, they have very particular religious customs, and they don't eat the same things as us or not in the same way.

To accept them with relative ease, we must first see them in our schools, together with our children. If they have attended them since childhood, they understand secularism better and are more easily assimilated. We don't expect them to become Catholic or Protestant or atheist, but only that they don't make their otherness weigh too heavily in the religious field.

If they don't carry out terrorist or criminal acts, we tolerate them calmly, even if we don't frequent them that much, because we Westerners like to remain a little racist, to make our cultural, techno-scientific superiority, etc. weigh on us.

However, with the issue of the genocide committed by Israel in Gaza (but this has been going on since 1948) our attitude is changing. We are nourishing sympathy, understanding, indeed admiration towards the Palestinian Muslims. And we are asking ourselves, without wanting to feel hatred towards the Israelis, how it is possible to resolve this age-old question peacefully, that is, whether it is really possible to grant the Palestinians their own autonomous state, without this leading to a new war against Israel.

We need to understand how not to fall back into the mistakes of the past. There's no point in hating. We must solve the problems by setting the basic conditions so that they do not arise again. The longer we let them fester, the more painful the solution will be.

Given that no problem has been solved so far, we Westerners should ask ourselves whether it is not more our fault than that of the populations living in the Middle East. It would be a great thing if we Westerners stopped interfering militarily in that geographical area. It would be a significant first step to dismantle all our military bases.

Ukrainians and chemical weapons

By now the Ukrainian armed forces are so desperate that they are starting to use chemical weapons provided by the USA, in violation of the Chemical Weapons Convention ratified by the Americans themselves on April 25, 1997.

On the other hand, it is difficult to think that the Ukrainians could really do something against the Russians without the total support of NATO, especially the Anglo-Americans.

February 21

The crisis of the collective West

Collective Western capitalism has probably become so aggressive in the last 30 years (but perhaps we could start from the first Gulf War), because capital needs to control in an absolutely secure way the energy resources that nourish it, the resources that other countries, especially Middle Eastern ones. Without these cheap sources, our system very quickly ends up in dramatic crises, with no outlets, which it is unable to deal with, in internal politics, except in a violent, authoritarian way, which is most suited to it.

Capital cannot defend itself from this continuous decrease in energy resources, transforming itself from productive to financial, since finance expands (generally without shocks), if production expands, otherwise it is subject to safe and ruinous "speculative bubbles", which in a short time they lose what has been earned over many years. One of the most catastrophic ones was to do with real estate, the *subprime* of 2008.

Investment in stock market securities is based on the illusory assumption that one can easily get rich by making bets, as in the game of Monopoly. But on the stock market, those who do not have confidential information easily lose their investments. There are too many of us for everyone to win.

Or one could say that the industry goes to the stock market to look for the capital it needs to survive in a world that is increasingly poorer in energy resources and where competition is increasingly stronger, as all countries want to become capitalists in an international market. And the last arrivals do not need to retrace the great and tiring stages of those who left first.

Furthermore, since the birth of information technology, companies have been listed on the stock exchange that are not productive in the classic sense, i.e. in the material sense, but are productive in the immaterial sense, based solely on services that could disappear, for any reason, from one moment to the next.

From this point of view it is clear that capitalism cannot survive if everyone wants to be exploiters of other people's human and material resources. Someone has to play the part of the "exploited". And it is not simple, since capitalism is not like classic slavery: it must guarantee a certain formal or juridical freedom, otherwise it makes no sense to talk about "democracy". Only those who have this freedom try to take advantage of it to emancipate themselves. This is why wars are inevitable.

The new capitalist countries entering the scene are making the problem of the progressive lack of energy resources increasingly difficult to solve.

It cannot be ruled out that the managers of large capital are wondering how to renounce formal democracy and legal freedom, in order to maintain a certain level of material well-being at a social level, in the absence of which some sections of the population, the most oppressed, could arise. Capital must remove the mask of pseudo-democracy and transform itself into a clear dictatorship, as they did in Rome in the transition from republic to empire, when the emperors demagogically presented themselves alongside the people against the senate and the landowners.

At the time of the Romans, the empire was based on slave labor for the large landowners, so winning the periodic colonial wars was fundamental, so much so that when it was no longer possible, they began to transform the slave into a colonist, that is, into a worker. which legally enjoyed certain freedoms or a certain autonomy of action on an economic level, characterized by a contractual agreement. Settlers had to provide landowners with a quantity of goods or hours of free labor or a certain amount of rent money. However, this did not at all imply that the empire was more democratic than the republic; in fact, the opposite: the dictatorship was more ferocious.

Today, however, the wealth of industrial capital is the energy resources that make machines work. The fewer they are available, the more aggressive capital becomes.

It was once said that the well-being of the collective West is closely related to the malaise of the global South. But it is even more so if this South wants to free itself from our colonialism.

February 22

The alternatives envisaged by the collective West

Capitalism is aiming to replace classic energy resources (fossil ones) with new resources based on so-called "rare materials", which should guarantee the transition towards electricity, considered (naively?) less polluting.

In practice it has already been understood that tools such as wind turbines and solar panels are absolutely not sufficient to replace hydrocarbons, not even as complementary energy: at most they are good for domestic, family use.

But perhaps it would be better to say that it is the "strong powers" who want to convince us that our well-being would be better guaranteed with electrical. Ecology based on electric batteries is obviously a new business.

At the moment, however, we are convinced that nuclear power is not a viable alternative to fossil fuels: power plants are too dangerous, both when they operate and when disposing of their waste. Chernobyl and Fukushima terrorized the whole world.

However, the fact that resources for electricals are "rare" makes the transition very difficult. Western capitalism is no longer able to guarantee the colonialism of the past. It has to buy such resources on international markets, and they are very expensive.

Furthermore, the disposal of spent materials in the electrical field is very complex and not at all eco-friendly. Batteries, solar panels[2], computers, cell phones, power plants and nuclear weapons... are becoming an environmental curse for all of humanity, especially for those countries that the West exploits as real open-air landfills.

Now, if for these reasons we must be subject to periodic wars, we should at least be clear about what possible alternative to pose to the development of capitalism, otherwise each war will be followed by another, with possible even more catastrophic effects.

Nine Russian-Ukrainian lessons

Questions to find answers to:

---

2 In theory, glass and aluminum from solar panels could be recycled, but under private capitalism, if it's not convenient, no one will do it.

1. What are the most reliable sources for sufficiently truthful information?

2. What are the most disastrous consequences on the West caused by this war?

3. What can democratic socialism expect from multipolarism?

4. How can this war end, avoiding the use of nuclear weapons?

5. What are the minimum conditions to ensure a sufficiently stable peace in Europe?

6. What relationship can there be on a legal level between national sovereignty, political independence and self-determination of peoples?

7. How can the presence of NATO bases in Italy be reformulated?

8. In what sense is a possible reform of the UN?

9. What relationship can there be between Local Territorial Authorities and the national State in view of the next elections?

Answers

1. With this war in Ukraine we have understood that we cannot trust simple sensations or impressions or perceptions (typical for example that which divides the contenders into the semantic pair of attacked and aggressor), but we must exercise the intelligence of things, making use of them from many sources. We must test the sources themselves, constantly verify them with a cold, rational, detached approach, capable of seeing if space is given to historical analyses, to motivations of an economic, social, political, ideological or military nature. We need to compare all the causes, explanations and theses that support each other, avoiding fact-checking like Mentana's Open, which believes it plays the role of judge superior to everything and everyone.

To me Giulietto Chiesa sometimes seemed exaggerated when he talked about WWIII starting from the Ukrainian conflict, already in 2014. Over time I changed my mind and also gained a military culture with this war. But he had clear ideas because he read US sources, and he said that Americans are so arrogant that not only do they lie constantly, but they don't even bother telling the most embarrassing truths, because they know that no one can challenge them.

The most reliable sources are many, almost unlimited, because they continually grow outside the dominant media mainstream. They can be found on Youtube: see the channels of Stefano Orsi, Alessandro Orsini, Giacomo Gabellini, Nicolai Lilin, Paolo Borgognone, Giuseppe Masala, Il Vaso di Pandora by Carlo Savegnago, Pangea Grandandolo by Manlio

Dinucci, Casa del Sole Tv and Levante by Margherita Furlan and associates, Border Nights by Fabio Frabetti, Massimo Mazzucco, Roberto Quaglia, Alessandro Di Battista, the authors of Radio Radio Tv, Il Fatto giorno, Visione TV by Francesco Toscano (who often pairs with the communist Marco Rizzo), Dazibao by Davide Martinotti on China, Lafinanzasulweb by Arnaldo Vitangeli, Fabbrica della Comunicazione by Beatrice Silenzi, Una Voce Libera by Tiziana Alterio, 100 Days of Lions by Riccardo Rocchesso, ByoBlu by Claudio Messora, even Pubble (i.e. Paola Ceccantoni) is a reliable source, albeit ironic. I would say to definitely forget about The Mine and Parabellum, but also, in some ways, Dario Fabbri. The interviews with Fulvio Grimaldi, but also with Enrica Perrucchietti, are interesting.

The most popular social networks, full of channels or rather useful groups, are, as usual, those of Meta/Facebook and X (formerly Twitter), but it is also good to follow Quora because it does not have the censorship of Facebook.

Then obviously there is the big news for everyone: Telegram (the annual subscription, to have immediate translation in all languages, costs very little). The Russian channels, that of Lilin and many other Italians (such as Giubbe Rosse, L'Antidiplomatico, Idee&Azione, L'Ineditore, Controredazione, etc.) are fundamental. Many of these channels have their own blogs online.

In the paper world, fundamental are the books by Orsini, Gabellini, Dinucci, Fracassi, Lilin, Travaglio, Bonelli, Mussetti, Bifarini, Reginella, and many many others (e.g. Andrea Zhok, Demostenes Floros, Fulvio Grimaldi etc.). Indeed, a list of all these books should be made and distributed to everyone. Among the geopolitical magazines I would point out Eurasia, Sicurezza Internazionale by Orsini, L'Ineditore, Marx21 by Sorini, Prospettiva marxista and Limes by Caracciolo (the latter with a grain of salt, since it is financed by the Gedi Group, but has important collaborators). Among the newspapers is "Il Fatto Quotidiano" (the "Manifesto" split with Dinucci is shameful. No one in Italy knows NATO better than Dinucci). MicroMega's anti-Russian position is incomprehensible.

All these sources seem like too many. They often intersect with each other, overlap, repeat the same things. The problem is that the dominant mainstream does not take them into consideration, because from the beginning it has supported a Russophobic and warmongering thesis, aligning itself with the Anglo-American position. But they are overflowing sources, which enrich like never before, infinitely surpassing the news broadcast on radio and TV. The only "normal" one in RAI was Marc Innaro: the others, in general, are all corrupt, intellectually limited, full of prejudices, rhetoric, clichés on a conceptual level. If you don't listen to them, you lose nothing.

2. The most disastrous consequences for the West are first of all the economic ones, then the political ones, as is inevitable in a system where the economy is more important than politics, and today finance is more important than the economy itself.

The inevitable economic consequences are the increase in inflation, which we try to remedy (unnecessarily) with the increase in the cost of money, which depresses productive investments and causes mortgages to skyrocket. Lack of investment reduces employment. Inflation erodes savings. Public debt will become increasingly out of control. More and more fiat money will be printed, i.e. without underlying assets. There will be an incredible hoarding of precious metals. Governments will control citizens' bank accounts down to the last cent: they will end up withdrawing money from these accounts and will force us not to spend too much per day. We will be prevented from freely accessing bank or post office branches. The use of Paypal or other forms of online payment that are beyond state control will be banned. All payments will be traced, with the excuse of eradicating tax avoidance and evasion. Only a few super-rich companies will remain on Western stock exchanges. The large international financial funds (BlackRock, Vanguard, State Street, IMF etc.) under the pretext of efficiency, ecology, energy saving etc. they will buy the family jewels (everything relating to tourism and food from us), they will force us within a decade to completely renovate our homes, otherwise they will lose value, but also to buy electric cars and other nonsense that will be of absolutely no use to nothing for the purposes of the true alternative to a productivist and consumerist system. Finally, if the US defaults, the EU and the UK and Canada and the collective West will follow suit. At that moment we will need to have clear ideas on how to proceed with a real alternative, which cannot be the entire nationalization of the means of production, because we have already seen in the Soviet system that in the long run it does not work. It took 70 years for everything to collapse. We can't take anything from that experiment. We'll have to invent something new. And the first thing we will have to do is to overthrow the military dictatorship that will fall on our heads. Because there is no doubt that in the face of economic and financial collapse, the system will defend itself by entrusting powers to the military. Civil war will be inevitable, just as the system's attempt to divert attention from internal problems towards the outside, favoring war against a State defined as "enemy" or "rogue", will be inevitable. If there is civil war, the occupation of the levers of state will be a priority objective. But the state serves to coordinate the resistance against the reactionaries. It cannot be used to rebuild the economy, except at the level of direction or coordination. Here the Local Territorial Authorities must assert themselves, who must manage local resources in a social way, taking away their property from private individuals. Then the Regions will make mandatory agreements or agreements with other Regions to eliminate disparities.

But we must carefully prevent the State from monopolizing the production and distribution of products. The State must favor national defense and foreign trade, but in internal politics it must delegate the management of the territory to peripheral bodies, because only in this way can the intelligence of things be developed and bureaucracy eliminated. However, this means that financial resources will be needed. That is, the taxes cannot be sent to Rome and wait for part of it to come back from here. That part of the taxes will go to Rome to make what is needed at a national level work, for example. the construction of interregional infrastructures.

3. The concept of "multipolarity" has come to global public attention, but let us not delude ourselves. Is it necessary to defeat neoliberal globalism? I do not know. The state capitalism of Russia, China, India etc. Can Western private capitalism win? Perhaps. But the point is another. Let's ask ourselves a question: is multipolarism perhaps the antechamber of a finally democratic socialism? I have my doubts. In itself it is only about mutual respect for existing civilizations, diversified interests, the need to use one's own national currencies, without having to depend on the petrodollar. It will certainly be right to link national currencies to actual internal resources, such as energy reserves, precious minerals, rare earths, industrial production... But it will soon be realized that one nation has more assets than another, and what will be done within BRICS? Will the weaker nation claim to have more power so as not to be swallowed up? Perhaps a common virtual currency will be created to carry out some forms of commercial exchange. But then, ultimately, what does it mean that money should be linked to useful goods in a capitalist context? Why force states to think about such constraints? What if exchanges took place on the basis of bartering? Wouldn't they be less tiring, less expensive, freer from the needs of the markets? Are securities and securities markets and stock exchanges so indispensable? Are we sure that self-consumption is an opprobrious thing, to be absolutely avoided? Without a doubt, multipolarism is a concept that favors the independence of the political state, the end of neocolonialism. But this cannot be enough to achieve substantial democracy, real and non-mercantilist socialism like the Chinese one.

Who likes a Russia so tied to the religious tradition of Orthodoxy? Who likes a president who frequents Orthodox circles so closely in a multi-confessional Federation? Not me. In this respect I prefer the Chinese: they are more secular, more indifferent to religions, more equidistant.

And what about Islamic civilization? It is even further from secular-humanistic ideas. Multipolarism will certainly mean that the racist, warmongering, cynical and materialist unipolarity of the West will die. So what will the alternative be? The burqa? The confessional state? Indian polytheism? Or will everyone have to keep their own traditions? Their own identities? Your own values? So does it mean that gigantic ghettos will be created worldwide that will communicate with each other only on a commercial level? Is this all that those who are social-communists want for all humanity?

4. How will this war end? Falcone said that everything has a beginning and an end, and this one will have one too. But it will not end well either for Ukraine or for NATO or for Europe or for the collective West. By now things have become gangrenous and are proceeding on their own, like a train without an engineer. Russia's initial objectives were very clear: denazification of the Kiev government, demilitarization of the country (reduced to having purely defensive weapons), NATO out of Ukraine, even if the country could join the EU. Putin also wants to dismantle all NATO bases on his country's borders, as he realizes that they can threaten him on a nuclear level.

From this point of view, I have my doubts that Moscow wants to accept the Korean solution, in which the western part of Ukraine passes under NATO and Donbass is kept by Russia, leaving the country to remain divided, more or less, by the great river Dnper. In fact, this is a solution that will re-propose a new war in a few years, even if Moscow obtains a demilitarization zone of 200-300 km from Donbass, and also if the current neo-Nazi junta is replaced with a more moderate one , which respects the rules of formal democracy, while retaining the necessary Russophobia. This is because Ukraine is destined to lose any form of political and economic independence, regardless of what the neo-Nazis in Kiev want.

Now that Finland and soon Sweden have also joined NATO, the security problem has become incredibly complicated. After the involvement of the collective West, Moscow needs Kiev's unconditional surrender. There can be no negotiations with Washington regarding the current line of contact. Unless Moscow proves that it is incapable of occupying Kiev, though it is very doubtful that it will fail to do so. At first it hoped for a direct and quick negotiation with Kiev so as not to cause Ukraine to lose its independence, to limit human and material losses as much as possible. Now the situation is completely different: Russia feels at war against the entire West, which continues to boycott and sanction it in every way. Moscow actually needs a regime change in Washington, which in turn brings about a radical change in the war posture within the EU.

In the Korean War, China was induced to accept the freeze because it did not have sufficient forces to win it with certainty (as Russia does today). Indeed, today China tends to put an end to everything that separates it from Taiwan. If it succeeds, it will then demand the reunification of the two Koreas, complete with the forced closure of all American military bases. For all this to happen it is only a matter of time.

Certainly in a Korean solution Moscow will not give a ruble to rebuild western Ukraine. Indeed, it cannot be ruled out that before accepting such a solution, Moscow will make sure to prevent Western Ukraine from doing harm for a long time, to the point that the EU will have to discuss whether to accept a completely destroyed country within itself.

Moscow cannot even allow Poland to take back Galicia and Volhynia, because it would be too humiliating for the pro-Russian Ukrainians. Also because Poland would not give anything in return. At most, Moscow could agree to grant something of Transcarpathia to the Hungarians, in order to allow them to reunite with the Magyars residing in Ukraine, persecuted by Kiev's neo-Nazis just like the Russian-speaking people of Donbass. It may make this concession as a reward for refusing to comply with anti-Russian sanctions. I also don't think he will cede part of Bessarabia to Romania, which is eager to join Moldova to become a large NATO state. Indeed, for me, Putin will end up occupying Odessa to unite Donbass with Transnistria, realizing the wishes of the Russian-speaking people of Transnistria. After that Moldova or Romania would think twice before threatening Transnistria. It cannot be ruled out that Gagauzia, an autonomous region of Moldova, not recognized by the central government, may not ask Turkey or Russia for help to be recognized as such.

If Russia occupies Odessa, it will deprive Ukraine of its access to the sea and take it back to the Middle Ages. I don't think it will get that far if Kiev accepts unconditional surrender.

The United States, Germany, France and the United Kingdom have almost completed work on a draft framework agreement on Ukraine's security obligations: the G7 and EU countries are expected to join it. That is, Kiev, in exchange for the promise of NATO membership, could be persuaded to negotiate peace with the Russians, admitting the loss of Donbass and Crimea. This is because in Europe the large states are starting to get tired of the war. In short, it is important for NATO that a piece of Ukrainian territory remains which, like a cancer, can weaken Russia, allowing NATO to deploy military contingents and weapons in the territory left free from the Russian presence.

However, after the many dead soldiers it has had, will Moscow be able to accept such a conclusion, which will not solve the security problem of the entire Federation at all? Absolutely not.

Another solution hypothesis: the Israeli model. Israel is not a member of NATO and therefore is not obliged to help its allies in the event of an attack by an enemy, as required by the art. 5 of the North Atlantic Treaty. But at the same time the country is considered an important partner of the United States, which provides it with significant military and financial assistance.

In particular, Kiev should not expect the agreement to be "legally binding" or wait for military exercises to take place on Ukrainian territory. The agreement will contain the notion of "obligations" but not of "safety guarantees". However, it is not clear whether the agreement will be long-term or short-term. Military aid is likely to remain at current levels and decline if the conflict ends. Ukraine will certainly not be able to join NATO at the moment, as there is no unanimous consensus among the members of the alliance. The United Kingdom, Eastern and Scandinavian countries would be in favor, but others would not. The EU is discussing, as possible obligations for Ukraine, the continuation of the financing of arms supplies through the European Peace Fund, the expansion of the training possibilities of the Ukrainian army, the sending of military missions to that country under suitable conditions. The draft statement from European leaders spoke of the long-term nature of a possible agreement.

It is clear that with this proposal the West wants to catch its breath, after the resounding defeats in the field, to replenish its military supplies. And we all know that Israel has been the main misfortune of the Middle East since 1948.

It cannot be ruled out, seeing Zelensky's irrationality, that the more moderate Ukrainian politicians decide to abolish presidentialism and return to parliamentarism, ensuring that the prime minister is elected with full powers by the population, but is subject to parliament. Today he is just a puppet in the hands of the President of the Republic.

Once this war is over, it is impossible for Russia not to want to intervene in the Baltic countries, where Russian speakers have begun to suffer harassment of all kinds; it is impossible that it does not want to settle accounts with Sweden and Finland, now that they have joined NATO, for the issue of border security and access to the Baltic Sea (fundamental for supplying Kaliningrad); it is impossible for the situation in Transnistria to remain so precarious and undefined on the international level; it is impossible that in Syria, a nation allied with Moscow, American bases continue to rob it of its oil with the complicity of the Kurds; it is impossible for Moscow to remain indifferent to the Serbs' request to resolve the absurd issue of Kosovo; it is impossible that the age-old conflict between Armenians and Azerbaijanis will not be resolved once and for all; it is impossible that Moldova and Georgia can claim to join NATO; it is impossible that the responsibilities for the sabotage of the Nordstream are not definitively ascertained and that light is not shed on all the acts of terrorism carried out by Kiev with the complicity of Western intelligence. It is impossible for Moscow not to make clear to the whole world, in as much detail as possible, how dangerous the biolaboratories that the US secretly operates in many parts of the world are.

If this Russian-Ukrainian war is not won by Russia, it will be lost by the whole of Europe, since nuclear power will inevitably be used. But if it is won, Moscow will necessarily ask to resolve all the other tense situations that risk provoking new wars in the future. And in this constructive attitude it could find allies or supporters in Europe willing to restore economic cooperation.

5. The conditions for achieving stable peace in Europe are very simple, and therefore probably unachievable, because we are designed to complicate our lives.

This war cannot end with a simple peace negotiation. The criteria of mutual security must be reset. The West has never understood the principle that security is either mutual or exists only for the strongest. Since NATO's aggressiveness has become unsustainable for Russia's security, it will demand that the EU has its own army that is not dependent on American hegemony. Negotiations to dismantle nuclear power from the entire European theater will take place later. From the Pyrenees to the Urals, the continent must be denuclearized. And this will never be possible until the EU renounces its role as an American colony.

In Europe, to guarantee a minimum level of security for future generations, we should first of all demand the limitation or reduction of strategic and medium-range nuclear weapons, to the point of foreseeing their definitive destruction.

Two prohibitions should be included within this objective: 1) any type of experimentation that increases the power of nuclear weapons; 2) being able to use the atomic weapon first in the event of conflict (the so-called "preventive attack" or "first strike"). Two things that, if they are not removed from the way, any other discussion becomes useless.

Now, given that NATO and Russia already have so many nuclear weapons that they can annihilate each other, it should be relatively easy to agree on the elimination of all other weapons of mass destruction: chemical, bacteriological, space, laser, particle beams etc. It makes no sense to think of disintegrating each other using different weapons, when we have understood that only one is enough to do it and that we have more of this than necessary.

What is certain is that if NATO continues to install bases close to Russia's borders, these proposals make no sense. NATO only understands the balance of power, so Russia (and in time China will too) will be forced to install its nuclear bases as close as possible to the USA (Caribbean? Central America? North Korea?).

You don't need to be an expert psychologist to understand that when two nations are at war and hate each other to death, the one firmly convinced that its military strength depends on weapons that the other doesn't have will be more inclined to launch the attack. first shot. And we know well what this means in the nuclear field (or in any case in the weapons of mass destruction sector).

Those who possess atomic weapons want to use them first, ensuring that the enemy is unable to react. The first nation to declare that it would never use them first was the USSR in 1982. The USA has always refused to make a similar commitment.

Even a child understands that if all nuclear nations refused to fire the first shot, there could be no subsequent shots, and thus a nuclear war would be virtually averted. The Russians probably made that common-sense statement because they believed that no first strike could be so devastating as to prevent the enemy from reacting equally catastrophically. They had essentially come to a realistic conclusion: there is no impenetrable anti-missile defense.

From this aspect we must be convinced that the more space is militarized, the more likely it is that a nuclear war will break out on Earth. Any army would like to wage war while looking at the enemy from above. Today there is nothing better than doing it with satellites (military, espionage, telecommunications, meteorological, etc.).

For these reasons it is difficult to think that any peace treaty between Russians and Ukrainians does not provide for an expansion of security criteria in which the entire Atlantic Alliance is involved (which also goes beyond the EU countries). There are too many military bases on Russia's borders. By "bases" we do not mean only those on land, but also those located in space. Not to mention the fact that an American aircraft carrier is a base in its own right, capable of controlling large portions of the ocean, commercial straits, airspace, and managing land landings of marines, and launching intercontinental missiles.

There must necessarily be military conditions capable of offering more or less security. One might be this: no state should possess weapons that could prevent another state from reacting. That is, not only should surprise attacks be avoided, but also that such attacks should be so devastating as to prevent a retaliatory strike. This means that any super-fast, long-range, mass-destructive weapon should be dismantled. No army should aim to have a clear superiority in means and men over another army (at least for the same geographical extension or demographic density). The security of a State should be established at a reasonable level of armaments, sufficient for its own defense. If it were possible to put effective controls on such conditions, then perhaps we could talk about peace. Which obviously must be guaranteed with fewer and fewer or less dangerous weapons, creating increasingly larger totally demilitarized zones.

6. We see the concept of self-determination of peoples, a principle recognized by the UN and the international community. We talked a lot about this concept already when Catalonia claimed it against Spain. But in the past it was also claimed by the Basques against the Spanish, the Scots and Irish against the English, the inhabitants of Corsica against the French motherland, and so on. Ukraine itself separated from Russia in 1991 in the name of peoples' self-determination. In Italy we had to deal with the South Tyroleans, at the time when they were terrorists because they wanted to pass under Austria. The Christian Democrats allowed them to keep 100% of the taxes and they stopped throwing bombs. Today they are so happy and content that not only do they not ask to pass under Austria but they don't even know what to do with dual citizenship. In fact, Austria would certainly not do them such a great favor.

Since the end of the coup in 2014, the Minsk Protocols I and II, put in place before this Russian-Ukrainian war began, were never upheld. They confirmed clearly that the strongly centralist neo-Nazi state of Kiev never accepted the idea of granting a special status to Donbass, which would allow it to equip itself with its own autonomous police force and judicial system, and linguistic self-determination. Russian-speakers of the two Donbass republics (Donetsk and Lugansk) also wanted the participation of local self-government bodies in the appointment of heads of prosecutor's offices and presidents of courts of autonomous areas. For all these things they were considered "terrorists". I remember that these two regions, combined by geographical extension, were as large as Lazio and that Ukraine is twice the size of Italy. Today, in order not to grant decentralization to these two small regions, Kiev risks losing the entire nation.

The various neo-Nazi Ukrainian governments have never accepted neither the ceasefire of their regular army, nor the use of weapons of a certain caliber, nor the agreement of a demilitarized zone, nor the obligation to disarm the ultranationalist and neo-Nazi groups (Azov battalion and military apparatus of Pravij Sektor) who fought illegally against the separatists, much less bothered to try them when they were guilty of atrocities (such as that of Odessa). Naturally they rejected Russia's military support for the two republics of Donetsk and Lugansk. The OSCE recorded 200 violations of the ceasefire between 2016 and 2020 and over 1,000 from 2021. In short, Kiev signed the agreements knowing a priori that it would disregard them and could not wait to launch a deadly attack against the two republics. They wanted to do it because they knew very well that they had NATO's backing.

The protocols were also signed by France, Germany and Poland, not only by Russia, Ukraine, OSCE and separatist leaders. They also obtained the approval of the UN Security Council. France and Germany have admitted that the Protocols were signed only to give the Nazis in the Kiev government time to arm themselves and train properly.

A strong point of disagreement was the order of implementation of the political and military points of the protocols. Russia considered the order of points to be implemented chronologically: Ukraine had to first guarantee the separatists in Donbass effective autonomy and representation in the central government; only afterwards would the military vehicles be withdrawn and Ukrainian control of the border restored.

Zelensky, on the other hand, demanded the opposite: first the restoration of national borders, then regional elections. Furthermore, he refused to guarantee true autonomy to the pro-Russian regions, since he considered them "occupied" by Russia, which over the years had granted citizenship to over 800,000 inhabitants. He was convinced that autonomy for the breakaway regions could be a means for Moscow to obtain a sort of veto over Ukraine's foreign policy decisions, especially in relation to its intention to join NATO. In fact, if Moscow has never opposed Kiev's idea of joining the EU, it has never accepted the idea of having American missiles capable of hitting it in a few minutes. In 8 years there have been 14,000 deaths and 1.5 million displaced people.

In Crimea the referendum on independence was won by the separatists with 97% of the votes. In the Donbass regions the referendum achieved 79% of votes in favour.

The West does not want to hear about the self-determination of peoples, unless this self-determination serves to destroy a socialist or non-globalist or Islamized state, that is, unless the insurgents serve the interests of the West, as happened with Kosovo (where the fascists of the KLA went from terrorists to patriots in an instant), with South Sudan, with the Kurds, with the Tibetans, the Uyghurs in China, the Libyan tribes... The disintegration of Yugoslavia itself is the result of a concept of self-determination favorable to Western interests. Speaking of South Sudan: this country acquired definitive independence on 9 July 2011, following a referendum passed with 98.83% of the votes. Well the UN recognized it on July 14th! If he had had the same speed towards the two Donbass republics, perhaps all this slaughter would not have happened. It is evident, in fact, that if a State is not recognized as separatist or secessionist, the other, from which it has separated, is authorized to continuously fight it.

In the West, if the State is fully capitalist, Westernized, formally democratic, the principle of territorial integrity and national sovereignty and independence of a centralized political State applies, which is such even when it is federated, since the recognition of regional autonomy is very relative, purely formal, concerning only some restricted fields of intervention. In fact, it is one thing to consensually separate into two distinct nations (such as Czechia and Slovakia), both capitalist, with different traditions and languages (they separated peacefully on 1 January 1993 and 18 days later were recognized by the UN); another is to break away independently, reducing the borders of a nation or even ending up under another nation (as for example the Magyars of Transcarpathia in Ukraine would like to do, who would like to pass under Hungary because they feel very discriminated against).

In short, with this war we understood that when a people claims their autonomy, independence, self-determination, we must listen to them very carefully, we must find an effective agreement, an effective, convincing compromise, otherwise we risk a civil war, and if the people ask for intervention of a foreign state, there is even a risk of a regional war and even a world war (as happened in World War I, when the various ethnic groups, nationalities and regions of the Austro-Hungarian empire wanted to separate from Vienna. In order not to grant this autonomy, the entire empire was blown up and today Austria is a nation with almost zero geopolitical weight).

7. The NATO bases we have in Italy, regardless of European intentions and American will, must be nationalized, eliminating their legal

extraterritoriality, and must be denuclearized, that is, reduced to a conventional defense system, and its American presence in Italy must be concluded, since defense must be placed under the control of an independent national state, a state which, in our case, also belongs to a European Union, for which defense is also a supranational topic, but always within the context of a collective chosen to consensual contract. Defense criteria cannot be imposed by a foreign state by virtue of its military strength. We cannot do without defense, but neither can we give up the freedom to defend ourselves as we want. Nor can we accept the idea that our bases have such an offensive capacity that neighboring states do not feel safe with us. We cannot have weapons that prevent a potential enemy from defending itself or firing a retaliatory shot, because no state will accept being put in a position where it is constantly afraid of its neighbor. We must avoid as much as possible creating conditions that favor an arms race.

NATO is scary, not only because it is extremely aggressive, but also because it aspires to an international role. It is no longer a merely European anti-communist alliance. It is an instrument of death in favor of US domination, against anyone who challenges it, whether communist or Islamist or capitalist, rival or colonized insubordinate.

However, if NATO does not dissolve, as the Warsaw Pact did, Russia will aim most of its nuclear missiles at the EU. Indeed, Russia and China will build military bases in Central America and fill North Korea with hypersonic missiles, capable of hitting any area of the USA.

NATO clearly dominates the European Union: the European Commission, the Council of State, the European Parliament itself take orders from NATO or the USA. Even the International Criminal Court, which the USA has not joined, cannot express autonomous sentences.

Not only that, but the USA tends to prefer the former Soviet bloc countries within NATO because, being poorer, they are more easily blackmailed.

Even the European Union is forced to demand that those states that want to join this economic bloc also join NATO.

In short, either Russia itself joins NATO, and then we can think about mutual security, or the war will go on until the USA, EU and NATO come to a more lenient opinion.

Putin said in an interview: "We will die like martyrs, but you will die like dogs."In the sense that the Russians, as usual, will consider themselves victims of a situation that they did not favor in any way, while we Westerners will suffer such a retaliatory blow that we will not be able to recover so easily. The destruction of the two Japanese cities should be considered a trifle compared to what can happen today. Just to give an example, the Russians are capable of submerging the whole of England with ocean waters with their atomic weapons.

Of course, someone like Gorbachev would never have said that phrase, but because he was naive, an idealist, a do-gooder. Putin, on the other hand, is a tough guy, but among the tough guys in the Russian leadership, he is perhaps the most moderate (Medvedev, Surovikin, Patrushev are much less so). He was very disappointed by Europe's attitude and is now no longer willing to make concessions. Even if we wanted to resume trade relations with Russia by restoring Nordstream, they would reply that we all have to pay for the damages, given that they are not at fault.

8. UN reform is essential. The Security Council cannot be more important than the General Assembly, at most it can perform the task of an executive body that monitors compliance with the decisions taken in the Assembly (for which a 2/3 majority would be sufficient). It is true that it has been extended to other nations, but the right of veto has remained with only five nations. Today the Security Council is made up of 10 other countries elected by the General Assembly for a two-year term, not immediately renewable. They are divided among the geographical groupings of the UN (3 seats for Africa; 2 for Asia-Pacific; 2 for the countries of the Western Group; 2 for the countries of Latin America and the Caribbean; 1 for the countries of Eastern Europe).

To expel Russia from the Security Council – as Zelensky requested – it would take the unanimity of the countries with the right of veto (probably also a majority of no less than 2/3 of the other 10 countries) and above all Russia's refusal to participate in the meetings of the same Council (which occurred only once in the early 1950s, when the UN, during the war in Korea, supported the pro-American South against the communist North. But no one had ever made such an absurd request).

It must also be said that the three Western countries of the Security Council have always opposed the idea of expanding the Council to other countries of considerable importance, such as Germany, India, Japan and Brazil, granting them the right of veto (today there are also in the running Nigeria, South Africa and Egypt). Consider that the UN Secretary General himself, who presides over Security Council meetings, has no right to vote.

The only possible reform should take into account the fact that while in 1945 the United Nations had 51 member states, today it has 193, so the distribution of seats of non-permanent countries in the Security Council makes no sense. And perhaps it doesn't even make sense that there is a Security Council infinitely more important than the entire General Assembly. If the Security Council were abolished completely, we would have been spared the ridiculous speech that Biden made to the General Assembly on 21 September 2022, in which he assured, hoping to remove consensus from the BRICS, US support for the increase in the number of permanent and non-permanent representatives in the Security Council itself, with particular preference for the countries of the global South.

This war has shown that the Assembly has always been more objective than the Council itself. In all anti-Russian resolution proposals, the Assembly has never given a majority. And when it gave it, at the beginning of the conflict, the states that abstained or opposed had a population that was decidedly higher than that of the other states. In all its resolutions the UN tends to be pro-West, or, if the West intervened militarily without an explicit mandate, the UN does not react negatively (even the OSCE in Ukraine was pro-Kiev and not Donbass). So either the UN agrees to be reformed, or it is better to leave, since it is just a waste of time and money.

At the beginning of the special operation in Ukraine, African countries seemed a bit indifferent. At the UN they had not voted in favor of anti-Russian sanctions, but not against them either: they had abstained. They had attributed a regional dimension to that conflict. Then, with Moscow's great diplomatic activity, they understood that the world was changing. And the litmus test of this epochal change was in the fact that the collective West wanted to maintain its usual colonial relationship with Africa. That is, to have the continent on its side against Russia, the West would have tried to blackmail and threaten it in every way (even starving it, if necessary). At a certain point Africa said enough. A continent rich in resources of all kinds cannot continue to live in a very poor manner, it cannot have to deal with a development model that is contrary to its interests, it cannot be forced into continuous migration for economic or war reasons. It was Africa that gave the Russian-Ukrainian conflict an international dimension.

9. Let's now look at the role of Local Authorities at a national level. This is the most difficult point, because it is the operational one and I am not the most suitable person to deal with it, but an urban, local, provincial Committee with regional projection must be.

As a premise I would say not to repeat the mistakes of the past state socialism, both the industrial-Soviet type and the rural-Chinese type.

Naturally here we must exclude a priori that a mercantilist or liberal or capitalist socialism can exist or that state capitalism is a form of socialism. Otherwise any discussion becomes meaningless.

The ongoing war between the collective West on the one hand and Russia and China on the other is a war between two forms of capitalism:

one private, the Western one, and the other State. The private one is destined to succumb, because, even if it may appear more advanced in certain techno-scientific sectors, overall it is more inhuman, more hypocritical, more false, less attentive to welfare, to social needs, to the common good. Over time it cannot hold up, as it creates discontent, intolerance, rebellion not only outside oneself but also within oneself, favoring great governmental instability. The center of gravity of history is moving from west to east, and will move even further from north to south, or in any case from the Euro-American area to the Asian one and from this to the Afro-South American one. The Anglosphere is dying and does not want to die without a fight.

Here we have now reached a point where the simplistic alternatives have become two: either all these conflicts (in Ukraine, Israel, Taiwan or elsewhere) are resolved with tarallucci and wine, that is, in a stalemate, or a world war breaks out. There is no middle ground, such as regional wars.

It depends on what the United States wants to do: they are the main terminally ill patients. Indeed, it is a fact that the proxy war is lost in Ukraine. That this defeat remains independent of what will happen in the Middle East is equally obvious. It is probable that after this defeat the USA wants to go to war with China over the Taiwan issue.

But there are other options, including the financial default of the American state and the risk that after this default some federal states want to break away from the central government. The United States must then face enormous migratory flows from South America, much greater than ours. It is not excluded that the USA transforms its pseudo democracy into an explicit military dictatorship.

Whatever the next scenario, in Italy (or rather in Europe) we have the duty to free ourselves from this dependence that chains us to NATO and the USA, and consequently we must free ourselves from all our collaborationist governments, which do not question this dependence.

What to do? Take roots in the local territory and national coordination of these local territorial units.

What is the purpose? Perhaps create a centralist state like the current one, obviously revised and corrected? Or create a federalist state like the Swiss or German ones? Or simply replace the current parliamentarians with other elected ones, always within the current national representative democracy? Or favor a decentralization or devolution of state functions, possibly to a regional level?

For me these are all solutions that do not allow us to avoid the risk of creating a new formal democracy.

A substantial democracy can only be direct, that is, local, where all economic resources are managed by the local, territorial community. The State must progressively wither away, dissolve, as the classics of Marxism have always said. It can be maintained for defense needs, to encourage foreign trade, to promote a certain balance between the different local and regional realities. But the most important decisions, in everyday life, must be taken at a local level, that is, the administrative sphere must become political, and the political-national sphere must be subordinated to local-regional needs.

Is it possible to build a direct democracy without making a revolution that overturns the national political system? No, you can't. This is why the idea of the Five Star Movement failed.

Can a direct democracy be built, after having made a political revolution, when there are aggressive states abroad that would like to occupy ours? Stalinism said no. We, however, must say yes. We must say that the more local communities are autonomous, master of their resources, that is, self-managed (at least in fundamental resources, those that reduce dependence on markets to a minimum), the more they will be willing to defend themselves. They will also defend themselves better against organized crime, which must be eradicated without many scruples.

If we want to build a popular movement over time, it cannot only be anti-government, it must also be *antisystemic*. We were supposed to be anti-systemic at the end of World War II, but the partisan, proletarian, democratic, social-communist forces were disarmed. The left preferred compromise, fearing the outbreak of a civil war: a left that even accepted the art. 7 in the Constitution because it feared a religious war between Catholics and communists. Even at the end of World War I we could and should have been anti-systemic, but after the failure of the occupation of the factories due to conformist socialism, the right took advantage of this to march on Rome. Every missed opportunity is lost and not for a short time. The decade 1968-78 was also a lost opportunity, and since then there has never been a favorable moment like that again.

We certainly need to put an end to a consolidated practice, that of a state living on debt. We must stop giving so much importance to GDP: it is not a criterion that explains the well-being of the population. It is a purely quantitative criterion which mainly concerns private companies, which in order to restructure ask to be financed by citizens' taxes, on the pretext that, by closing, they could increase unemployment or decrease wealth.

When a country has 140-150% public debt of its GDP, it is taken for granted that it is no longer able to repay it, therefore it is a country close to bankruptcy, and cuts to the welfare state will not save it from this fate. Also because all it takes is for it to go to war and the public debt will skyrocket.

Those who govern are not at all concerned about these risks, for a series of reasons: both because they think that the GDP is too high to make the State go bankrupt; both because they cannot perceive the gravity of a public debt when they see it spread at a national level (i.e. they do not perceive it as a danger that concerns them personally or that directly concerns the territory from which they got the votes to be elected to parliament); both because they are convinced that Italians, in order not to see the State and their savings fail, will continue to buy government (or bank or postal) bonds; and because those who govern have the opportunity to export their capital abroad without having to undergo any controls.

Direct democracy means becoming responsible for the budgets of the community to which one belongs. Democracy can never be a political condition that is granted from above. If it is granted from above, without also being an achievement from below, it will certainly be a fictitious thing. A state that guarantees democracy automatically denies it. Democracy can only be guaranteed by itself. It can also be conquered with weapons, if necessary, but it cannot coincide with a national parliamentary representation similar to that of today, which is democratic only in name. The powers that a parliamentarian can have must be inversely proportional to the distance that separates him from the community that elected him, and the smaller the longer he has been away from that community.

We must create a new version of democratic socialism, a version that has nothing to do with the temptations of the bourgeoisie (liberal, globalist, social democratic, populist) nor with the limits of multipolarism, which has nothing socialistic about it, in the sense that it does not have a model of socialism to propose. Multipolarity means that everyone has the right to exist for who they are, without having to suffer impositions from others, but it does not affect the right to choose the model of social system that best conforms to the needs of democracy, human rights and environmental protection.

This means that we must totally, integrally rethink the criteria of productivity, well-being, consumption and also the exploitation, or rather the use of natural resources. Nature must be given the opportunity to reproduce, otherwise we will not escape the logic of looting, the practice of pollution. We must not be afraid to talk about "degrowth" if this term is seriously associated with socialism. Socialism does not mean "having nothing and being happy", it does not mean "socialism of poverty", it does not mean "nationalising or nationalizing everything", in such a way that no one is responsible for anything anymore. It means collective management of common resources, found first and foremost locally, in order to reduce dependence on markets to a minimum.

If this is true, it is clear that local territorial authorities acquire a strategic importance, far superior to that of the State and its central bodies.

Do we need to occupy the State to carry out this project? Yes, we need to, because the State will certainly hinder it with violence, being an instrument in the hands of the bourgeoisie, entrepreneurs, multinationals. And we must occupy it with a centralized direction of war operations, otherwise we will repeat the mistakes of the Spanish civil war, which failed due to the autonomist tendencies of anarchism and Trotskyism.

Do we perhaps need the State to defend ourselves, once we have occupied it, from the violent reaction of those who will not accept being put into oblivion? Yes, we will still need it, because without a centralized direction of anti-systemic defense, we would be easily defeated.

Will we still need the state when the counter-revolution has been defeated? No, we won't need it anymore. We will ensure that it is gradually dismantled. We cannot make the mistake of Stalinism again, when, under the pretext that Russia could be attacked at any moment by the capitalist states, it took advantage of this to eliminate every form of democracy and impose the dictatorship of the party and the centralist state, which made it rain from above the five-year plans (which everyone at the local level lied about when the set objectives were not achieved. Not only that but they let the companies fail, they knew that the State would assist them). State does not coincide with social, indeed the state instance, once the counter-revolution of the exploiters and those who want to make a living from income has been won, becomes the strongest enemy of the social instance.

February 23

Croce on Marx must be trashed

Sometimes it takes very little to understand whether a book is worth reading or not. Let's take for example. *Historical materialism and Marxist economics* by Benedetto Croce.

In the Preface he outlines the reasons why he liked Marx in his youth. Well, there isn't one that is true. If you understand this, you will also easily understand why Croce stopped harboring such sympathy rather quickly.

First of all, for him Marx was a simple Hegelian "much more concrete" than those who reduced Hegel to a Platonizing theologian or metaphysician. It was because he had given a lot of importance to the economy.

In reality, the European bourgeoisie (especially the English one) was full of theorists who gave importance to the economy, including the political one. At the beginning of the twentieth century, if anything, it was the provincial Italian intellectuals who didn't know it, with a few exceptions (Pareto, Mosca, Michels...). But this ignorance depended on the economic backwardness of our country.

Marx had started studying economics thanks to the French utopian socialists. But it was only in London that he was able to study a myriad of texts by bourgeois economists.

However, this interest in economic science means absolutely nothing. Hegel also knew some texts of classical political economy, but he did not draw the same conclusions from them as Marx.

You don't become more "concrete" by studying political economy or the history of economic doctrines. Marx had noticed that the liberal economists themselves often fell into mystical absurdities coming from Christian theology, even if taken in a secularized form (think for example of the providential "invisible hand", which in Smith resolves, almost magically, all the distortions of the market capitalist).

All of Marx's economic texts stand as one *criticism* of bourgeois or liberal political economy. And if you don't understand why, it is useless to consider Marx more "concrete" than Hegel.

In *Capital* Marx outlined in detail the laws of the functioning of capital, especially of *surplus value*, and the structural contradictions within the capitalist system, which cannot be resolved peacefully. Croce will never understand these laws, or, even if he understands them, he will reject them.

Croce will never say anything original compared to the classical economists of the Anglo-French bourgeoisie. He was provincial, even if he boasted of having read and appreciated Marx in his youth, following in the wake of his university teacher, Antonio Labriola.

Marx was not a "Hegelian", albeit a more "concrete" one. Despite having adhered to Hegel's use of the category of "necessity" (which Hegel had also taken from Spinoza), he believed that the political revolution of the industrial proletariat was also necessary. Something that Hegel would never have admitted, as for him all the contradictions of capitalism could be resolved without needing to overthrow the system: the mediation of the inter-class State was sufficient, *super parts*.

Marx had accepted the unscrupulous, revolutionary use of *dialectic* Hegelian, but to direct it against the Prussian state and states in general, when they defended the interests of the property-owning social classes, sworn enemies of the propertyless proletariat, only willing to exploit its workforce.

Marx's "concreteness" did not depend on his studies of political economy, but on the fact that he began to theorize an *alternative* to the capitalist system. If anything, he was not "concrete" enough when he avoided questioning the power of the bourgeoisie's techno-scientific and industrial revolution.

In his opinion, to best develop this production, it would have been sufficient to socialize its ownership. This was an error of perspective which today, in light of the ecological disasters of the environment, we are paying dearly for.

Capitalism cannot be contested only on the level of the socio-economic exploitation of the workforce, legitimized by an arbitrary private appropriation of the main means of production. But it must also be contested in and of itself, as a "social formation in general", as an "industrial way of producing", as a "form of civilisation" based on machinery.

The industry that replaces craftsmanship and self-production in agriculture was a need of the bourgeoisie: it does not necessarily need to be safeguarded. That is, it is not essential, in order to achieve socialism, that there is an industrial proletariat, master of the means of production. Even supposing we could achieve a complete replacement of the factory worker, making all production processes automatic, the question would always remain whether this is permissible from the point of view of nature's reproductive needs.

Socialism cannot be just state-managed capitalism, nor capital without wage labor. It does not necessarily have to be a society that, after eliminating the cumbersome presence of the State, uses industry to self-reproduce. This prevalence granted to industry over craftsmanship is up for debate, and whether it is managed directly by the State, or by a company that deprives itself of the State, does not make much difference.

Marx only laid the theoretical foundations for a definitive overcoming of the exploitation of propertyless labor. He understood that legal freedom does not in itself prevent a citizen from becoming a wage slave. But his idea of industrialized socialism is not necessarily the best solution to the problems of capitalism.

On this topic Croce is of no use. A few words of a Preface are enough to understand that the book is not worth reading. The other nonsense he wrote immediately after the aforementioned sentence about Marx's "concreteness" confirms this.

In fact, it is absolutely not true that Marx wanted to make the "new workers' society" a sort of "aristocracy". The working class had to emancipate itself to emancipate everyone else. If she, who owned nothing, could do it, why couldn't the peasants or the lower middle class, who suffered, albeit in other forms, the oppression of capital?

Marx criticizes bourgeois democracy because he considers it hypocritical, but he would never have dreamed of making the proletariat a new "aristocracy" above any other social class. If anything, it is the bourgeois unions that transform the metalworkers into a "worker aristocracy", snubbing the other categories of paid workers.

Marx simply limited himself to saying that, by emancipating itself from the bourgeoisie, the industrial proletariat would emancipate the entire population. Lenin would later add that in a backward country like Russia, the alliance of this proletariat with peasants without agricultural property was absolutely fundamental to winning the revolution.

If anything, one can ask why, in places where the industrial proletariat has come to power, it has not been able to eliminate the protection of the State. The "real socialism" of some countries was in reality a state socialism managed by intellectuals, who inevitably issued their directives from above. That is, what is the reason why a nationalization of the means of production is of no use in achieving truly democratic socialism?

Is the system perhaps made more democratic by behaving as the current Chinese do, who authorize the development of the bourgeoisie on a social level, without renouncing state control of the economy? Does the fact that there is a communist party in power make a society "communist"?

This too is all nonsense. A truly democratic socialism cannot bet its cards on the State, nor on the market, nor on industry. It shouldn't even be interested in a representative democracy at the national level. The very concept of "nation" no longer has any meaning. If the state is eliminated, the nation must necessarily be eliminated as well. If dependence on the national state is eliminated, it makes no sense to do so to affirm dependence on an industry managed at a supranational or suprastate level.

If a population wants to obtain greater sovereignty it must not only abolish the State, abolish the centralized management of representative democracy; it must also eliminate private management of the economy and finance, be it management conducted at a national or supranational level.

Any idea of a national state or a national people, but also of a supranational state (such as the European one), must be overcome. How any idea of an international market or supranational industrial production must be overcome.

From the point of view of democratic socialism, less bombastic concepts are sufficient. We need local communities that own the means of production, who alone decide how to relate to the surrounding nature. We are still very far from realizing this type of socialism.

A war against children had never been seen

According to Save The Children, "Israeli forces have killed and maimed children in the Gaza Strip at an unprecedented rate and scale."

It should be noted that approximately 12,400 children have died and thousands more remain missing.

Furthermore, 100 Palestinian children were killed in the West Bank.

On average, about 10 children a day in the Strip have lost one or both legs. Many of these amputations were performed without anesthesia.

On the other hand, all Palestinian children in the Gaza Strip "should be killed", declared Republican MP Andy Ogles, from the state of Tennessee, in response to a question from a pro-Palestinian activist about the atrocities that the Israeli army is committing in the Gaza Strip. 'enclave.

Faced with these things one can ask: who supports Israel in terms of food? According to the Israeli Ministry of Agriculture, the most important countries exporting agricultural products to Israel from October to today have been, in order of importance: Turkey, Jordan, the Netherlands, Italy and France. Egypt is completely absent. So who is supporting the war?

The UN does not seek the truth

The Office of the United Nations High Commissioner for Human Rights (OHCHR) said it had received information that Palestinian women and girls had been "arbitrarily executed in Gaza, often together with their family members, including their children, in places where they sought refuge or during their escape."

The UN report also raises the alarm over the arbitrary detention of hundreds of Palestinian women and girls, including human rights defenders, journalists and humanitarian workers in Gaza and the West Bank. Many were reportedly subjected to inhumane treatment, multiple forms of sexual violence, stripped naked, and searched by male Israeli officers. An unknown number of Palestinian women and girls have reportedly disappeared after coming into contact with the Israeli army in Gaza.

Faced with these very serious accusations, which would have required at least an investigation *super parts*, what did Israeli government spokesperson Eilon Levy respond to? These kinds of accusations are "disgusting"; the experts who wrote the report are unreliable, as they are moved not by a spirit of truth but by their hatred towards Israel and the Jewish people.

We just missed him concluding with the words: "Amen, peace be with you".

The showdown in Ramadan

If Hamas does not free the 130 hostages, Israel will bomb Rafah in the month of Ramadan, around March 10. 1.4 million Palestinians are at risk, who find themselves there as internal refugees. They no longer have anywhere else to run.

The threat of this inhuman catastrophe even came from Benny Gantz, Netanyahu's political opponent, as if the two wanted to show the world that they are united in view of an attack against which Western countries are already protesting.

There are no negotiations that can prevent this development of events. In Cairo everything is blocked. Israel justifies itself by saying that it cannot grant an autonomous state to terrorists, and in any case, before making any concession, Hamas must free the hostages.

Meanwhile, the Israeli minister of national security, Itamar Ben Gvir, one of the leaders of the far right, intends to place strong restrictions during Ramadan on access to the mosque esplanade in Jerusalem, a point of reference for Muslim Palestinians. A move rejected by the Palestinians of Israel, who, unlike the inhabitants of the occupied territories, have rights as citizens of the Jewish state.

There are only two scenarios in which the fighting could stop. The first is one in which Israel believes it has achieved its objectives and can claim victory, but this does not appear to be the case. The second is the one in which international pressures are finally felt, but this too is only a hope.

In recent days, Israel has also attacked the Nasser hospital in Khan Yunis, where it claims to have captured some Hamas fighters.

But these attacks against civilian structures occur first and foremost to terrorize the population and induce them to leave the Strip. That they are hiding terrorists is just a pretext.

Israel does not know what to make of the recommendations of the International Court of Justice, which ordered it to take all measures to avoid acts of genocide.

It is more concerned that because the military had to recall

300,000 reservists, its GDP fell 19.4% year-on-year in the fourth quarter. In the same period, private consumption fell by 27% on a quarterly basis, exports fell by 18%, while imports fell by 42%.

Furthermore, Palestinians can no longer go to work in the Jewish state, which is particularly affecting the construction sector.

If Israel is not supported by the US, its economic collapse will be inevitable.

Meanwhile, the G20 foreign ministers reached a unanimous agreement during the Rio de Janeiro summit: immediate opening of humanitarian access to Gaza leading to a ceasefire and support for the creation of a Palestinian state.

But, as we know, hell is paved with good intentions.

That damn depleted uranium

When the Bosnian Serb leader Milorad Dodik met Putin in Kazan in recent days, he reiterated to him that the Republika Sprska (the Serb-majority entity in Bosnia-Herzegovina of which he himself is president), not only remains opposed to sanctions on Russia and a possible membership of NATO, but also pointed out to him that Serbia is still suffering today from the depleted uranium bombings carried out by NATO in 1999, during the Kosovo war.

After a quarter of a century, still "a large number of young people, even newborns, suffer from the consequences of depleted uranium, with the level of radioactive contamination increased in the region by up to ten times," Dodik told Putin.

Has anyone condemned NATO for the use of these anti-human and anti-natural projectiles? Nobody.

February 24

Two countries clearly in favor of Nazism

The UN Third Commission approved a resolution banning the glorification of Nazism with 125 votes in favor, 53 abstentions and the United States and Ukraine voting against.

The latter two countries once again reject the project which is put to the vote every year and which aims to combat any form of Nazism, neo-Nazism, racial discrimination or xenophobia.

The document recommends that countries take concrete measures in the legislative, educational, human rights and other fields to eliminate racial discrimination and avoid revising the history of the Second World War.

The authors of the resolution firmly condemn the glorification of Nazism, in particular with writings and insults to the monuments dedicated to the victims of World War II.

The resolution also warns against the spread of racism, discrimination, hatred and violence based on race, religion, nationality, gender, membership of a particular group or political opinions, in schools.

Once put to the vote with the following title: "Fighting the glorification of Nazism, neo-Nazism and other practices that contribute to fueling contemporary forms of racism, racial discrimination, xenophobia and related intolerance" saw the following results in the commission, pending to be voted on at the General Assembly next month.

121 Yes to the motion:
Algeria, Angola, Antigua-Barbuda, Saudi Arabia, Argentina, Armenia, Azerbaijan, Bahamas, Bahrain, Bangladesh, Barbados, Belize, Bhutan, Belarus, Bolivia, Bosnia-Herzegovina, Botswana, Brazil, Brunei, Burkina Faso, Cambodia, Cameroon, Cape Verde, Chile, China, Colombia, Comoros, Congo, Ivory Coast, Costa Rica, Cuba, Ecuador, Egypt, El Salvador, United Arab Emirates, Eritrea, Eswatini, Ethiopia, Fiji, Philippines, Gabon, Ghana, Jamaica, Djibouti, Jordan, Grenada, Guatemala, Guinea, Equatorial Guinea, Guyana, Haiti, Honduras, India, Indonesia, Iraq, Israel, Kazakhstan, Kenya, Kyrgyzstan, Kuwait, Laos, Lesotho, Lebanon, Libya, Madagascar, Malawi, Maldives, Malaysia , Mali, Morocco, Mauritania, Mauritius, Mexico, Mongolia, Mozambique, Myanmar, Namibia, Nauru, Nepal, Nicaragua, Niger, Nigeria, Oman, Pakistan, Panama, Paraguay, Peru, Qatar, Central African Republic, Democratic Republic of Korea, Republic Dominican, Russia, Rwanda, Saints Kitts and Newis, Saint Lucia, Senegal, Serbia, Sierra Leone, Singapore, Syria, Somalia, Sri Lanka, South Africa, Sudan, Suriname, Tajikistan, Tanzania, Thailand, East Timor, Togo, Trinidad and Tobago , Tunisia, Turkmenistan, Uganda, Uruguay, Uzbekistan, Venezuela, Vietnam, Yemen, Zambia, Zimbabwe.

2 No: United States, Ukraine

53 Abstentions: Afghanistan, Albania, Andorra, Australia, Austria, Belgium, Bulgaria, Canada, Cyprus, South Korea, Croatia, Denmark, Estonia, Finland, France, Georgia, Germany, Japan, Greece, Kiribati, Ireland, Iceland, Solomon Islands, Italy, Latvia, Liechtenstein, Lithuania, Luxembourg, North Macedonia, Malta, Moldova, Monaco, Montenegro,

Norway, New Zealand, Netherlands, Palau, Papua New Guinea, Poland, Portugal, United Kingdom, Czech Republic, Romania, Samoa, San Marino, Slovakia, Slovenia, Spain, Sweden, Switzerland, Tonga, Turkey, Hungary.

It is likely that many abstained because the motion was presented by Russia. In any case, when faced with such a topic, abstaining is equivalent to being against it.

An alternative to everything

Where there is talk of the primacy of *use value* on that of exchange, we must necessarily speak of the primacy of *barter* about money.

This also means eliminating international markets (or greatly reducing their importance), to the benefit of *self-management* local or regional, which includes the *cooperation of self-managed businesses*.

The foundations of capitalism are broken. The very idea of "exploitation" of natural resources must be rethought, since these resources must be given all the time necessary to reproduce.

The question of the machinery remains pending. What to do with industry when, to respect the reproductive needs of nature, we should be very careful not to waste anything and above all not to pollute anything? Nature should be left as it is, or in any case, if a landscape is modified, it must then be given time to reconstitute itself.

It is inevitable that at a certain point we realize that industrialization makes no sense. Or we can go so far as to say: the mass production of certain goods makes sense only to the extent that it does not become the goal of production. In fact, if it becomes one, the real aim, in reality, is another: to accumulate capital in an indefinite (or in any case abnormal) manner.

In this way we return to the fundamental limit of capital, which continually needs to valorise itself through the market, otherwise it fails, implodes, succumbs to the competition of others. Capitalism means individualism, which remains so even when monopolies are formed.

However, even if industrialization must be completely rethought, any idea of socialism, which limits itself to managing state intervention in the economy or to socializing the ownership of the fundamental means of production, is an idea incapable of laying the foundations for a true alternative to capitalism.

The future of humanity will need neither capitalism (private or state) nor state socialism, nor even industrialized socialism. We will only need one *self-managed socialism*, without the cumbersome presence of the two entities that cause dependence: State and Market.

Production will be managed by *local communities*, who will use local resources, and who will practice barter as a form of exchange for the surplus goods they produce.

The theories of scientific socialism will have to be rectified a lot, while all those in favor of capitalism will have to be completely removed. Theories of utopian socialism based on mechanization will also be of no use. Not to mention those theories of self-managed socialism that think they can create happy islands within dominant systems favorable only to the primacy of the State and the Market. Before we can talk about "self-management" or "self-consumption", the system must be overthrown.

The final objective is to understand that we will only be freer if we increase the management autonomy of our natural resources, duly socialized.

February 25

Our relationship with nature

Nature's fundamental resources should never be privatized. When air, water, forests, solar energy, etc. make entire communities live, not only does it make no sense to privatize them but it doesn't even make sense to pollute them.

Natural energy sources, on which human life depends, must never be prevented from reproducing in the times that nature requires and which certainly do not depend on our will. Nature has its reproduction times: if we do not respect them, not only it loses out, but also us, since we are beings or entities of nature. That is, even if we can consider nature as a means at our disposal, in fact nature is made up of its own laws, which we must know and respect.

If for example a human being is born after nine months of gestation, it is nature that imposes it on us. If we prevent him from being born, by procuring an artificial abortion, we are making an act against nature (short of any social motivations that may exist). Which doesn't mean that nature doesn't know about miscarriage. Indeed, faced with such a decision of nature, we should ask ourselves why. It cannot be ruled out that nature prevents us from reproducing because it perceives us as enemies. We are not its enemies when, after nine months of gestation, it seems better to induce birth in some way.

But, apart from these particular cases, it must be admitted that, left to itself, nature is infallible, or in any case much more perfect than us, since it preserves the memory of processes that took millions of years to stabilize. We too, as time goes by, through trial and error, create increasingly perfect (performing) artificial means. But this does not mean that they are more compatible with the needs of nature.

The problem is that we don't know how to leave nature to itself. For example, it would be inconceivable for us not to work the land to allow it to regenerate from the production stress we impose on it. If farmers protest in the face of this environmental request from the EU, they must be understood, also because competition from multinationals is killing them. But this does not mean that, in the abstract, the request is not right.

That is, in order not to prevent nature from living an autonomous life, we should reduce to a minimum the artificial tools with which we use it, or at least we should ensure that these tools do not have such a strong impact that they cannot be absorbed in a reasonable time. Every time we use an artificial medium, we should ask ourselves: will someone after us use it? Can he do it in the same way? If he does it differently, will it be a problem for nature? If he doesn't use it in any way, how long will it take for nature to completely reabsorb it?

It makes no sense for someone to leave this planet forever, leaving future generations with the problems caused by the means they used. These irresponsible attitudes must be prevented in the bud, otherwise, when added together, they eventually become unmanageable, creating unsolvable problems.

We cannot always hope that nature will ward off the effects of our madness. That doesn't mean it has the strength to do it. Above all, it is not certain that we will be able to do it while we are still alive. In fact, it is probable that nature will take back what belongs to it when we no longer exist. We are amazed that entire populations, disappearing from the face of the Earth, have left nothing of themselves. Instead we should rejoice about it. It's a sign that they were perfectly done *naturally*.

If nature is "living", it is impossible for it not to look at us with great concern when we go looking for energy sources in the depths of its bowels, or when we disfigure the environment or modify the integrated processes (osmotic, symbiotic, holistic) that maintain into life, according to a certain frequency and regularity, natural phenomena.

However, there is no doubt that we have caused the greatest problems for nature since the birth of slave civilizations, which, where they could, have been responsible for the desertification of a large part of the planet, to achieve which it was sufficient to eliminate the forests.

Today we are responsible for the (especially chemical) pollution of the planet, that is, not only do we continue to deforest it, but we fill it with non-recyclable, non-reusable, non-absorbable waste. For about 6000 years we have not only been creating deserts, destined to last much longer than our single existence, but we have also been producing waste that will last even longer than our deserts. Let's just think about nuclear waste, electric car batteries, electronic components, etc. If we no longer existed, perhaps nature would be able to recover our deserts. But how long would it take for it to reabsorb our artificial means?

We complain that energy resources are limited. It's actually our luck. If anything, the problem is that, faced with this limit, we are not led to rethink our lifestyle, but, rather, to conserve it, looking for new energy sources, even more dangerous than the previous ones, even more impactful on natural processes. Now we no longer know how to distinguish the natural from the artificial: everything seems natural to us because everything is artificial. This is called "cognitive distortion".

We use natural resources as if they were unlimited, and when we realize that they are not, we kill each other, at least until we find a way to replace them with others that we believe are equally unlimited. Neither history nor nature teaches us anything useful. It seems that not even when faced with the risk of our extinction we can accept the idea of radically changing our lifestyle.

We modify the tools with which to live life, but always within a fundamentally violent framework, towards ourselves and our relationships with nature. We are no longer able to recover a natural lifestyle, prior to the birth of slavery.

February 26

It's not just a problem of quantity

James O'Connor is considered a great eco-Marxist, but sometimes I don't understand him. Let's take for example. this sentence of his: "there would be (almost) no environmental problem if the bodies from which natural resources are extracted and the receiving environmental bodies had no dimension *limited*" (cfr *Capitalismo, Natura, Socialismo*, ed. Jaca Book, Milano 2006).

Due to these limits, the production of human goods depletes reserves of natural resources and worsens the quality of the environment, since our waste takes its toll.

This is wrong reasoning. It is as if he were saying: unfortunately we live on only one planet, but in the future, when we have colonized other planets, we will have solved all our problems (those inherent both to the procurement of energy resources and to the placement of the most harmful waste).

With such a setting of things, it seems that the solution to the problem is only one type *quantity*, when instead it is of type *qualitative*.

That is, our planet is not only the structural (objective) limit within which we can move and which we cannot ignore, but it is also a "test bed". It is a kind of laboratory in which to test all the experiments that make a life worth living possible, compatible with human and natural needs.

When we are ready to colonize other planets, we will have to do it with full knowledge of the facts, knowing exactly what is necessary to reproduce to live at our best. We will need to know first. It makes no sense to colonize the universe by repeating the same mistakes made on Earth. We cannot waste the time we have: we don't just need it to test the worst of us, but also the best, precisely so as not to repeat mistakes already made.

In this respect we are not yet ready to settle on other planets, precisely because we cannot guarantee the survival of our own. Indeed, if we were already able to colonize the cosmos, we would certainly worsen our lifestyle on Earth, as we would have the illusion of being able to obtain unlimited energy resources, with equally unlimited possibilities of long or very long-lasting waste storage.

Today we are carrying out explorations in cosmic space that serve no purpose other than to procrastinate over time the failure to resolve our most absurd contradictions. In fact we are trying to export the worst of us, so much so that our experience in cosmic space cannot be considered simply scientific. The satellites we are using do not only have a meteorological or communication function, but also a military and espionage one. And there are already so many of them that we have transformed the space around the planet into a real landfill, a harbinger of risks and dangers for our orbiting stations, spacecraft, robotic probes, artificial satellites... The wars we will wage in the future will probably resemble those that we see in science fiction films.

If we have to spread the limits of capitalism (private or state) or those of socialism (market or planned from above) throughout the universe, it is better to end up like the dinosaurs, it is better for a natural cataclysm to take us back to the Stone Age, living in caves, when we certainly weren't doing any harm to nature.

By this, of course, I do not mean that we will be able to colonize other planets only when we stop misusing our free will. Freedom of conscience is a human characteristic, which no one can take away from us. However, we will have to be fully aware of what favors the use of this freedom and what instead hinders it in a dangerous way.

In fact, one thing is the contradictions for which it is necessary to find a mediation, the key to the problem. Another, very different, are social antagonisms, those that prevent us from finding practicable, definitive solutions to our problems of identity, of normal liveability.

What of our science and technology is not useful to make us more human and natural, we must throw away without many scruples. If we turn to look at Sodom, with a nostalgic attitude, we will transform into a horrible pillar of salt. It makes no sense to think that one day our technology will be useful to us. There are problems that cannot be solved by any technical means, not now or ever. We cannot have a mystical or magical attitude towards technology, also because we developed it by hating religion.

If "surplus value" means "exploitation" of labor power, the problem cannot be solved by replacing human labor power with that of machines (the automatism of robots). This is because exploitation will also exist in the construction of robotics itself. Everything artificial that exists is produced by human beings, even when there are machines that build other machines.

Our first real problem is to establish what is human and natural and what is not. We must do this regardless of the type of technology we use. Today we do not have this awareness not because of technology itself, but because we live in highly conflictual human relationships.

The technology we use is inevitably a product of such relationships; and the fact that it is unable to resolve in the slightest the inhuman antagonism that characterizes us (and which is also reflected in our relationships with nature) demonstrates that today's technology has fundamental, absolutely insurmountable limits.

All this discussion must not lead us to think that the criterion for establishing the human and the natural can only be given to us by our earthly condition. It is in fact evident that, when we live in an extraterrestrial condition, the parameters will change, just as those of the newborn compared to the maternal fetus. However, it is equally clear that if on this Earth we are unable to respect the conditions we are given to live in, we will not be able to offer any guarantee that we will succeed in another existential dimension.

Human beings cannot be "eliminated" (this is just an illusion we have on Earth). Whether we like it or not we are eternal. There is no superhuman entity that can establish which people have the right to populate the universe and which do not. Myths such as the universal flood or the destruction of "sinful" cities such as Sodom and Gomorrah are only symbolic operations of the human mind, which feels limited in the face of certain macroscopic problems. But to populate the universe we need something else.

Anyone who is not able to offer guarantees of substantial, authentic correctness, experience or expressibility of the human and natural dimension will risk living a marginalized life in the universe. The so-called "greats of the Earth", those who have held top roles on our planet, will probably be the least suitable to populate the universe, to establish rules of conduct.

February 27

Resources and population

The question that as the population increases, natural resources decrease, so it is easy to expect wars, I have never understood it well. In fact, it should be the opposite: the more people are willing to work, the more resources increase, precisely because human beings are able to transform them.

Or we should say that with the technological means we have today, we are able to easily satisfy everyone's needs. If this does not happen, it is only because we keep work separate from property.

If anything, the discussion should focus on other topics. One concerns the excessive use of chemical agents with which the land is exploited. These fertilizers not only impoverish the yield of the land in the long run, that is, by dint of "drugging" them they become impoverished, but they are also a problem for human and animal health.

Lately we have come to produce partially or completely artificial foods, capable of growing at any time of the year and in any conditions. In the not too distant future we will certainly suffer physical consequences.

How long has it been known that the excessive use of cereals is related to the increase in dental cavities? How many pathologies does the excessive use of sugars create? And what about meat? Nowadays we should say that we do not "eat" something, but we "poison" ourselves with something.

If biochemical products are used that modify the genetic structure of foods, how long will it take to return to a normal situation? The excessive use of chemicals is likely to make the fate of agricultural land's death irreversible. We do not desert them only because of deforestation, but also because of the type of production we practice, which no longer has anything natural about it.

This shows that producing food for market needs is a contradiction. A market cannot decide the reproductive needs of a population. It makes no sense for people to eat more than they should, just to satisfy the mania of accumulating capital. The spontaneity of action is lost.

A population should decide for itself what it needs, based on e.g. demographic growth or changing needs. It should independently find the resources with which to feed itself. And it should go to the markets to exchange the surplus or to buy what it cannot produce and which it considers important to have.

What is certain is that if someone goes to the market because only there can they find something absolutely necessary for their survival, they end up immediately losing their autonomy. He becomes dependent on an external factor, which he obviously cannot control. He acts like a drug addict.

From this point of view it must be admitted that it is above all urbanized people who need to obtain supplies from a market. Those who live in the countryside are more free to practice *self-consumption*.

Today we have reached the point that capitalism has turned the entire world into an open-air absurdity, like the prison in Gaza. Billions of people are concentrated in a few cities, while billions of hectares of land are cultivated by a few people who have large machinery and many chemicals at their disposal. Then it becomes inevitable to tell ourselves that there are not enough resources to satisfy everyone's needs.

Rebalancing things means not only returning to the land, but also doing so on the basis of methods not aimed at production for the market. It is not the market that satisfies human needs first and foremost. First of all, the market satisfies the needs of entrepreneurs, whether public or private.

The market is there to make money and to keep buyers in a state of perpetual subjection. There is an economic, financial and even political use of the market. And these are not *human* uses.

February 28

Human and natural capitalism

Thinking of making capitalism acceptable or better just because you want to be more careful about environmental problems is simply illusory. And not because it is not right to do so, but because it is clear that in capitalism there are such aggressive forces that will also turn ecology into another business.

Whether it is right to be interested in ecology does not depend on the goodwill or sensitivity of some government or political party, but is precisely a necessity caused by the objective disasters that capitalism causes for the environment and the lives of human beings.

They are disasters evident to all, which capitalism thinks it can resolve without questioning the type of industrialization that supports it. That is, not only does one tolerate the *surplus value* (which is the structural need for capital to exploit the work of others in order to reproduce itself), but it is also taken for granted that machinery can only be modified in some of its formal aspects, not in its substance. Let's just think about the ridiculous meaning of the word "hybrid" when referring to our cars.

Undoubtedly capitalism was not born together with machinery. In Italy we have been "capitalists" ever since the bourgeois municipalities were born. Industrial capitalism is the penultimate manifestation of capital. The first is the commercial one; then came manufacturing, which, in turn, became industrial. The last manifestation is the financial one, the worst of all, since with a lot *nonchalance* it does not look at anything or anyone, even though it wants to make people believe that it does not carry out any violence towards the workforce.

In reality, no financialisation of the economy could exist in Western countries of advanced capitalism if there did not exist, in other parts of the planet, an economic exploitation of labor power, for which Western capitalism is largely responsible.

We Westerners want to live on income, investing our money in real estate, in usurious loans, in stock market speculation and in other financial devices (typical of the tertiaryization of the economy), which give the impression of making us earn quite well with minimal effort.

The work of others as a source of wealth is no longer our only dogma. The other dogma is: money makes money. That is, we need to learn to make them profit without committing to setting up a real industry, based on machines. The latter has become a low-level need, which makes sense to satisfy in a backward country, where the cost of labor is minimal and where all the other classic conditions exist to make an investment in machinery very profitable.

The West always needs wage slaves, but since in advanced countries workers are unionized and therefore more expensive, it prefers to export the exploitation of labor abroad to more backward countries, where there is no talk of "environmentalism".

The countries of the global South (as they are defined today) can continue to be exploited in a classic way, as cheap labor, as cheap raw materials, as unlocking markets for our goods, as landfills for our waste, as centers of debt international, which allows us to benefit from interest on credit, etc.

Until the global South emancipates itself, capitalism may appear acceptable in the West. It is evident, in fact, that the less the global South intends to be exploited, the more life in the West will become unlivable, in the sense that it will become impossible for capital to guarantee certain consolidated standards of well-being. Someone has to lose out. And since people, accustomed to consumerism, do not accept becoming impoverished (at least not to a certain level), governments will necessarily have to become more authoritarian. And when they become authoritarian, all ecological or environmental discourses disappear, or are imposed by force, exploiting them as a new profit opportunity for those who produce certain goods (for example electric car engines, replacing fossil combustion ones; condensing boilers in homes; photovoltaic or wind systems in buildings, air conditioners and so on).

Ecology is a luxury of advanced capitalism, which can become a misfortune for those who cannot afford it.

February 29

Let us have no illusions about ecology

One of the main deceptions of modern ecology is to make people believe that electricals are less polluting than fossil fuel.

We limit ourselves to looking at the exhaust pipes of cars or the chimneys of factories or the chimneys of houses. We look at the effects visible to the naked eye, not the causes that generate them. And we don't realize that solar panels and electric batteries are highly polluting, not only because they are produced with materials that are not so easily found in nature, but also because they are not recyclable or reusable. They are not as dangerous as nuclear waste, but almost. And in any case, when they work, they last much less than a nuclear power plant.

In capitalism there is nothing that is not polluting or poisonous. Toxicity is a characteristic of the industry itself, regardless of how it works. The only non-polluting one was the lithic one of primitive man. Even forestry could be dangerous if the forest was not allowed to self-regenerate.

The mere fact of producing objects in series, which have a limited lifespan and which, in order to be sold, need to be promoted, is a harmful attitude. The market only partially satisfies real needs; for the most part, in fact, it must create them. The goods first of all satisfy profit needs, therefore they inevitably pollute. Indeed, it even alienates, deforms the mind, makes it other-directed, dependent on external entities, which the markets are unable to control, since in the markets there is no equivalence between producer and consumer. It is the producers who command the markets.

Consumers, who cannot even benefit from the constitutional right to self-produce their own food, can only defend themselves from abuse, scams and continuous deception. At most, competition is between producers, but the larger one tends to swallow up the smaller one and become more or less a monopolist. Today the large monopolies have the entire planet as a market in which to sell their products. For them the concept of "nation" is ridiculous. Their "religious temple" is the hypermarket.

Consumers will never have equivalent power to defend themselves internationally. Consumers, at most, can defend themselves on a national level. They can nationalize their resources. They can stop multinationals from plundering their countries. But, in order to do so, these consumers must transform themselves into subversive citizens, politically committed to fighting the state of subjugation in which they live. They must transform themselves into guerrillas willing to carry out political revolutions. Only in this way can the power of monopolies protected by the States be overcome.

And if they manage to defeat the states and monopolies, they have only taken the first step. The second is in fact much more challenging: finding an alternative not only to capitalism, but also to a certain way of conceiving industry.

Today the global South needs the industry with which to produce weapons to defend itself from those who want to dominate it. But it must be careful not to have an exploitative attitude towards its natural resources, otherwise emancipating itself is useless.

The industry must serve to defend itself from external enemies, who want to deprive an entire country of its autonomy. But it cannot be used to attack nature. Citizens must seek an alternative way of life to the one imposed by capitalism.

Unfortunately, countries that want to free themselves from the weight of capitalism can only do so by using its own industrial means, which are largely harmful to nature. They must use great foresight, great far-sightedness, since they must lay the foundations for future generations. Living in wartime is one thing: paradoxically it is easier, as we tend to use only two colours, black and white. Living in times of peace is something completely different: here it is nature that must dictate the laws of self-government of human beings.

That is, on this planet, when human beings were born, the natural resources with which to live and reproduce were within reach. There was no need for a particular industry to use these resources: even when the craftsman built terracotta containers, the mud was found on the earth's surface. All that was needed were the hands, the manual work, individual and collective, and the artisanal skill that was acquired through trial and error.

Water, fire, wood, stone, bamboo canes etc. they were enough. There was no need to dig deep or drill into mountains or divert river courses or create artificial lakes. Being "natural" meant making the laws of nature one's criterion of life. It was sufficient to become aware of these laws, act on them, taking care not to overturn them, not to modify them in an irrecoverable, irreversible way. The deserts already widely present on our planet are the most striking demonstration of our inadequacy.

If we turn the entire planet into a desert, we will not be able to populate the universe. We won't be able to do this even if we had many more powers to transform matter. In fact, the real problem is that we wouldn't have the right mentality to do it, the correct predisposition.

On this planet we must learn to live with the means that nature makes available to us. Only in this way will we be able to live in another dimension with other means and in other ways.

Throwing stones

On Facebook, Biden is often portrayed as a dotard. But the American Secretary of Defense, Lloyd Austin, is not far behind. On February 29, he declared that if Ukraine is defeated, NATO troops will fight against Russia.

In reality, Ukraine is already defeated: it just needs to take note of it and accept the conditions that Russia wants to impose on it. If it surrendered immediately, it could come to negotiations. Now, however, it has before it, as the only possibility to survive, unconditional surrender. Otherwise it will disappear from the maps, especially after the Russians have occupied Odessa to unite Donbass with Transnistria.

If NATO declares war on Russia, nuclear war will be inevitable. But this will mean that the EU will return to the Stone Age and the USA will suffer colossal damage, *with great joy* from China, which will eat Taiwan in one bite, which will push Japan down, which will occupy the entire Pacific, and so on.

Even Biden's idea of using frozen Russian assets to finance Ukraine's budget and restore the country is an idea not against Russia but against Europe. In fact, Moscow would certainly carry out 360-degree retaliation. Anyone who lives in a glass house cannot throw stones.

It is better to leave the EU

In a resolution on EU defense and security policy approved on 28 February, the EU Parliament – with the PD voting in favor – condemned "the Israeli army's disproportionate response" taking place in the Gaza Strip and called for a "permanent ceasefire to be able to provide aid to civilians in the Strip." It didn't talk about genocide. Indeed it supported "Israel's right to defend itself".

In particular, however, it tied the truce to the release of all the hostages and the dismantling of Hamas.

Then the same parliament voted for total war on Russia, up to the reconquest of Crimea, with maximum spending on weapons, as Lady Genocide Ursula von der Leyen wants.

March

March 1th

Environmental problems and world markets

Is it possible to solve the planet's environmental problems in the presence of international markets? No, it's not possible. It makes no sense to buy products that come from countries very far from those in which they are consumed. Their transportation is an incredible source of pollution. Not to mention the fact that food products can be devoid of significant nutritional values because they are harvested unripe, or even toxic because they are chemically treated without the consumer's knowledge, for their preservation or storage. Today, with biochemistry, there are food products with a modified genetic structure. Many of these products are checked by those who purchase them only by sampling, randomly choosing the container that transports them. And so on.

World markets serve primarily multinationals. The end user needs it only because he has been deprived, in advance, of the possibility of being self-sufficient, that is, of self-producing what he substantially needs to live with.

Environmental disasters are not only those of oil tankers which, from time to time, due to particular accidents, spill their goods into the sea (in Italy we remember the two serious accidents to oil tankers off the coast of Genoa and Livorno). The most serious disasters are those that are not talked about, because they are everyday, but which produce monstrous effects, such as for example. the seven islands of plastic floating in the oceans (only the Great Pacific Garbage Patch is larger than France[3]).

But there are disasters caused by the use of fuel for navigation. The largest cruise ship in the world, the Icon of the Seas, recently left Miami, five times larger than the Titanic, 365 meters long (more than three football fields lined up), has 20 decks, 250,800 tons of gross tonnage and can carry 7,600 passengers, plus 2,350 crew; it consumes 10 tons of fuel

---

3 To tell the truth, it is estimated that its extension varies between 700,000 km^2 and up to more than 10 million km^2, i.e. from an area larger than the Iberian Peninsula to an area larger than the United States: it increases 10 times every decade starting in 1945. Over 90% of its mass is made up of objects that have not yet fragmented into microplastics.

every hour, that is, it pollutes like a million cars. Then they ask us to scrap the old car, forcing us, even if it works perfectly, to buy a new, more "ecological" one.

The fish products we eat are all polluted by international trade. Poisons do not have an immediate effect on us only because, like Mithridates, we take the poison in small doses. But if we add it to all those found in other foods, the final result is obvious. Also because, before we become intoxicated with the products of international markets, we are already intoxicated where we live, due to the use of hydrocarbons. It is not only our digestive system that breaks down, but also our respiratory system. And both, inevitably, influence the reproductive one.

We are destined for extinction, since we are essentially self-destructive. But, what is worse, we Westerners, with our frenzied capitalism, make all the inhabitants of the planet sick, including those who have worked for us and produced goods for our markets, and who have not had the same well-being as us.

We are the scourge of humanity, also because we force everyone to imitate us, pushing the countries of the world to compete with each other, to produce more and more goods at ever lower costs, until someone, unable to keep up, allows themselves to be enslaved or deludes themselves of being able to survive by declaring war on some competitor. Even our farmers are forced to resort to the poisons of the world if they want to compete with multinational competition.

We have been living on international trade for a thousand years, that is, since the end of the High Middle Ages, which was, moreover, a parenthesis after the great global trade of the great slave civilizations, which desertified a large part of the planet with their deforestation.

Where do we want to go? What is the maximum endurance limit of our planet? Haven't we already surpassed it by far? What kind of alternative should we look for? If we leave it to the pseudo-enlightened minds of profit, there is only one solution: greatly reduce the earth's population, either with wars or with pandemics.

March 2

The rights of nature

In *Capital* Marx wrote that human societies are not "owners" of the Earth, but only "usufructuaries", and have the duty to pass it on, improved, to subsequent generations. He said this because he had foreseen a capitalist degradation of the land.

But in his time there was certainly not the pollution of today. Therefore he could easily cultivate the cult of machinery, limiting himself to demanding the socialization of ownership of the means of production.

Today, however, we are convinced that even this socialization cannot solve environmental problems. It is industrialization itself that needs to be rethought, and unfortunately we don't know how to do it, also because we do not agree to pit the rights of nature against those of labor, and industry is very happy with this position of ours, so it can extort from work as much added value as possible.

We live in a completely artificial world, submerged in mountains of waste, where everything is potentially carcinogenic. Our civilization is essentially based on hydrocarbons and plastic (and the latter is simply a synthesis of oil and chemistry).

We have understood that replacing fossil fuels with nuclear power is too dangerous, as accidents last too long and we don't know where to put the waste. We therefore desperately try to opt for electrical, but with results that leave a lot to be desired. In fact, electrical seems to be too expensive, since it depends on "rare earths", then it is not as safe and above all not as ecological as they want us to believe. Battery disposal will remain a major problem.

As for plastic, replacing it with biodegradable elements is easier said than done. Just enter any supermarket to realize that packaging is a mortal enemy of humanity.

On the other hand, they have accustomed us to comfort, to waste, to the illusion of believing that well-being means being able to choose a product from a thousand different brands. The idea of a few dispensers replacing dozens of plastic packages for many products is still very remote. If we do separate waste collection at home, the plastic bin fills up at the same speed as the organic one. We can't even accept the idea (which once existed) of returning the glass vacuum to purchase a new product. Absurdly we go to throw glass in perfect condition into the relevant recycling bins.

We are convinced, rather naively, that we can solve the plastic problem by placing the waste in the appropriate public containers, which will then be emptied at an incinerator or waste-to-energy plant or waste recycler. We delude ourselves that the problem is solved downstream, at the time of disposal, and we are not concerned that it is especially so upstream, at the time of packaging.

Around 80% of what we buy in the EU is packaged in paper (41%) or plastic (19-20%) or glass (19%) containers. Glass and aluminum are reserved for what you drink, with the exception of water, which is strictly bottled in plastic containers, which inevitably makes it unhealthy from all points of view.

Contrary to what you might think, paper packaging for food and drinks is poorly recyclable, as it is made of composite materials. Paradoxically it is easier to recycle plastic.

Not only that, but paper packaging contains substances that are harmful to the health of consumers. And all this without considering that every year 3 billion trees are cut down around the world to produce paper-based packaging. The paper industry is the third largest consumer of water in the world (e.g. the production of a single sheet of A4 paper requires approximately 10 liters of water). The paper industry is also the world's fifth largest energy consumer. Large quantities of water and energy are needed to recycle paper and make it suitable for creating new packaging products.

From time to time we should go to an ecological station, where our most significant waste (televisions, household appliances, computers, furniture...) is collected in special, large containers. Well, in that moment we realize very easily how absurd our way of life is. We tend to throw away what still works or what in theory could be repaired, simply because progress forces us to do so.

Even when you buy a new car, you can benefit from scrapping incentives only if the old one is completely destroyed, even if it is in perfect working order. Which suggests that the approach we have towards ecology is not practical but ideological. In the context of capitalism, ecology is also in the hands of the strong powers, who decide for us what is good or bad, that is, more or less convenient for them.

We are unable to make ecology a value higher than that of the economy. Selling is more important than saving, reusing, recycling, repairing etc. On the other hand, the first country in the world that put the rights of nature in its Constitution was Ecuador in 2008.

We still fail to understand that the true value of a material good should not lie in its market price (the more widespread it is, the less it costs), but in the raw materials it is made of, i.e. the higher the less we have used it. Because this is what nature asks of us.

Not to mention the fact that the use value of a product should be infinitely more important than its exchange value. We Westerners have imposed exchange value (decided on the markets) as an economic parameter throughout the world. The weaker countries must produce only what we need. Wars are only an infernal consequence of this unnatural mechanism.

Articles on nature in the Constitution of Ecuador

Art. 71. Nature, or Pachamama, where life reproduces and occurs, has the right to integral respect for its existence and to the maintenance and regeneration of its life cycles, its structures, its functions and its evolutionary processes .

Every person, community, people or nationality will be able to demand from public authorities the observance of the rights of nature. To apply and interpret these rights, the principles established by the Constitution will be observed, according to the circumstances.

The State will encourage natural and legal persons, as well as communities, to protect nature, and will promote respect for all the elements that form an ecosystem.

Art. 72. Nature has the right to restoration interventions. Such interventions will be independent of the obligation of the State and natural and legal persons to compensate individuals and communities that depend on the damaged natural systems.

In cases of serious or permanent environmental impacts, including those resulting from the exploitation of non-renewable natural resources, the State will establish the most effective mechanisms for remediation and take appropriate measures to mitigate or eliminate harmful environmental consequences.

Art. 73. The State will adopt precautionary and restrictive measures for activities that may lead to the extinction of species, the destruction of ecosystems or the permanent alteration of natural cycles. The introduction of organisms and organic and inorganic material that could permanently alter the national genetic heritage is prohibited.

Art. 74. Persons, peoples, communities and nationalities will have the right to enjoy the environment and natural riches that make good living possible. Environmental services will not be susceptible to appropriation; their production, supply, use and enjoyment will be regulated by the State.

March 3

There's still a long way to go

When private capitalism forcefully imposed itself in Western Europe (let's say with the second industrial revolution and therefore with the birth of imperialism, especially of the Anglo-French brand), the theorists of socialism (utopian and scientific) immediately understood the great defects of this system, even if they were dazzled by the great progress of machinery, which was going to definitively upset the last traces of late-feudal or pre-capitalist modes of production.

Capitalism was criticized for the violence with which it imposed itself, for the clear subordination of wage labor to the private ownership of the means of production, for the irreversible overcoming of use value orchestrated by exchange value, for the imposition of markets and currencies international, for the colonial subjugation of many non-European countries, which could not boast a force of the same level.

The antagonistic contradictions of capital were very clear, but it was thought, very naively, that it would be enough to send the proletariat to power and socialize ownership of the means of production to make machinery something we could count on with confidence. They wanted to extend the benefits of industrialization to the entire community.

Today we must note that things have gone very differently, not only because in the West the bourgeoisie did not allow the proletariat to take political power, but also because industrialization, where the workers had taken power, gave the environment colossal damage. The eastern area of Europe subjected to state socialism has proven not to be a convincing alternative to private capitalism either on a social or environmental level.

Not only has criticism of the system proven to be very limited, but so has the attempt to find a practical alternative. There was a lack of real intelligence about things. We have allowed ourselves to be influenced too much by the mirages of progress. We have allowed ourselves to be influenced by prejudices towards pre-bourgeois societies, judging them to be crude and primitive, dominated by serfdom and clericalism. And so we threw away the dirty water with the baby inside.

Today all over the world, with a few small exceptions, we are dealing with all variants of capitalism, both private and state. The private capitalism of the collective West is about to be replaced, as the leader of the planet, by the state capitalism of the Asian area. Once again we will delude ourselves that we have found the solution to all our problems. In reality we will have greater control over the population and with increasingly sophisticated weapons.

In reality, we must escape from this mystique of great empires, from this senseless cult we have for States and Markets, from this fatal attraction to well-being, consumerism, comfort, merely economic and financial development. We should focus more on the essentiality of things, on the simplicity of habits and customs, on what makes us transparent in our attitudes and above all in our intentions. We should use weapons against those who want to enslave us, but to put them away immediately after defeating them. A society is safer if disarmed.

The expulsion of the merchants from the Temple is false

The Sunday Gospel is a column in "Fatto Quotidiano" held by the Jesuit Antonio Spadaro.

Today the topic was the expulsion of the merchants from the Temple.

These exegetes should get it into their heads that there is no point in being scandalized by the presence of animal traders and money changers in the courtyard of the pagans. Simply because it was completely normal for the Jews to make sacrifices by killing animals, and since the faithful came from everywhere, it was inevitable to convert their different currencies into the one used in Judea to pay the priests.

Jesus could not have done anything against this consolidated tradition. They wouldn't have understood it. He couldn't have overturned the money changers' tables, frustrated the merchants or freed the animals from bloody sacrifices.

The real problem of the corruption of the Temple did not lie in this nonsense, but in the fact that the high priests and the aristocratic class of the Sadducees, responsible for managing the Temple, collaborated with the Romans. Theirs was a theological-political power, strictly confessional, highly mercantile and prone to Pilate's diktats, which represented the power of the emperors in Palestine (particularly in Judea and Samaria).

If on that occasion Jesus did something subversive, which according to the fourth gospel concerns not the end of his political career but the beginning, it was rather much more, so much so that immediately afterwards he was forced to emigrate to Galilee. It was something that the evangelists kept quiet about, since for them Jesus was not a revolutionary politician but a religious preacher.

On that occasion he tried to lead a kind of insurrection against the managers of the Temple. He must have had part of the Essene movement led by the Baptist on his side, certainly the Galilean zealots and probably counted on the support of the Jewish Pharisees, who in the Knesset were opponents of the Sadducees. All anti-Templar and anti-Roman religious and political formations.

The attempt, however, was not successful, and not because it was prevented by the Temple guards or by the Roman forces present in the Antonia Fortress, who were caught off guard, but because ultimately the most significant support, the Pharisaic one, failed. So much so that the next day Nicodemus, one of the most democratic leaders of the Pharisees, had to apologize to Jesus.

March 4

Long and painful processes

State capitalism in Western Europe is in irreversible decline. In Italy it was born with fascism and continued during the half century of Christian Democratic government. Paradoxically he began to enter into a crisis with the Craxian socialists, who hated the communists to death and who, rather than govern with them, preferred to do so with the Christian Democrats.

State capitalism was a bourgeois response to Soviet-style state socialism. Nazism also put it into practice. Ultimately, Nazism and fascism were two petty-bourgeois by-products of proletarian socialism. However, once they came to power, they had to submit to the diktats of big industry, traditionally favorable to economic liberalism and political liberalism.

In their first phase, fascists and Nazis had and nurtured illusory aspects, useful for enchanting the masses; in the second they cultivated profoundly reactionary attitudes with which they disillusioned them.

The progressive dismantling of state capitalism went hand in hand with some phenomena: 1) the increase in economic well-being, especially for the middle classes; 2) the end of the worker-student protest that began in 1968; 3) the crisis of Soviet state socialism; 4) the growing influence of the American model.

In Western Europe, state capitalism was also due to the fact that the two world wars enormously devastated the European populations. To avoid the outbreak of civil wars, which could have been managed by social-communist formations, the bourgeoisie thought it best to protect itself, promising the satisfaction of many socio-economic rights.

The USA, on the other hand, did not need to resort to this trick, as it did not internally suffer the devastation of the world wars, so much so that it became the leading power in the world, replacing the Anglo-French hegemony.

Today in the EU the end of state capitalism goes hand in hand with the acceptance of US private capitalism. Europe is becoming Americanised. The dependence on the North American model is no longer just military, as at the time of the Cold War, but also economic, financial and ideological,

The Russian-Ukrainian war has clearly shown that we are a colony in all respects, with a vast scope, to the point that we are willing to deindustrialize ourselves to do the Americans a favor, or in any case to completely depend on their market. The Israeli-Palestinian war reaffirmed this. This means that if US private capitalism wants to wage a third world war, we Europeans will follow it.

War will be inevitable, since US private capitalism can no longer exercise the world hegemony of past decades. Countries that experiment with state capitalism or market socialism prevent them from doing so. And they have the military strength to do it.

The collective West is digging its own grave. The time it has ruled the world has been too long to be able to calmly accept the idea of *multipolarity*.

If anything, the problem for us Westerners will arise on a two-fold level. We will certainly emerge defeated from the clash with countries that prefer to have a state that controls the economy. But after this defeat we will have, within our own countries, a bourgeoisie which, in order to survive, will remove the mask of formal democracy to show the true face of the dictatorship of capital. These will be long and painful processes.

March 5

True and false environmentalism

Any intellectually honest environmentalist position must necessarily criticize the logic of capital, especially its idea of maximizing profits by selling as many goods as possible, and obviously at a price such that competitors are eliminated from the market.

The fact that many simply get rich by speculating financially on the sale of such goods does not make finance, from an ecological point of view, less dangerous than economics, if only because the existence of a capitalism without goods to sell is unthinkable. Someone necessarily has to produce them: it is not important whether the workforce resides in a hegemonic or subordinate country. What matters most is that it is exploited at the lowest possible cost.

A logic of this kind cannot have so many scruples towards nature. In capitalism the exploitation of labor (whether direct, through machines, or indirect, through stock exchanges) always goes hand in hand with the plundering of natural resources. This is why honest environmentalism cannot say enough about looting without placing its finger on the wound of exploitation.

Here, however, ecology ends up in a dead end. In fact, if it is not possible to solve the problems of looting without calling into question those of the exploitation of labor, it is even less possible to solve both problems without addressing that of mechanization, that is, the processes of industrialization that make collective well-being possible ("collective" , of course, in a broad sense: the countries of the North compared to those of the South or certain social classes compared to others both in the North and in the South, etc.).

We have arrived at this conclusion because, even if we wanted to take away from the bourgeoisie the private ownership of the means of production, which enriches it in a frightening way, the problem of the plundering of natural resources would remain unsolved, which also occurred in the time of the USSR and which today occurs in Chinese-style mercantile socialism. Without considering the fact that for a worker, being "salaried" by a private individual or by the State does not change his life substantially.

However, today in the West the problem is yet another. In fact, the entrepreneurial bourgeoisie is taking advantage of environmentalist ideas to impose certain types of consumption and behaviors that only have the appearance of being ecological, but which in reality favor large-scale industry. When we talk about separate waste collection, we favor semblance, as in reality nothing is done to solve the problem upstream (just think of the massive packaging of goods in plastic containers).

When we talk about electric or hybrid cars, or condensing boilers, or solar panels, etc., we clearly favor the interests of big industry, which is certainly not concerned with protecting nature, nor when it produces these new pseudo-ecological goods, nor when it comes to disposing of them once they have become obsolete.

We in the West are aware (at best) of the problems we ourselves create, but we have absolutely no idea how to solve them. Not only do we not have the will, but even if we do, we lack the right tools to deal with them.

In fact, any industrial production seems to be in itself incompatible with the reproductive needs of nature. Cutting down a tree is a matter of a few minutes with an electric saw, but regrowing another tree, to the same size as the previous one, takes many years.

This is why today, when Western statesmen talk about environmentalism, they lie knowing they are lying. Not only that, but they also make statesmen from non-Western countries lie, who do not want to be crucified by beautiful words without objective evidence. Behind the "beautiful phrases" lies interests of a completely different nature.

The only thing that statesmen manage to do, to satisfy the popular masses, is to promise that one day (but always postponed) the problems will be solved.

In the meantime, they impose additional burdens that erode private savings, also because they demand them from those who, in a highly competitive market, have fewer means to survive.

Today's example of small agricultural businesses is apt: they can protest as much as they want, they can complain about having been forced to purchase very expensive machinery, to suffer penalizing regulations compared to foreign competition; they can also force governments, with their demonstrations, to give in on the tax issue or on the cost of hydrocarbons, but their fate is sealed. Only multinationals must operate in the markets. The alleged ecological precautions will serve precisely to make them dominate better, and not because they will have more means to implement them, but precisely because other companies will not have them.

p.s. A fairly argued objection was made to this post. The following: "If on the one hand it is obvious that environmentalism must necessarily radically rethink the economic and productive system, one cannot realistically think, outside of the anarcho-primitivist bubbles, of a society that gives up means of transport, heating and energy production. Electric cars decarbonize and eliminate pollution due to private transport. Yes, public transport and alternative mobility must be strengthened first (also electrical), but a certain number of cars will certainly remain, and they will have to be EVs. Heat pumps (not boilers) have an efficiency that essentially makes all other forms of heating ridiculous; as well as allowing us to decarbonise. Zero reasons not to install them. Solar panels have a low and plummeting cost, a rapidly growing efficiency, they are already more than 90% recyclable, they produce electricity. Here too it is not clear what the criticism is. All these technologies, it is worth remembering, serve to get rid of a sector (that of fossil fuels) which is based on the devastation of entire ecosystems, and on the release of enormous quantities of greenhouse gases. So yes, we reduce consumption, we reuse and recover, but if we reject technology like this out of bias, or on the basis of the fact that someone can profit from it (which is quite normal in a capitalist regime), it is not clear what alternatives we have left to mass suicide."

So I replied: I could share your observations on only one condition, that they were formulated, after extensive discussion, within an already anti-capitalist society. That is, I would like them to be the result of a common decision by a local community, owner of the means of production and therefore capable of direct democracy. Outside of such a society, I don't trust anything or anyone, precisely because one can easily predict that the best ideas would sooner or later be exploited by the strong powers.

Having said that, I have nothing against, in principle, towards anarcho-primitivism. And in any case I want to tell you that whatever objection you may make to me, I remind you that you would do so from a privileged position, the Western one, which lives on the shoulders of others. It is too easy to make such objections after 500 years of colonialism. I would like to hear them from those who provide us with the raw materials for our ecological transition.

When it was thought that hydrocarbons had a limited time, they aimed straight at civil nuclear power, even in Italy. Then the Chernobyl disaster convinced us that we were doing something stupid. We needed a tragedy to understand it. Now we're focusing on electrical. Who knows how long it will take before we discover that this too is disastrous for nature. But the Global South will have to tell us, because we in the North are deaf and blind.

The first question we should ask ourselves is: since I don't want my well-being to depend on someone's discomfort, how much energy do I need to live? The second, more difficult question is: can I get enough energy where I live, without having to ask for anything from those who live outside my community?

Is abortion an absolute right?

The French boast of having put the right to abortion in the Constitution, so no doctor will be able to be a conscientious objector (780 votes in favor and 72 against in parliament).

This will mean that within a few generations France will be made up only of immigrants, who, being predominantly Islamic and therefore against abortion, will certainly be the most prolific.

Apart from this demographic consideration, the underlying error is another. Abortion is always a personal drama, there is little that can be done. It is absurd to think of making it less dramatic by limiting it to the legal sphere of constitutional rights.

It can be a relative, private right, subject to various conditions, objective (e.g. allowing it within the first 90 days of gestation) and subjective, for which there could be discussions between the interested person, intending to make use of her right, and others entitled to dissuade her, such as naturally the partner, but also the psychologist, the social worker, the doctor, the employer...

A truly democratic society should favor conditions that prevent unwanted pregnancy or that minimize the social and professional consequences of a pregnancy in general (especially those that predominantly affect women).

That is, a woman cannot be penalized precisely because she is female. It cannot be left alone in making a decision which, ultimately, concerns the demography and social development of an entire population. Nor can she submit to the diktats of a dominant culture or ideology which, making use of its political power, wants to interfere with her private choices regarding her own body.

However, the birth of a new member of the community should be a commitment that the entire community takes on. It is evident that the rights of a woman are superior to the rights of those who have not yet been born (any religious discussion on the matter makes no sense), but the rights of any citizen must always be placed in relation to the rights of all the others. We are not isolated monads. The survival of a population cannot depend on the exercise of an absolute right, confined to the individual and private sphere.

Perhaps the only case in which a woman should be left absolutely free to decide what to do with the fetus in her body is rape. We cannot accept the idea that a woman should suffer the prolonged effects of a personal drama of such exceptional gravity. This is of course regardless of the fact that, at the time of giving birth, the woman must always be left free, whether there has been rape or not, not to recognize the unborn child.

In all other cases it should come down to a negotiation between the interested party and the institutions (obviously taking it for granted that officially banning abortion means relegating it to a clandestine sphere with all its risks and dangers).

Let's take for example. a country like Russia, the first nation in the world to legalize abortion in 1920. It is very vast and with a rather small population (practically the number of births is still at the levels of the Second World War). In this case it could be completely normal for the State to have an interest in preventing abortion from being practiced, even though it admits the right to it. It would be completely normal for institutions in a country like this to provide women with all the subsidies and assistance they want to convince them to give birth (even if they want to give the newborn up to foster care or adoption); then no one should be able to object if, despite this, the woman insists on making use of her right to have an abortion.

Guaranteeing women an absolute right, to be exercised exclusively, without interactions of any kind, in a field as important as that of the reproduction of the species, means affirming the most extreme individualism, and exempting the State from the duty to invest in social issues.

Here there should be only one absolute principle, and that is that motherhood, childhood and the family must be placed under the protection of the State or in any case of the community to which the woman belongs.

March 6

A new global South

It is common ground that the global South is increasingly escaping the neocolonial control of the collective West. Since the Second World War we have witnessed this progressive emancipation. At first it happened on a political and partly military level. Today it is also happening on the socio-economic level. But the processes are long and tiring, also because the West uses financial leverage to get these countries into debt, continuing to keep them subjugated.

On the other hand, with classical colonialism they had become accustomed to producing only those goods that were attractive for international markets. Having lost their autonomy, they now need funding to survive.

The Global South will sooner or later be forced to rethink itself. In fact, those natural resources that were previously exploited by Western colonial plunder, and then, after political emancipation, remained closely connected to world markets, are running out. They have made the fortune of the West, but only to a very limited extent are they able to do the same with the national forces of the country in the process of emancipation: generally only a small minority benefits from it.

However, the problem is not only this. The countries of the Global South, if they want to stop forced migration for economic and environmental reasons, must overcome the Western idea of producing monocultures or certain strategic raw materials for the needs of world markets. Also because the cash income they derive from this trade does not feed the national populations, but only enriches the privileged elites, who are furthermore protected by the State, that is, by corrupt governments, which certainly do not serve national interests.

To produce monocultures or particular raw materials, these countries have seen biodiversity impoverish and desertification increase; they have suffered the establishment of Western companies that are highly harmful to the environment; they have been treated as landfills for the

West's non-recyclable waste.[4]

Going forward at this rate, forced migrations towards the richest areas of the planet will never end, especially if the national populations are unable to overthrow their corrupt governments and completely reset the criteria of economic production, which cannot in any way ignore distributive justice, from social equality.

The global South must redeem itself from all points of view. In this sense, it is not a good choice to replace Western companies with Chinese ones. These countries need autonomy, that is, to be left in peace, to rediscover their original identities, to recover their traditions prior to Western colonialism (or in any case antithetical to this slavery).

It remains to be demonstrated that their destiny is to industrialize like the most advanced countries in the world. Whether they do this by adopting capitalist or socialist forms themselves changes nothing in substance. These are countries that must take advantage of the crisis of global capitalism, which is expressed in periodic regional wars, financial collapses and above all in increasingly frequent and massive environmental devastation, to totally rethink themselves.

It is no longer enough to emancipate oneself, to claim rights. We also need to reconstitute ourselves, restore lost foundations and recover the essential foundations of a pre-colonial past.

*

The ambassadors of EU countries in Russia refused the meeting with the Russian Foreign Minister, presumably following some advice from Brussels. This goes totally against the very idea of the existence of diplomatic missions and ambassadorial posts.

In reality all these ambassadors should be kicked out of Russia and the level of diplomatic relations should be lowered. These are not ambassadors, but political imbeciles who do not understand their real tasks.

Europe is dead.

So said Dmitry Medvedev, vice-president of the Security Council of the Russian Federation.

Impossible to blame him.

---

4 From the EU alone, every year around 20 million containers containing old electronic devices, scrap metal and plastics are exported which contain toxic materials that are very dangerous for human and environmental health. Every year hundreds of old cargo ships and oil tankers are sent from developed countries to India, Bangladesh and other Asian countries for scrapping.

Faces of bronze and hearts of stone

If Germany had won the First World War, would it have started the Second? A Germany that had a few colonies scattered around the world and that had entered the Middle East (like the Anglo-French) to exploit its energy resources and trade routes would have had much less reason to occupy Western Europe.

However, since France and the United Kingdom already had large empires, the Third Reich would certainly have declared war on Bolshevik Russia and, perhaps with the help of some Western powers, would have tried to occupy it.

If it had succeeded, that is, if it had taken the largest part of Russia, would the history of humanity have been very different? I would say no. Instead of a US-led world capitalism, we would have had one led by Germany, as well as France and the United Kingdom (and the US would also continue to play its part in Latin America and the Pacific).

Then, after dividing Russia, the bourgeois West would have tried to do the same with China, while India would have remained in English hands. At least until a global need for emancipation from Western colonialism arose.

This is to say that the Europeans would have been as aggressive as the Americans, since we are of the same "race". Indeed, we would almost certainly have declared war on the United States itself if they had not allowed us full freedom of access to South America.

This is because capitalism is like this: it is greedy, it is never satisfied with what it has. And the strongest nations (or multinationals) don't want to have competitors.

So let's not be surprised if in this Russian-Ukrainian war the USA tried to transform the EU into a colony with no say in the matter. If Germany had won the First World War, if it had occupied a good part of Russia, and if there had not been the Second World War, Western Europe would have continued to dominate the world for a long time to come.

The great thing is that we Europeans today behave as if things had actually happened like this, when in fact the entire Western brand of private capitalism is in decline.

We don't realize the reality, we don't want to admit the evidence of the facts. While we are aware that the USA behaves towards us like a hegemonic country, we believe that, as the "collective West", we continue to dominate the world. And we are willing to demonstrate it with military force, being willing to declare war on Russia and China: which we will do when we feel adequately ready.

In fact, first of all statesmen must prepare the populations for this great commitment, which will certainly involve enormous sacrifices. They will have to reinstate compulsory conscription and transform the industries into a war economy. Great conflicts cannot be won without risking losing one's life or being permanently mutilated or falling ill with some serious pathology.

To this end, democracy is destined to become a useless burden. To make the world understand that we dictate the rules for everyone, we ourselves must be the first to adopt intolerant attitudes. Faces of bronze and hearts of stone: we must educate ourselves to become like this.

*

The NATO Treaty denies the possibility of signing bilateral agreements with a country in a state of war. This means that all agreements signed independently by the English, French, Germans and Italians with Ukraine must be considered null and void, unless we want to admit that NATO no longer exists.

*

Donatella Di Cesare, professor of theoretical philosophy at the Sapienza University of Rome, wrote the following words of condolence towards Red Brigade member Balzerani in X: "Your revolution was mine too. Different paths do not erase ideas."

The post - later deleted - sparked a hornet's nest on social media, but all in all it is shareable for those who lived through the 70s.

In fact, the teacher herself then clarified: "I have always been far from any form of violence. My life, my writings, my teaching testify to this. I remembered the death of Barbara Balzerani from whom I have always been distant. In that context I mentioned the radical transformation that my generation aspired to. Some have chosen armed struggle; I took the path of feminism. I experienced the violence of those years firsthand, that of many fascists."

Well done Donatella! You have all my understanding and solidarity.

March 8

The reasons for a worldwide success

Sometimes I wonder where the collective West has this incredible ability to deceive the popular masses. That is, what is the cultural substratum that has allowed capitalism to become an economic system of global relevance.

The identification of this substratum is not immediate, since, if we stop at the slave era, we find that Roman law was no more important than Egyptian or Greek religion or Indo-Buddhist philosophy. And it has never happened anywhere that the slave system was able to give birth to the capitalist one. Of course in the USA there were so-called "niggers" on the southern plantations, but only because capitalism already existed in Europe, and in any case the industrialized north won in the Civil War.

Marx gave birth to industrial capitalism in the 16th century, but if he had studied in Italy, he would have anticipated it by at least half a millennium. Of course, not the "industrial" one, but certainly the commercial one, that is, that of the merchants who went to the East to purchase those goods that were not found in Western Europe, and for which those merchants knew how to arouse a "voluptuary need" in the wealthy classes. .

It will be said that this type of trade was also known to Jews and Muslims. It's true, but only in Western Europe did it have the strength to create a "bourgeois" social system, in which the urbanized individual was legally "free", that is, not subject to the constraints typical of the slavery and feudal era (slave or tax).

Only in Italian bourgeois municipalities does it occur, for the first time, that a serf can feel protected after fleeing from a fiefdom; only here can he transform from an enfeoffed peasant to a legally free salaried worker in a private company (especially textiles), whose production means were owned by a merchant who had accumulated capital through long-distance trade.

Marx managed to understand, without ever deepening the thesis, that the most suitable culture for the development of industrial capitalism was that coming from the Protestant world. However, when we talk about the "birth of the bourgeoisie" in Western Europe and particularly in Italy, the dominant culture was certainly not the Protestant one (which did not even exist), but the Catholic one, a religious culture which after the year 1000 began to clearly oppose the Christian one. - Orthodox of the Greek-Byzantine area.

In fact, capitalism was not born in the very rich Byzantium (or Constantinople), but in the newborn Italian maritime cities which traded above all with the Byzantines, and which, at a certain point, had understood how to set up factories free from any state control, in which a private entrepreneur, master of the means of production, could exploit the work of several formally free paid workers. These workers were initially scattered around their homes and used the looms they had available; then they were concentrated in factories or factories.

The key question at this point is the following: how was it possible for the Italian municipal bourgeoisie to develop an idea of this kind, which would shock the entire world over the centuries, without encountering firm opposition from the aristocratic class, then clearly dominant and protected by sovereigns?

There is only one reason, easily verifiable on a historical level. The bourgeoisie was able to be born and develop successfully thanks to the support it found in the papacy, which firmly intended to use the bourgeoisie itself in an anti-imperial function, that is, to create a theocratic system in which the only true emperor was the pontiff himself, while the two others (the Byzantine basileus and the western one of the Holy Roman Empire) were conceived as its secular arms.

This theocratic claim with universal ambition came to an end at the end of the 14th century, when national monarchies began to develop, within which the idea of linking private capitalism with the Roman Catholic religion continued (for a while time), but under the centralized management of an independent sovereign.

In other words, the absolute individualism that Catholicism had initially affirmed on the political level, inventing the figure of a pontiff-emperor, had progressively extended, on a social level, up to the point in which the bourgeois class of Northern Europe completely escaped the ecclesiastical control, transforming (starting from 1517) from Catholic to Protestant.

Strengthened by its economic success, the bourgeois class had come to believe that it could impose itself with the same individualistic criterion of the papacy, but emancipating itself from any form of protection. As is known, in Italy the papacy reacted to this claim by imposing a counter-reform which brought the country out of the impetuous processes of capitalist development. But this is another matter.

Rather we must say that in the last half millennium the Protestant culture has become enormously secularised, and has had all the time necessary to impose even on non-Christian countries the idea that capitalism can only be born if the private exploitation of labor is carried out on workers legally free, abstractly protected by various rights.

Today the epochal clash we are witnessing is between two forms of capitalism, having the same military, economic and financial power: the Western-style private capitalism, in which economics and finance consider politics and law as their operational tools, and the Asian-style state one, in which politics and law claim to exercise a certain control over the economy and finance. It's easy to understand who will win.

March 9

Destined to collapse

Every social formation identified by the classics of scientific socialism has had centuries-old periods. Just think of slavery and serfdom. Primitive communism even lasted millions of years. So not even capitalism can escape this typical trend of civilizations based on social antagonism.

When he decided to emigrate to London, Marx was so disheartened by the ineffectiveness of the proletarian revolutions in Western Europe that he went so far as to say that capitalism is destined to survive until it has exhausted all its driving force.

Lenin, on the other hand, will say that, since capitalism was still weak in Russia, having been born only recently, it would have been easier to overthrow it, especially if the world war had been taken advantage of, transforming it into a civil war. And history proved him right, although, given how things went with state socialism, up to a certain point.

At the time of Lenin, the European socialism of the Second International was unanimously convinced (in the wake of the late Engels) that, before realizing socialism, it was necessary to develop capitalism to the maximum: in this way a powerful industrial proletariat would be formed, which would manage a welfare socialism, thanks to the development of industry.

The transition to socialism would have been, in a certain sense, inevitable, precisely to prevent barbarism, that is, the absurdity of private ownership of the means of production in the face of great collective work in the factories.

Lenin was seen as a heretic, not because he was against industrialization, but because he spoke of a proletarian revolution (made by workers and peasants) in an economically backward country like his.

He defended himself by saying that if in Russia it would have been easier to carry out the revolution and difficult to carry it forward, precisely because of its economic backwardness, in Western Europe instead it would have been very difficult to start it (due to widespread corruption), even if it would have been easy to continue, given its high level of industrial development.

As can be seen, both in one way and another, there was an almost reverential attitude towards the industry. It was considered the fundamental parameter to avoid the creation of a socialism of poverty.

Unfortunately there was little awareness of the environmental disasters that the industry itself could cause, regardless of the social formation in which it could develop. This is demonstrated by the fact that, while Western Europe devastated both its own continent and that of the colonized countries, in Russia it was its European area that devastated itself and its Asian area, penalizing its primitive populations.

The collapse of state socialism did not constitute a U-turn at all, on the contrary the energy industry developed even further.

Today capitalism, both in the private Western form and in the Asian state form, is widespread throughout almost the entire planet. But, if you notice, the same general argument is made everywhere: as long as the classic energy resources (oil, gas and coal) are easily available, it makes no sense to pose the problem of building a new social formation, a new lifestyle. At most, if we really want to talk about ecological transition, let's look for the so-called "rare earths" (those that should be used to develop electric against fossil fuels).

Does it make sense to think about such a transition by focusing on the concept of "rarity"? I do not think so. In fact, we are also forced to focus on other things regarding energy saving: solar panels, thermal insulation, double glazing and condensing boilers and green building in general. But there is also talk of wind turbines, fusion (not fission) nuclear power plants, the use of hydrogen separated from the oxygen present in water, the construction of dams for hydroelectric energy, and so on.

In all these cases, the industry is never questioned, nor a lifestyle based on well-being/development/economic growth. Not only that, but weapons continue to be built whose destructive potential is deadly for nature, to the point that those who survive the bombings are destined to a life full of diseases.

Ecology is used only as a patch for the disasters of capitalism. It has not yet been understood that, without ecology, no economy has a future. At this rate, mankind is destined to suffer a catastrophic collapse. Nature itself will take care of it.

March 10

From the Neolithic revolution to today

We all know that the Neolithic revolution began about 10,000 years ago, at the end of the last glaciation. It consisted of the transition from hunting and gathering to agriculture and livestock.

It did not happen all over the planet, but only in some of its areas, those near the large rivers, devoid of forests, swampy due to recurring floods, and therefore little or not habitable by humans.

One may think that the misfortune of mankind is related to that revolution, but that would be a mistake. In fact, it took another 4,000 years for the first slave civilizations to be born. As long as agriculture and livestock were activities managed collectively, they did not constitute a problem for the survival of mankind and nature; indeed, they seemed to be the only possible solution for those populations that emerged from the forests.

Of course, one might think that without those new activities slavery would never have been born. This is because those activities created wealth (food was more abundant and safe). But the fact remains that the first slave civilizations (along the Nile, the Tigris, the Euphrates, etc.) date back to around 6,000 years ago.

The real problem is that we haven't gotten rid of it since then. In fact, from slavery we moved to serfdom and from this to capitalism (private and state). Each time we were convinced that we had solved the problems of the previous civilization. Even with Soviet-style state socialism it was thought that we had overcome the contradictions of capitalism, but it was a failure. Today we are thinking of doing it with Chinese-style mercantile socialism, but it will inevitably be another failure.

There is something fundamental that isn't working. This something is the relationship with nature. With hunting and gathering you do not "exploit" nature; with agriculture and livestock farming yes. And when this exploitation becomes intensive, resources decrease: there are not enough for the entire population, which in the meantime has grown significantly (2,000 years ago the population of the entire planet had only reached 200 million inhabitants).

Agriculture and livestock farming had accustomed us to unexpected well-being, they had helped us overcome the precariousness of a life outside the forest. The loss of certain certainties has affected the relationships between farmers and breeders, between sedentary living and nomadism. The legends speak clearly: the farmer Cain kills the farmer Abel; the same with Romulus and Remus, etc.

Slavery is linked above all to agriculture. The first cities arise where agriculture is intensive. Agriculture of this kind conflicts with large sheep, goat and cattle farms... which need open spaces, not subject to privatisation.

When you specialize in a particular economic activity, and there is not room for everyone, serious problems begin to arise. In fact, nature, as long as we limit ourselves to exploiting it on the surface, cannot give much.

The native North Americans were neither farmers nor breeders, unlike the inhabitants of the three slave civilizations on the other side of the continent: Inca, Mayan and Aztec. They were hunters and followed the periodic, spontaneous movement of the bison herds. When they clashed with the Europeans, farmers and intensive breeders, their fate was sealed.

We started talking about "progress" when agriculture not only eliminated hunting and the spontaneous gathering of the fruits of nature, but also when it eliminated the power of nomadic breeders. To date, 3/4 of the world's food depends on just 12 plant species and 5 animal species.

Permanence, intensive agriculture and urbanization laid the foundations for the birth of slavery, that is, for the progressive deforestation and desertification of the planet (which currently affects 1/3 of all emerged lands).

The size of the resources, in the face of an ever-increasing population, has led to the search for increasingly sophisticated means to try to obtain them, but these are completely unnatural means, the result of technical-scientific experiments.

Today violence against nature has spread to the entire planet. From time to time human beings, in order to obtain exclusive exploitation of the last remaining resources, are willing to exterminate each other. But even after doing so, we continue to have the same violent attitude towards nature as always.

The anthropization of nature has become so strong that we no longer know the difference between natural and artificial. Even today we think that forests, in the best of cases, should be protected because they offer oxygen. It has been completely forgotten that for millions of years they have guaranteed life.

March 11

In what sense is a new development model?

In the book by Manlio Dinucci and Carla Pellegrini, SOS Environment, the need for a new development model is invoked and two fundamental parameters are outlined: 1) it must be centered on the human being in his totality; 2) it must satisfy the needs of current generations without compromising those of future generations.

What do the authors mean by "totality"? Something quantitative/extensive: all peoples must be creators and beneficiaries of their own development. This seems to be an anti-colonial concern. Commendable but insufficient.

In fact, the concept of "totality" must also concern qualitative aspects. The "total" human being is an "integral" entity, that is, an indissoluble, inseparable composite of human and natural aspects.

From this aspect it should be said that the manipulative (or transformative) abilities of humans should never go to the point of subordinating the natural aspects of human life.

The human being is certainly responsible for transforming things in such a way as to have no equal in the animal world. However, this ability should be exercised within the space-time and environmental limits that nature imposes. Otherwise the notion of difference between artificial and natural is lost. Everything begins to appear natural even if it isn't at all.

Nature cannot give us the parameters in which to exercise our freedom of conscience and our consciousness of freedom. However, it tells us what the necessary, objective laws are in which to develop the sense of humanity that characterizes us. If with our freedom (unique and unrepeatable) we claim to change these laws, we inevitably lose our humanity, that is, we become worse than animals.

The second aspect, that relating to generations, is a consequence of this. In the sense that, if the reproductive needs of nature are respected, it will necessarily not jeopardize in any way the exercise of the freedom and creativity of future generations.

However, if this is true, a generation can expect to have from the previous one only those knowledge and skills (or competences) that it really considers useful for itself. That is, not only must it feel free from having to solve the problem of disposing of waste from the previous generation, but it must not even have the obligation to inherit all the intellectual works, artefacts and artificial means of the previous generation. This is because it is absurd to think that we necessarily have to retrace the exact same path as those who preceded us. Freedom of choice would collapse. What you inherit must not be such as to absolutely constrain your life choices. And in any case it is one thing to inherit a spade and a hoe; it's quite another to inherit a tractor or a combine harvester.

When the so-called "barbarian populations" entered the Western Roman Empire, they inherited the urban sewers, the aqueducts, the baths, the lead water pipes, and many other things, which they then abandoned to themselves, since they did not they considered them useful for a life in the countryside. The cities were almost completely dismantled. The concepts of "development" or "growth" were understood in a completely different way.

March 12

Quantity before everything

All productivity and profitability indices used in capitalism (capital, materials, workforce) are quantitative (economic, financial, statistical...).

Capitalism has led to the triumph of mathematics, which, combined with propositional logic, has produced information technology, and this has evolved as telematics: all together they are producing artificial intelligence, which is abstract thought, vaguely humanoid, as limited ability to interact with those who question it.

In all the macroeconomic calculations that can be made (the most frequent are the gross domestic product, the public debt and deficit, the rate of unemployment, inflation, interest on money, etc.), environmental damage is not not even counted. This is because they spill over into the community. Paradoxically, while we are very precise when it comes to money, we are incredibly approximate, superficial and minimalist when it comes to nature and the environment in general.

Criticizing capitalism only on the aspect of the capital/labour relationship, without adding the issue of the environment, is the stupidest thing that can be done today. Keeping economic problems separate from ecological ones is irresponsible to the highest degree. To the point that today we should completely overturn the dominant priorities: ecology comes before the economy. That is, an economic system deserves to exist only if it is compatible with the ecological needs of the natural environment.

Today, environmental disasters are so great that they should be considered a sufficient reason to carry out an anti-system revolution. In fact, there is no point in guaranteeing employment or a decent salary if you then get sick easily, have to deal with very expensive treatments, or die early.

Environmental problems are so serious that they are passed on to subsequent generations in increasingly serious forms, and do not seem solvable in the presence of industrial activity.

The population is destined to decline, not only because the toxicity of the environment reduces reproductive capacity, but also because an economy disconnected from ecology makes life increasingly expensive. In Italy the demographic boom only occurred in the years 1963-65.

When capital wants to make people believe that well-being is unlimited, the prices of goods inevitably tend to rise, while wages do not keep pace. We live in such an absurd system that prices go up even when there are environmental concerns. In fact, ecological needs are exploited to do business.

When scientists say that respect for the environment would have positive repercussions on the economy, private entrepreneurs ask the State to intervene with the taxes of all citizens. Not only are profits privatized and losses socialized, but the costs of environmental protection are also nationalized. For example. the purification plants are all public, while the private ones concern water for domestic use.

Is there a zero-emission, i.e. non-polluting, production cycle? On an industrial level, certainly not. In fact, the term "emission" should not only mean the release of dangerous chemical agents into the atmosphere (e.g. a greenhouse gas), but any unnatural waste produced by the manufacture of a commodity, its use and its disposal when it is exhausted. .

We all remember when scientists told us that CFC gases in refrigerators, sprays, etc. contributed to widening the ozone hole. Has anything changed after we purchased new generation refrigerators and freezers? In part yes, but it is not enough. If we were really worried about getting skin and eye tumors, we couldn't wait for the polar ice to disappear so we could exploit its seabed, which is certainly rich in hydrocarbons.

March 13

An autonomous development model

When in Western Europe people began to understand, at the time of the Romans, that slavery no longer made sense, as it was no longer possible to expand the borders of the empire by colonizing new populations, the figure of the colonist was established, that is, a worker who, despite being dependent on a master (usually a landowner), enjoyed certain freedoms and a certain margin of autonomy.

The colonist then became a serf in the Middle Ages, when the Germanic and Asian populations occupied the western area of the aforementioned empire. And in turn the peasant serf was transformed into a legally free wage worker under capitalism.

He moved from one condition of subjection or submission to another, without interruption. There was never a time when a worker could say he was completely free. To be so, he still had to exploit someone: for example. in the artisan world the master exploited the apprentice, in the monetary world the banker exploited the employee, or the usurer exploited the debtor, in the agricultural world the landowner exploited the farmer, in the manufacturing world the entrepreneur exploited the worker, and so on .

In Europe it was never possible to rediscover the freedom that preceded social antagonism and class conflicts. Even when state socialism was achieved in Eastern Europe, there was always a certain dependence (ideological, political, administrative...) on the part of citizens towards a father and master State, mostly managed by a single party and union or prevalent. The construction of a completely self-managed society, devoid of the paternalistic and authoritarian protection of the State, was postponed to an unspecified future.

Today we do the same thing towards nature. When we tell ourselves that we must progressively replace fossil energy sources (which are running out) and nuclear ones (which are too dangerous) with renewable ones, we always remain within the limits of the industrialization that largely characterizes our time.

We can talk as much as we want about hydroelectric, wind and solar resources... But to set up structures that exploit renewable sources, we need knowledge, means and methods that are not within everyone's reach. Even today, billions of people are without electricity not so much or not only because they do not know what the technical-scientific revolution is (which led for example to thermodynamic energy), but above all because they live in conditions of subordination compared to the dominant powers.

The most advanced countries in the world, paradoxically, can talk about ecological transition precisely because they experience a privileged situation on an economic level, the result of colonialism that began half a millennium ago.

We Westerners look at things only from our point of view, and since we know that if other large nations claim to achieve the same well-being as us, energy resources will not be enough for everyone, wars are inevitable for us.

In any case, even if there were no wars, the problem of how to exploit water, wind and solar energy for very long periods, millennia, by the most backward nations, lacking industrial capacity and skills, would remain unsolved. They would necessarily have to depend on someone, even just to replace individual components that have failed or worn out, or to replace obsolete systems or machines.

This is to say that we must stop associating the word "wellbeing" with the word "industry". We must rather associate it with the word "autonomy", which, in turn, presumes full social equality between citizens, and which implies the shared management of common resources, the natural ones available and those produced by the human transformation of these resources.

Each country must find its own development model. One must not feel in awe of other people's models.

March 14

A paradoxical world

Today we live in increasingly larger, increasingly polluted cities, using increasingly sophisticated technologies, which when we stop or replace them, we don't know where to put them, we don't know how to prevent them from damaging our environment. We have fewer and fewer children and we get older and older. Not only that, but we tend to deindustrialise, without recovering anything from the pre-bourgeois past, preferring instead to stake our last cards above all on services and finance. There is no real future for Europe, so much so that we are becoming too warmongering: we are becoming Americanized.

Yet due to our well-being, the result of centuries-old robberies of other people's resources, we are constantly subject to the desire for redemption of massive migratory flows coming from all over the global South.

Paradoxically, these poor people come to live with us hoping to become, sooner or later, wealthy like us, without realizing that, already with their work, they participate in the exploitation of the same countries of origin from which they come, even when, with their remittances , they somehow help their distant relatives survive.

Everyone wants to become like us, instead of fighting to be different.

In the past, nomadic populations were forced to become sedentary. But among the settled populations there have always been those who had advanced means and those who did not; indeed, those who had natural resources often could not use them independently due to some form of colonialism suffered by other populations. This is still the case today, so much so that for many, living a somewhat dignified existence means becoming nomads again to find a different sedentary lifestyle.

We live in an absurd world, which does not allow us to perceive the origin of things, much less the origin of problems. Isn't it incredible that countries richer in natural resources make countries that lack them wealthier? Is it possible that those who have industrial, financial and military means should determine the fate of countries that only have human and natural resources to exploit?

If we think about it, all the speeches that are made today by the lovers of multipolarism represent the bare minimum to be able to survive in a dignified manner, without having to submit to the diktats of others. Multipolarists are not offering the Global South the socio-economic recipes for how to achieve equality and social justice. They are simply talking about autonomy towards the collective West, which for centuries has been used to living on the shoulders of others.

The management autonomy of its own resources should be the starting point for any state in the world. Instead, for those in the global South it is an objective to be pursued, a goal to be achieved.

Paradoxically, even Western countries are not aware of what "management autonomy" means. In fact, they make it depend, internally, on resources that they do not have. The very fact that they are always tempted to relocate their businesses to save on goods costs proves this.

We Westerners like to talk about an integrated, global world, of interdependence between nations, of interconnection between the various functions and roles. But we say these things to make others feel as important as us. That is, to deceive them. In fact, we are in charge, and since we are becoming a small minority, we fear that someone will notice.

March 15

A deadly virus

One of the most illusory things in the American way of life is the idea that strength can inspire fear. They still use the death penalty in the belief, absolutely unjustified as it is contradicted by statistics, that it can dissuade people from committing heinous crimes.

They impose very long prison sentences to make it clear that even if the State allows you to do what you want, in the face of every mistake it can use ruthless harshness (except of course towards those who have huge means with which to ensure a successful defense).

But above all they use increasingly lethal, sophisticated weapons, with such devastating effects that they last well beyond the end of the conflict: this is because they are convinced that, by doing so, the enemy will not only surrender more easily, but will also think twice before returning to the fight.

The USA is an anti-pedagogical country by definition: it does not understand that more security is obtained not from terror that instills fear but from mutual trust. They don't understand that if you want to set yourself up as a model to be imitated, you can't behave like arrogant people but like democratic people, who know how to make peace a universal value and who don't pretend to believe in the values and needs of others only on a temporary basis, showing magnanimity and indulgence with that unbearable paternalistic attitude which, when necessary, is denied in a flash.

Peace cannot be a value that the strongest imposes or grants to the weakest, keeping them subjugated, since this instills resentment, frustration, fuels the spirit of revanche, vengeance which leads to extreme, unilateral actions.

It is clear that if the USA has such hypocritical and aggressive attitudes in foreign policy, it is because within them they experience very acute, paroxysmal social conflicts, which the media naturally pass off as conflicts of an ethnic or racial nature.

The antagonism between those who have a lot and those who have little or nothing is stellar. The idea that everyone can get rich is a myth spread by the rich. In fact, any human value is seen in the light of interest or convenience. Only the naive can be altruistic. And there can be no repentance or self-criticism on the part of those who commit shameful abuses or are accustomed to lying. A minimum of humanity can perhaps be found in the inmates on death row, awaiting their execution, because they know they have nothing left to lose.

In order to accept such a world, dominated by the Latin principle homo homini lupus, it is evident that society must be continually induced to dream. Hollywood cinematography, television advertising, lotteries, quizzes and prize games, unbridled sporting competition, the use of any type of drug and sexual license, music and dancing in all their forms...: all this is a big dream factory.

But also the idea that, by arming themselves, the common citizen feels safer, only to then witness senseless massacres precisely because of those weapons in the hands of deranged people. Not to mention the possibility that is offered to any citizen to punt on the stock market, in the belief that getting rich is the easiest thing in the world (a belief that was held throughout the country even shortly before the collapse of 1929 and 2008).

And what about the idea of getting up to your neck in debt, believing that in the richest and most powerful country in the world only a fool can fail? As if the USA weren't the clearest example of what it means to fail when you least expect it...

This is a country that needs to be stopped, which has no merit in continuing to exist. The only people who really had anything to teach humanity were the Native Americans, but they largely eliminated them and many survivors were relegated to reservations (where quite a few run casinos and gambling games).

Today the USA has nothing to teach anyone. Indeed, they must be isolated from the rest of humanity. They have become a deadly virus, capable of infecting the entire world population. Doing business with people with forked tongues, who do not keep their promises, who betray the agreements signed, who are used to lying and stealing, who do not respect the needs of others can lead to catastrophic consequences for one's safety and security.

March 16

Go back to having peaceful dreams

Of course, if we start looking at our time from an ecological point of view, the countries that are indebted to nature are not only the Western ones, but all the industrialized ones, that is, including those that today talk about multipolarism, in contrast to Western-style globalism.

Countries in the Global South should care little about which side they are on. However, this would be a superficial attitude. We all know that the BRICS countries are not able to guarantee true environmental protection, but we also know that, at the moment, they are the only ones who can offer the countries subject to Western colonialism true national sovereignty, which also includes socio-economic and financial.

It is therefore a good idea for the global South not to be too picky and to be content with taking one step at a time. Also because it remains to be demonstrated that the countries that have been subjected to colonialism for half a millennium now have an exact awareness of how one should live in a world that respects the reproductive needs of nature.

So much time has passed. Western conditioning has been so strong that it would be naive to take for granted that the Global South has an ecological intelligence superior to that of any other geographic area on the planet. In fact, if they demand full national sovereignty just to be able to industrialize according to our own life criteria, multipolarism will have been of no use. Indeed, for nature it will be the knockout blow.

From this point of view, it is useless to complain that the well-being of the West was obtained with unprecedented violence towards the colonized countries. If you want to industrialize like us, if you want to follow our same "bourgeois" path, nature will continue to be plundered and, sooner or later, the nations that have acquired true national sovereignty will fight each other, and history will begin again as before, except for some variations that obviously we cannot know.

If mankind wants to go back to having peaceful dreams, this nightmare must be resolved once and for all.

Differences between globalism and imperialism

It is quite curious that today, in the presence of a dominant capitalism on a world level, we talk about anti-globalism and in a certain way we succeed in overcoming it thanks to the idea of multipolarism brought forward by the BRICS, when, at the time of Soviet-style state socialism, there was talk of anti-imperialism, without ever managing to overcome it. Why this paradoxical situation? The reason lies in the fact that the crisis of private capitalism, typical of the collective West, today suffers from much more acute contradictions, as the South of the world is increasingly refractory to being exploited on a socioeconomic level.

At the time of the Cold War, the Third World looked favorably on the state socialism of the Soviet bloc, but this, at most, allowed it to emancipate itself on a political and not at the economic level. Indeed, on an economic level the introduction of elements of state socialism into the economies of the Third World was, overall, quite unsuccessful.

When the USSR imploded in 1991, the disappointment of the Third World was truly great, as it was feared that the neocolonial dependence on the collective West would be definitive and worse than before. However, a glimmer of light came from China, which managed to penetrate the global South on an economic level, without having any colonial claims.

Today the glimmer of hope also comes from Russia, capable of standing up militarily not only to Ukraine but also to the entire collective West, which with its proxy war and its inhuman sanctions has shown its great limits.

March 17

Deodorants and sewage

At this moment a world war seems to be inevitable for a number of reasons:

1) the capitalism of the most advanced Western countries wants to seize the immense energy resources of the Russian Federation;

2) the collective West itself cannot tolerate industrial competition from China, which is now present, on a commercial level, throughout the planet;

3) the oil countries of the Middle East want to exploit in absolute autonomy the only real resource that could spread a high level of well-being to all their populations (without however considering the environmental repercussions of such exploitation);

4) the countries of the global South want to definitively free themselves from all the constraints that bind them, like a noose around their neck, to the development needs of those industrialized and neoliberal countries that want to exploit their resources.

When the last two world wars broke out, the motivations were mainly concentrated in a few capitalist countries. At the time, when people spoke of "poles of world imperialism", they meant Western Europe, the United States and Japan.

Today the situation has become so gangrenous that a possible world war would not happen just because some states would cause it to break out and others suffer it, but precisely because everyone wants to settle accounts with their historical enemies or with those who at this moment are seriously threatening their safety, their existence in life.

It is difficult to imagine where the madness of those who have dominated the world in the last half millennium and want to continue to do so can reach, even at the cost, using nuclear weapons, of making the entire planet uninhabitable, or inhabitable only in areas so limited as to make the return to a primitive or even prehistoric way of life inevitable.

Let's just think about one simple fact: when the Spanish conquerors landed on the American continent, there were around 70 million people; well, after about a century and a half the population had reduced to 3.5 million. Firearms and disease had caused a massacre of immense proportions, from which the natives never recovered.[5]

Today, colonial languages are spoken in Latin America; the natives are not at the head of governments, with some exceptions; and economic activities strictly depend on relations with the industrialized countries of the global North.

---

[5] However, according to the 2020 census, there are approximately 9.7 million North American Indians, including mestizos, to which must be added the almost two million residents of Canada. Furthermore, only 20% of the native population lives on reserves.

For just a few years, the American continent has witnessed a leading role for natives within the governments in office. Evo Morales in Bolivia, the first indigenous president to lead his own state, certainly deserves to be remembered; Sonia Guajajara, Brazilian minister of indigenous peoples; Debra Haaland, Minister of the Interior in Biden's government, responsible for the management of natural resources, forestry assets, national parks, programs for ethnic minorities...

Which obviously does not mean that in South America there have not been statesmen of European origin who fought against Western imperialism: think of very famous names such as Castro, Che Guevara, Chavez, Maduro, Ortega, Allende... But, if we want to be honest, It's like putting deodorant in a sewage tank.

Unwanted psychological effects

One of the most dramatic and little-known effects of the transition from state socialism in Eastern European countries to private capitalism in the EU is psychological. It is the acute depression that affects the migrants who come to us to work as carers and which also affects the children left behind in their respective homelands. This refers above all to Romania, Ukraine, Moldova, Poland and Albania. Over 57% of foreign domestic workers come from Eastern Europe. And around 90% of all these workers from all over the world are female, under the age of 40 and reside mainly in large metropolitan areas.

Due to the prolonged distance from their children and their homeland, they no longer perceive themselves as "good mothers" and are experiencing an identity crisis. They no longer know which family and which part of Europe they belong to.

Furthermore, they often leave a qualified job to come and carry out tasks that many Euro-Western women are no longer willing to do. In particular, Italy is the largest host country for carers, nannies and housekeepers.

Not only that but sometimes it happens that children abandoned at home attempt suicide. This problem could find some solution by very quickly encouraging family reunification, but also by guaranteeing psychological assistance and easy audiovisual communication between these mothers and the children they leave behind in their homeland.

In any case it must be said that since the aforementioned transition was started, the Eastern European countries, which previously lived in poverty, now suffer from poverty, except naturally for a privileged few.

Source: Slavia n. 4/2014

March 18

The destinies of history

It seems that the historical function of Westerners (first Europeans, then Americans) was to make all the populations of the world lose their virginity, that is, their innocence.

All those populations that we, with great arrogance and, ultimately, contempt, have defined as "primitive", we have brought out of the prehistory of natural relationships. In fact, when we talk about "history", we mean something violent, not just the use of writing, the rise of cities and markets, and so on.

Within certain "historical" populations, groups of people who rivaled each other were formed, with opposing interests (e.g. sedentary versus nomadic, farmers versus breeders, farmers and breeders versus hunters and gatherers, etc.).

Whoever wins exercises dominion and forces those who lose to contribute to conquering the territories of neighboring populations, in a process that seems to never end, as the empires that slowly formed (which at the beginning of history were of the slave type), they continually expanded, until they encountered stronger, more belligerent populations, capable of resisting and going on the counterattack. Think for example. to the expansion of the Persian empire towards Europe: if it had not been stopped by the Greeks, Europe would not have been dominated by private but by state slavery. And what about the Ottoman Empire? If we had not stopped it in Lepanto and Vienna, how many of us would be Muslims today? And if the Mongols hadn't been stopped in Poland, what languages would we speak?

We Euro-Westerners have created the most powerful slave empire in the world, eliminating any trace of "primitivism" from our continent.

With the arrival of the Germanic and Asian populations, who had not lost those traces, we transformed the slave without any rights into a serf with some rights. And while in Eastern Europe this form of servile work has been maintained over the course of many centuries, we in the Euro-West have instead been able to transform the serf peasant into a wage worker, legally free even if socially similar to the slave, in that he lacks everything or Almost.

And with the birth of bourgeois civilization and industrial capitalism we induced the whole world to change its skin, establishing processes that must have appeared irreversible.

We have brought humanity out of childhood, of adolescence, using brutal ways, deception of words and decoys. Everyone had to become like us, following a pre-established and very accelerated path, and they had to remain submissive, because those who "teach" how to be in the world must be respected.

We created a world in our image and likeness, we Europeans, even though we lived in a marginal area of the great Asian continent. We have conquered the entire African and American, Southern and Middle Eastern continents and a large part of the Asian continent with the strength of our weapons and with the cunning that has characterized us since the time of Ulysses.

Today we are witnessing a reversal of the situation, an epochal transition. Entire populations, long subjugated, are rebelling. They do it in Asia, in Africa, in Latin America, in the Middle East... Looking at the resistance of the Russian Federation towards over 30 NATO countries, which are waging a proxy war in Ukraine, the global South is persuading itself that winning is possible, i.e. that the collective West is not as strong as it seems. The courage of the Houthis is astonishing to the whole world.

Certainly we are realizing that Western ideology no longer has any credibility, that its democracy is false and its law is fictitious, purely formal. We are preparing for an apocalyptic clash, which will mark the destinies of the history of humanity for the next centuries. When the going gets tough, the tough stop playing.

March 19

Different chronologies of systemic collapses

The fact that Western private capitalism is collapsing after the end of Soviet and Chinese brand state socialism should give us pause for reflection.

In fact, one might think that the opposite should have been the case, that is, where politics (no matter how authoritarian it is) dominates the economy, the greater the resilience to its own implosion should be.

However, this was not the case. In China, the end of Maoism (1976) triggered a mercantilist process that produced impressive results on a global level. No one could have ever imagined that in the space of half a century an agricultural and, according to Western parameters, underdeveloped country could have become the first industrialized economy on the planet. Today, mercantile socialism seems to be becoming a model of development for the entire global South, intent on definitively emerging from the shallows of the neoliberal globalism of the collective West.

As for Russia, the turning point occurred with Gorbachev in 1985, betrayed by that wretched anti-communist Yeltsin, and salvaged into a corner by the pragmatic Putin, who, despite being far from any socialist ideology, was able to prevent the private capitalism of the oligarchs from disintegrating the Russian Federation. And, in doing this, he has taken up a certain religious nationalism and a vague Eurasian Slavophile tradition, which inevitably refers to the tsarist past.

In any case, neither of the two countries made other countries pay for the consequences of the failure of their own ideological-political construction (mainly focused on heavy industry by Russia, and on agricultural communes by China).

Yes, but why is Western capitalism only now starting to collapse? Is a system where economics dominates politics really stronger than a system where the opposite exists? Does material interest really matter more than political ideology?

Stalin and Mao had immense power on a political level, but it was not enough to stem the growing economic crisis, which became clear in all its drama after their deaths.

Today the progressive decline of the Western economy cannot be averted by any political leadership. In fact, Western statesmen are all half-figures, puppets manipulated by occult, industrial and financial powers, which act behind the scenes.

These powers, rather than surrendering to the evidence, are thinking of replacing formal democracy with the real dictatorship of capital. And they want to make the whole world pay for it.

They absolutely cannot bear the idea that two powers like China (economically strong) and Russia (militarily strong) are convincing the global South to emancipate itself from Western neocolonialism on the economic-financial and military levels, after having done so on the political level over the years 60s and 70s.

Because this is what we ultimately need to talk about. Western capitalism is collapsing because it cannot bear a complete liberation of those who have accustomed them for half a millennium to living on income, allowing them to exploit other people's human and natural resources.

Russia and China have never been able to do this. Authoritarianism was all within their nations. The collapse would have had no reason to trigger a third world war. Indeed today it is precisely these two nations, largely deserving for having been able to deal with their own structural limits, which can prevent the West from behaving irrationally.

March 20

Minimum and maximum objectives

A state socialism like the Soviet-Stalinist (industrialized) and Chinese-Maoist (agricultural) one, or a mercantile socialism (like the current one in China) are authentic contradictions in terms. This is because a truly democratic socialism must overcome the two main entities dominant today: the State and the Market. In the current capitalism of the collective West, multinationals and centers of financial power go even beyond states and organizations of international law, in the sense that they do not want to be controlled by anything or anyone.

Socialism, for which we must lay the foundations today, will have to be self-managed by local communities, based on common ownership of the means of production and direct democracy.

State socialism failed due to its own internal contradictions; today's Chinese capitalism will fail in the future, just as state capitalism will fail, which at the moment, in Russia, is opposed to Western-style private capitalism. Why do we say this? Are we perhaps maximalists? Do we only demand the best?

Let's say one thing first: human beings are not so stupid as not to see the problems that they themselves create. The fact is unfortunately that it will take centuries before finding any solution. And when you think you have found it, you realize that it is very relative, temporary, a kind of a patch on an old garment.

We fight to improve things only after having devastated them: we are not capable of prevention. And since we intervene with the treatment after allowing a lot of time to pass, the results we obtain are only temporary, even if, when we make our maximum commitment, they seem definitive, indeed "lifesaving".

We are always affected by "mystical" visions, even when we are atheists. Just think of the cult of personality attributed to Stalin and Mao, and the horrors we have tolerated in the name of this absurd cult; not to mention those permitted in the name of the idolatrous cult of money.

We are chronically deluded. However, since we must avoid nihilism, which would certainly lead us to worsen the quality of life, we must also advocate for those causes that appear minimalist to us. A proverb says: something is better than nothing.

And so, at this moment we must prefer Asian state capitalism to Western private capitalism; mercantile socialism to state capitalism. In the context of capitalism, we must prefer multipolar capitalism to unipolar capitalism. We must prefer national sovereignism to neoliberal globalism, because it guarantees greater autonomy to individual states. Personally, I also prefer a federated state to a centralized one, since I am in favor of the decentralization of responsibilities and functions, and I would be willing to give much more power to the Local Territorial Bodies. Then we would stop always blaming the State for everything we don't know how to do.

Is this perhaps the best that can be achieved? No, it's the minimum. But anyone who reasons with the categorical aut-aut: either all or nothing, for me is an infantile subject, closed in on himself, an abstract idealist who will never obtain anything useful from life.

Lenin said that, in order to overthrow capitalism in his country, he would have been willing to ally himself even with the monarchy. Let's take an example from him, who was very far from taking dogmatic positions, so much so that after completing the revolution and defeating the counter-revolutionaries, he introduced partial elements of capitalism with the New Economic Policy: the NEP which authoritarian Stalinism eliminated in no time at all.

March 21

Traumatic experiences

At the end of the 1990s the American professor Mike Davis wrote: "If Marx were alive today he would underline the hallucinatory character of the vision that galvanized the masses during the so-called revolutions of 1989. The mirage towards which millions of people were marching was the cornucopia of Fordism: that is, the mass consumer society, with high levels of wages and consumption, still identified with the American (and Northern European) lifestyle. The only emancipation achieved by the unfortunate citizens of the former Warsaw bloc is a sinister paleo-capitalism, combining all the most backward and most brutal elements of underdevelopment (including the accelerated robbery of natural resources and virgin forests by multinational corporations), with the most advanced aspects of global organized crime".

Those pseudo-revolutions were actually coups d'état organized with Western participation (the last successful one was in 2014 in Kiev).

The EU was looking forward to being able to expand so easily and acquire the assets of Eastern Europe. One of the heaviest prices paid by those former nations of state socialism was the entry into NATO.

When they tried to do the same thing in Ukraine (and Belarus), the intent, in reality, was to dismember the great Russian Federation, very rich in raw materials, hitting its vital nerve centers in the European area.

However, the collective West has done its calculations badly: Russia allowed itself to be colonized in the 1990s, but with Putin it said enough and went on the counterattack. No one expected it to be able to do so with such strength and speed, although obviously it was feared in terms of nuclear weapons.

Today it is difficult to say that NATO will resign itself to losing the proxy war unleashed against Russia in Ukraine. In fact, it is easier to think that it is preparing for a real direct clash. A clash that the West will inevitably lose again. This is because history is taking a specific direction: the unchallenged dominion of Western private capitalism over the entire planet is over. The near future will be in the hands of Asian brand state capitalism and mercantile socialism, where the state plays a significant role.

However, an observation must be made on one aspect of Davis' aforementioned sentence. The transition from state socialism to private capitalism in the former Soviet bloc countries was, in a certain sense, made possible by an important generational change. It was not wanted by those who had fought in the Second World War, but by their children. The illusion of being able to have everything immediately was typical of young people, who did not accept living in poverty and under the political-party control of the entire economy. Could this rebellious need continue to be prevented in an authoritarian or paternalistic manner? No, it couldn't. The Soviet repression of Hungary in 1956 and Czechoslovakia in 1968 had left heavy consequences.

Could the younger generations be persuaded by showing that Euro-American well-being was paid for by the malaise of the countries colonized by the West? It wouldn't have done any good. Any critical analysis made against the structural contradictions of capitalism was taken by young people as a form of propaganda. They wanted to eat the fruits of the maypole at all costs. Even today, those who carried out the coups and the so-called "color revolutions" of the 80s and 90s, and who are starting to reach a certain age, are not willing to admit having made a wrong choice. Rather, they insist on maintaining, in the most absurd way possible, that if their dreams have not come true according to their expectations, it is all the fault of Russia, which continues to threaten their country, to prevent the development of democracy, to break international rules.

Unfortunately we are made like this: to open our eyes and see reality for what it is and not for what it seems or what we would like it to be, we need traumatic experiences.

March 22

A priority objective above all

Why does representative democracy no longer work (and not just in Italy)? Naturally, I am referring first and foremost to the national-parliamentary type, but the voters' mistrust is also extending to the local-regional level.

Only half of those entitled to vote now go to vote, exactly like in the United States. So whoever wins only receives half of the total votes. Talking about "representative democracy", in these terms, no longer makes sense. The "party of abstentionists" is, in fact, the largely majority one over any other single party or coalition. The reason for this debacle is that democracy does not involve the masses, but only represents the interests of the elites.

The foundation of parliamentary representation, be it national or regional, namely economic democracy (or social equality), has ceased to exist even as a theoretical objective. It seems to be an unattainable mirage.

When it is said that in the West economics dominates politics, it means that private interest prevails over the public good. Even today it is largely finance that dominates the economy. And if official politics is placed at the service of private interest, it is clear that the population organizes itself outside the institutions.

This is very evident in the media. It doesn't take long to understand that the most objective information must be looked for on certain websites or in collective platforms such as Telegram, Youtube... and in some social networks where censorship almost does not exist.

Furthermore, this progressive disempowerment of that policy which, in theory, should be aimed at protecting the public good, leads to a very dangerous consequence: national states (not to mention local communities) are increasingly in the hands of international economic bodies - financial, public (such as the IMF, the World Bank, the World Trade Organization, etc.) and private (such as multinationals and investment funds: BlackRock, Vanguard, State Street...).

National sovereignty is subject to impressive limits. Even a military alliance like NATO, which should be subject to political powers, heavily influences the decisions of the European Parliament and of individual national parliaments.

Europeans have created a Union that deprives them of any decision-making autonomy, and to a much greater extent than the national states did before.

Representative democracy is becoming increasingly fictitious, indeed useless. Its function is only to promote the interests of the economic-financial powers, wherever they operate. The world is perceived as something "global" (i.e. interconnected, interdependent) only in the sense that strong powers have the privilege of being able to act, everywhere, without controls of any kind.

It is unthinkable to be able to restore national sovereignty at state level, without asking ourselves how to achieve true economic democracy, which involves social equality, environmental protection and which starts first and foremost from the local-regional instance.

Citizens need to see up close how their primary goals are being achieved. That is, even if they obtained Italy's exit from the EU and NATO, this recovery of national sovereignty could not be considered sufficient to obtain a strong popular consensus from the political institutions.

Citizens need to collectively manage local resources, those of the territory in which they live, and they need to make common decisions on this form of self-management, making use of all the tools of direct democracy, which must be exercised with a certain frequency. We cannot prevaricate on this objective, which takes priority over everything.

March 23

Ukraine and Gaza are not enough

It is clear that the United States is preparing for a war with China. This is demonstrated by the fact that they have just sold a 75 million dollar weapons package to Taiwan which includes a system known as Link 16, which allows the Taiwanese armed forces to share data with all the armamentarium of other countries, that is, to be able to fight alongside the United States, Japan, Korea, Australia etc. against China.

The Rand Corporation had already warned about 10 years ago that to prevail in the world it was necessary to go to war with China by 2025. Admiral Philip Davidson said that the war will be in 2027. For the neoliberal globalists to go to war is absolutely necessary. The reconstitution of fascism and fascist tendencies throughout the world becomes inevitable.

But why is the Chinese economy feared so much by the West?

Because the prices of their goods are too low, they are the result of too competitive labor costs. Even when industrial products do not have a quality comparable to Western ones, they still remain attractive for those who do not have many means. China's success in the markets of the Global South is overwhelming and is also affecting those in the West. That South that the West has wanted to exploit, subjugate, rob, impoverish, plunder for half a millennium is now turning its gaze elsewhere. Also because China does not want to impose ideologies of any kind: it refers to international law created by the West itself. It is exporting neither democracy nor socialism.

Furthermore, the mercantile socialism that it is currently experimenting with is not a post-Maoist invention. Lenin had already inaugurated it with the New Economic Policy. In Russia it was no longer restored, not so much on the mercantilist side (in fact with the decade of Yeltsin the system ended up bankrupt), but rather on the socialist side, since the horrors caused by the state system of Stalinism had been too extensive and deep.

The pragmatic Putin aimed at a sort of state capitalism, in the sense that the State opened up to foreign investments, while maintaining control of the Federation's strategic assets (energy and defense primarily, but also the mining, metallurgical and banking sectors). But in Russia light industry is in no way comparable to that of China.

Will it be the weak who want dictatorship?

It is evident that if the collective West continues to create external enemies, democracy will progressively tend to disappear.

At the time of the Cold War, enemies no. 1 were the so-called "real socialism" and the communist parties in general, wherever they were found. That was a kind of virtual world war that the American-led West conducted in terms of intelligence, coups d'état, excellent assassinations, artfully fomented opposing extremisms... Naturally, nuclear arsenals increased enormously. The USA significantly expanded the number of military bases around the world and began to place spy satellites in outer space (it is no coincidence that part of the "star shield" began with Reagan).

Once that war was won, the West created another enemy: Islamic terrorism. The self-produced attack on the Twin Towers was enough to unleash a twenty-year war on various Middle Eastern countries.

When the West suddenly armed to the teeth withdrew from Afghanistan, it was understood that the new enemy had become Putin's Russia, which, unlike Yeltsin's, did not accept being colonized.

The place to declare war was Ukraine, without excluding attempts at "color revolutions" in Chechnya, Georgia, Kazakhstan, Belarus... The objective was always the same: to dismember the Russian Federation, even at the cost of transforming a regional conflict into a global one. Even the current Israeli-Palestinian conflict serves the purpose. And the next one, already planned, between China and Taiwan will also have the same function.

Capitalism creates and destroys in alternating phases, because this is the best way to self-valorize, otherwise the tendency for the rate of profit to fall becomes increasingly dangerous. Constant capital, lavished on machinery, needs fresh meat every day and in large quantities, like the Minotaur in the Knossos labyrinth, and if it doesn't find it it becomes even more aggressive.

The West continually provokes, sowing terror, spreading mass massacres, forcing its own populations into total conformism, to accept the most absurd restrictions, to adopt habits that have nothing to do with democracy. It behaves this way because it is no longer able to guarantee what it promises: citizens, in order not to become anti-capitalists, cannot continue to demand too high standards of well-being. Only very few people can aspire to such a claim.

The vast majority of humans must suffer. And, for this purpose, everything can be used, from an ad hoc pandemic to a regional war, from obligations to quickly respect certain ecological parameters to the erosion of one's private savings, up to the forced transformation of cash into digital currency.

Until yesterday, capital had exploited the Third World to make its working class become a sort of middle class. Today, however, it is the entire middle class that must be proletarianized. This is because the Global South is raising its head and not without the help of the military and economic might of the collective West's two main adversaries: Russia and China.

Western populations must be kept under control, sent to die in various theaters of war, reduced in number, using artificial viruses and making healthcare increasingly expensive. Above all, they must be deprived of the possibility of freely using their properties. "You will have nothing and you will be happy", this is the main slogan at the annual forum in Davos.

The welfare state will no longer exist. The "poor" will be the one who will not accept to suffer subhuman working conditions in order to make a living. And the more the poor kill each other for a crust of bread, the more the system will demonstrate that dictatorship is necessary.

The narrative will be reversed: the dictatorship will not be requested by the strong powers, but by the weak ones, convinced, by doing so, that they will not weaken themselves even more. Dictators will be seen with messianic attitudes.

March 24

The sword of Damocles

We have seen in recent years with striking examples that the West is no longer used to looking at things as a whole and therefore in their complexity. During the pandemic the mantra was "Whoever doesn't get vaccinated, dies". With the Russian-Ukrainian war it was and is "There is the assailed and the aggressor". Now in Palestine it is "Israel has the right to defend itself" (and if Hamas terrorists are hiding in civilian structures, no one can do anything about it. Which in practice means genocide is tolerated).

Why do we interpret reality in such a schematic and one-sided way? It's very simple: in the West we live like alienated people. That is, everything is divided and, at the same time, hierarchized. The economy commands politics, finance commands the economy, the producer commands the consumer, the institutions command the citizens, the few who produce information command the many who receive it. And so on. Either you are on the side of the powerful or you are very weak. And even when you are with the strong, there is always someone even stronger.

The West is the civilization of private capital, which through formal legal freedom and mechanism dominates almost the entire planet. Its laws are irrational, producing conflicts and divisions of all sorts. Where there is competition, competition, antagonism, there can be no peace for anyone.

This is why we only see a small part of the reality that surrounds us, as if we lived in a prison with a tiny window. Each of us has a sword on our head tied to a very thin thread, which can break at any moment. In ancient times it was called the "sword of Damocles", but it had a moralistic meaning. The myth served to make ordinary people understand that even those with great power can never be safe. Today, however, it is the great masses of the people who must get used to living in chaos, in uncertainty, in temporariness.

When the Internet was born we deluded ourselves that with user interaction we could overcome the enormous distance that separates strong powers from weak ones. We thought that the enormous knowledge transmitted by the web could put a stop to the arrogance of power.

Instead, since power began to take over all social networks, transforming them into a new business opportunity and a tool for influencing the behavior of the masses, we are asking ourselves what are the most suitable tools to get out, collectively, from the system cage.

There are probably two ways:

- recover the physicality of human relationships (or in any case virtuality must serve this physicality);

- reclaim the local territory in all its aspects.

These are two basic conditions, starting from which, by looking up, one can begin to understand reality with greater knowledge of the facts. It is not important to know a lot of things: what is needed to defend ourselves from the interference of those who want to keep us divided, helpless, unaware of our true good.

March 25

Not all evil comes to harm

Every war, small or large, is always a colossal tragedy. However, not every evil comes to harm, in the sense that we should not worry too much if Western civilization, based on private capitalism, disappears following a nuclear war.

When we tell ourselves that, with such a war, the whole world will disappear, we are obviously exaggerating. We think, from the height of our egocentrism, that without us, nothing can exist.

In reality the real problem is what to do next. Assuming that we will live in much more difficult environmental conditions, we should now ask ourselves how we will be able to survive. That is, the survivors will have to create the conditions so that the apocalypse does not happen again. And it will certainly not be enough to tell ourselves that we will have to be "better". The conditions must be structural, capable of modifying people's subjectivity.

One of the examples to follow could be that of Pietro Laureano, architect and urban planner, described in his book The Inverted Pyramid. His model is that of the oasis, a human settlement in an unfavorable geographical situation that uses rare, locally available resources. The goal is to create a fertile and self-sustainable environmental niche.

The alternative certainly cannot be the industrialized world or the gigantism of great civilizations. Instead, we need small communities in close contact with nature. In this the global South is favored, provided of course that it frees itself from the weight of colonialism, old and new. And to do so it must act immediately, without waiting for an external event, such as a world war unfavorable to the West, to favor its emancipation.

If human beings want to stop being aggressive towards each other, they must first stop being aggressive towards nature. It is generally thought that to have a good relationship with nature, one must first overcome class conflicts and social antagonisms. In reality there is not one thing to do before and one thing after.

The human being is a natural entity. It makes no sense to try to achieve a truly democratic socialism, as opposed to any capitalist dynamic, without asking, at the same time, how to respect the reproductive needs of nature.

Even if we managed to create a true social alternative, the result would last very little time, in the absence of a balanced relationship with nature. An economic choice, which is not also an ecological choice, is worth nothing. Just as an economic choice of an industrial nature, based on the mass production of goods, on their sale in the markets and things of that nature, does not even deserve to be taken into consideration.

Those who think that the factories of the future will not have workers to exploit, but only machines to work 24 hours a day, and at the same time do not ask any environmental questions about the raw materials with which to operate the machines, nor about how they will be disposed of or how the goods produced by the same machines will be recycled, is thinking like a philosopher, that is, completely abstract.

We must carefully avoid the goal of immediate effectiveness. Nature's times are slow, sometimes very slow, but they are the ones that prevent catastrophe in the long term.

March 26

The humanization of the land

The Indian Vandana Shiva is an extraordinarily intelligent woman. She suggests that in the future India will have the greatest sensitivity to environmental issues and the importance of local communities.

In the context of capitalism she sees a line of continuity that is destroying the entire planet. In fact, while in its first phase capitalism was able to impose itself, transferring decision-making powers from local communities to national states, today the transfer has occurred from these states to multinationals and global financial funds, which have no borders whatsoever and which they are capable of influencing every country in the world.

The multinationals and the aforementioned funds are making the entire world their backyard, being able to move far and wide without any problem. Paradoxically, this attitude is similar to that of a prehistoric man, who certainly had no problems with borders. With one fundamental difference however: the primitive had his eyes wide open when faced with the diversity of the environment and respected it with care. Capitalism, on the other hand, in the name of industrial profit, land rent and monetary interest, exploits, plunderes and desertifies.

Today everything is reduced to a commodity and each of us is a mere consumer. The legal battles that Shiva led to obtain the revocation of the patents on Neem (the plant at the basis of Indian toothpaste) and Basmati (an important variety of Indian rice) are historic. This is because neoliberal globalism tends to privatize, through patent policy, biological and genetic commons. And national states are becoming complicit in this gigantic expropriation, which can easily be justified according to the formula of "public utility".

Statesmen have become half-figures precisely because the real power lies elsewhere. And the more the populations oppose these perverse designs of capital, the more authoritarian politics will become.

The solution proposed by Shiva is inevitable: local communities must return to take over the territories in which they live; they must self-produce what they need. Such communities must necessarily be democratic in every smallest aspect of their existence, otherwise they will not resist pressure coming from outside, from the strong powers. The local resistance itself will have to become the highest school of democracy at all levels.

On an economic level, the concept of "monoculture" must absolutely be overcome. We must not produce for a market but to satisfy real needs.

Let's get ready to understand something that will surely upset our lives: taking over agricultural land again, in a collective and democratic way, will cause a fatal blow to cities. The real war will be between the humanization of the land and urban alienation.

Where is the logic?

It can be understood that someone, like Erdoğan, incapable of undertaking any military initiative against Israel, would say senseless phrases such as "Allah destroy Netanyahu".

But one is a little shocked when Netanyahu responds with the words: "Israel observes the laws of war and will not be subjected to moral sermons from Erdoğan, who supports murderers and rapists of the Hamas terrorist organization, denies the Armenian genocide and massacres the Kurds in his own country."

In fact, even regardless of the fact that the Hamas organization could be defined as non-terrorist but resistance; even regardless of the fact that the Hamas raid on October 7th did not have the aim of killing and raping but of capturing hostages to be exchanged for the thousands of Palestinian prisoners in Israeli prisons; even taking it for granted that the Turkish government actually carried out the Armenian genocide and has always massacred the Kurds; so regardless of all this, what is the point of justifying one's genocide against the civilian population of Gaza?

On the basis of what human or religious logic can it be argued that since someone behaves in an inhumane manner, then I can do it too? What are these "laws of war" that Israel feels free to respect when it is exterminating completely unarmed civilian populations (including children)?

We are faced with these paradoxes

The Kiev government complains about not receiving military aid suitable for the current situation, but then says that the Russians have the ability to modify the response to new weapons arriving in Ukraine in real time.

They ask to be able to defend themselves against Russian drones with Western weapons, but then admit that they are completely helpless against hypersonic missiles.

On the one hand in Kiev they complain that weapons are not enough but more men are needed, on the other hand they complain that they don't know where to find them.

Ukraine is not a NATO country, but it asks NATO to enter the conflict with its troops. They ask Western countries for tens of billions, knowing in advance that they will not be able to pay them back.

They fear that they will not be able to withstand the Russian offensive for long, and therefore refuse to start negotiations to save what can be saved. They define themselves as more democratic than the Russians, and yet they refuse to call new parliamentary and presidential elections.

Ukraine is run by a former comedian, we know, but here all Western statesmen play comedic roles in the same comedy.

March 27

Two different forms of globalism

After all, the word "globalism", considered abstractly, could also seem positive. With bourgeois nations, feudal empires have been overcome, including the regional autonomies of aristocratic magnates, who lived on agricultural income.

Artisans, merchants, entrepreneurs felt freer within a nation, in which there were no insurmountable privileges due to birth, and where it was therefore easier to enrich oneself individually.

In a national state, citizens, at least theoretically, are all equal, subject to the same law. The national market does not know about expensive internal barriers (customs duties), and the currency, being single, allows you to save on transaction costs. Weights and measures also have unique parameters.

Half a millennium ago the expression "national state" seemed the optimal solution to overcome the limits of feudalism. However, being managed by a scientistic and developmentalist bourgeoisie, with its capitalist methods, this State was also the beginning of enormous disasters.

For example, the labor of a vast wage labor force, expelled from the land, was subjected to brutal exploitation in manufacturing and factories. The natural environment began to be devastated. When the market was firmly in the hands of the bourgeoisie, it was discovered that it was limited by national borders. Thus began the colonial conquest of the planet, which involved a strong rivalry between the bourgeois nations themselves.

The last two world wars marked the crisis of the traditional European national states, to the advantage of a gigantic federated national state, which in terms of geographical extension resembled an empire: the United States. No country in the world could compete with such a capitalist state. It was for this reason that the European national states thought of coming together, creating a European Union.

We look at things abstractly. Wasn't it preferable that the freedoms enjoyed by citizens at a national level could now be enjoyed at a supranational level? Who would have ever suspected that within the EU some states (Germany and France first and foremost) wanted to be more "equal" than others?

What an ugly Europe we have created! The economically strongest or politically most powerful or militarily most armed countries want to dominate all the others. The geopolitical lessons of two world wars thrown into the dustbin of history!

And in the midst of these absurd internal rivalries, those who have benefited most have always been the USA, which moreover boasts of not wanting to be "imperialist" like the Europeans. They are "globalists", that is, they claim to conquer the world only by virtue of mass consensus, consumerism, and dollarization. Their only ideology is economic liberalism. On a political and legal level they preach values acquired by Europeans: representative democracy and human rights.

In the abstract the word "globalism" seemed to be more democratic or less violent than the word "imperialism". American multinationals and their own financial institutions knew how to go beyond any national limit or difference.

It's a shame that the USA experiences social conflicts within itself that are so acute that they need to unleash, with a certain frequency, regional wars as a weapon of mass distraction. Today they are even thinking of a world war.

The fact of having a large territorial extension, a significant population density, a very respectable industrial production, a consolidated financial dominance in the world and above all control of the seas through their enormous naval fleet, has not made the USA a safer country than European ones.

The idea of a "globalized world" that they are flaunting is leaking from all sides. It does not arise from an effective equality of all nations, but from an unbearable arrogance, which now has to deal with two nations (Russia and China), very strong on a military and economic level: two nations that are moving at the "global" level in a very different way. And the South of the world has noticed it. The final bell for Western collapse is about to ring.

March 28

We dismantled a dangerous toy

In Western Europe, socialism (first utopian and then scientific) was born when rural life had been overturned by the penetration of capital.

The socialists themselves, when they saw farmers working the land without industrial means, and not willing to produce monocultures for the markets, considered them backward. If the farmers remained tied to outdated cultures, such as religious ones, it was very difficult for them to have relationships with the workers, who tended to be atheists and communists.

For the socialists the reference target was the factory worker, who after all was a former farmer, emancipated from religion, and devoid of any good other than the same working capacity as him. Socialism demanded that the industrial proletariat not limit itself to working with increasingly improved mechanical means, but also become its owners. The peasant class only had to help the workers carry out the political revolution against private entrepreneurs and the State that represented them.

Once the revolution was over, the farmers themselves would have obtained ownership of the land, managing it collectively and on the basis of advanced production tools. Hoe and spade had to be hung on a nail.

What didn't work in this project? In Western Europe the industrial proletariat has failed to carry out any political revolution (the only attempt, which lasted a few months, was that of the Paris Commune).

The failure of the working class and revolutionary socialism depended on two factors: 1) colonial exploitation of the Third World ensured high wages in Western Europe; 2) with high wages the workers tended to become bourgeois in their lifestyle, and their intellectual (political and trade union) leaders did even more so. Everyone tended to transform from revolutionaries to reformists. Socialism became a goal of an unspecified future, to be achieved when it would have been absurd not to.

In Eastern Europe, however, the political revolutions were successful. But all the enormous sacrifices made were wasted when the "social" was made to coincide with the "state". In other words, there was the illusion that by nationalizing all the main means of production, workers would feel socially satisfied. In reality, collective property, managed from above with authoritarian directives, ended up becoming nobody's property. Personal responsibility died. Production inefficiencies were passed on to the State, which ultimately had to save even the poorest companies.

The original socialist idea, according to which the State had to progressively wither away, had never been applied. And the State was unable to guarantee a significant market, either in quality or quantity. Indeed, for fear of the aggressiveness of capitalist countries, the levers of the state had been enormously strengthened. The centralization of power had become suffocating.

What alternative was opposed to this authoritarian and bureaucratic drift of state socialism? The return to capitalism and, moreover, in its worst form: the private one.

It didn't seem true to Western capitalism. It was the right moment to seize all the resources of the former socialist countries, still too weak on a mercantile level to put up solid resistance.

Only two large countries have resisted this triumphal march of Western private capitalism: China and Russia. The first with its mercantile socialism; the second was able to put a brake on its own oligarchies, re-storing some fundamental functions of control and direction of the state apparatus.

Having said this, let's get two illusions out of our heads: the first is that the definitive collapse of Western private capitalism is imminent; the second is that a multipolar vision, on a global geopolitical level, is in itself an incentive to achieve a truly democratic socialism.

At the moment we have only understood how things cannot work. Now we need to understand if there are pieces from the unipolar toy that we dismantled because it was dangerous that we can reuse for something different, or if we need to turn our gaze in a completely different direction.

March 29

It can be done

I have always liked the historian Pier Paolo Poggio, because I think he is very balanced and objective. In his best writings he had for example: understood that ecology is more important than economics. He demonstrated this by writing various articles and essays on the story of the ACNA (Azienda Coloranti Nazionali e Affini) which produced dyes and operated in the Bormida river valley (localities of Cengio, Cesano Maderno and Rho): an eloquent testimony to the failure of the idea of "progress".

That was an area subject to over a century of almost uninterrupted chemical pollution. The industry, born in 1929, was perceived as a deus ex machina of collective well-being, for which environmental and health controls were very poor, not to mention worker protection systems.

But already in 1882 the municipality of Cengio had authorized the construction of a dynamite factory (Barberi), while in 1906 a new company (SIPE) producing sulfuric acid, oleum and TNT explosives which supplied weapons to the Italian soldiers engaged in the wars of African colonialism. The river water for irrigation was toxic, and so were the wells for drinking it.

When the ACNA arrived the situation worsened drastically. In 1938 the company was sued for environmental damage, but the trial continued until 1962, when the farmers who survived the complaint lost the case and were even forced to pay the legal costs! It is no coincidence that in 1960 the Ministry of Agriculture and Forestry renewed ACNA's concession to use the waters of the Bormida for 70 years!

In 1974 the ACNA leaders were denounced, but four years later they were acquitted.

In 1976, after the Seveso disaster and the Merli Law, the Cengio factory, which produced 65% of the world's aluminum chloride, began to dump its waste at night or hide it in the surrounding land.

In 1982, various municipalities denounced the ACNA leaders, but that time too they were acquitted. Faced with the first cases of bladder cancer, the unions, for the first time, took action as civil parties, but the company convinced them to withdraw from the trial, threatening to close their doors.

We began to truly worry only when faced with the multiplication of carcinogenic diseases and inexorable deaths. Before this evidence we trusted promises and false assurances. Some magistrates even went so far as to say that ACNA had had a beneficial effect on the waters of the river, making them fertile! Surreal statements, like those we hear today from those media that justify the neo-Nazism of Kiev and Tel Aviv.

Within a few years the company top management decided to cease the production of dyes, maintaining that of pigments instead. But the illnesses did not decrease.

It took countless and tenacious popular, peasant and worker struggles to change the situation somewhat. Capital doesn't give anything to anyone, on the contrary, if you let it, it steals and plunders, exploits and kills, and above all lies, always and everywhere. It lied so much that corporate and political power, in order to keep the factory running, went so far as to transform it into a gigantic incinerator to recover the waste (sulfates) that the factory itself had produced. It planned to resell them to other industries. Practically we had gone from one form of pollution to another, with the addition, however, of criminal trafficking linked to the same waste.

Despite this, the local population managed to organize itself as a very combative movement against the opportunistic and indifferent positions of the parties in the left and unions, which tended to minimize the problem. The Ministry of the Environment even went so far as to say that ACNA could demonstrate the eco-friendliness of the chemical industry.

In reality, the pollution is still present, despite the many clean-ups started in 1999, when the company was finally closed. Now we are trying to recover some of the most ancient rural traditions (hilly and mountainous), in order to achieve self-sustainable endogenous development, compliant with the most solid ecological demands. But it won't be easy.

March 30

Russian-Chinese Asianism

What is Russian-Chinese Asianism? How does it differ from the bourgeois culture of Western private capitalism? Why is it destined to prevail in the future?

We shouldn't let ourselves be too impressed. Russia and China started out last on the path to capitalism: they were a sort of "weak link". The first to free itself from private capitalism was Russia with the revolution of 1917. China arrived in 1949, with the Maoist revolution.

What could they leverage to avoid being colonized by the West for hundreds of years? On two things: the great pre-bourgeois rural traditions and the ideology of scientific socialism. In the name of these two aspects they carried out their revolutions. India also had great peasant traditions, but remained foreign to socialist ideology in the modern sense.

The two aforementioned communist revolutions placed the all-encompassing functions of the State at the center of the interests of civil society; functions so pervasive that the results have been disastrous, which we have tried to remedy by reintroducing some typical aspects of capitalism, those linked to private initiative, into socio-economic life.

In Russia, accustomed to being "apocalyptic" (as the anti-Bolshevik philosopher Nikolai Berdjaev said), with the introduction of the wildest neoliberalism, at the time of Yeltsin, any socialist ideology was renounced. In China, however, the anti-capitalist rigors of this ideology were attenuated, allowing society to become bourgeois within certain limits. As is known, under Putin Russia had to backtrack, after losing millions of people along the way, literally reduced to starvation.

However, the socialist ideology was not restored, but simply an attempt was made to place society under the control of the state, giving life to a sort of state capitalism, ideologically nationalist and, in some respects, even confessional.

Such an operation in the West would be possible only in a few extreme cases: a disastrous defeat in a world war; a devastating financial collapse of the major stock exchanges, as in 1929; a catastrophic consequence of climate change.

In the past there were cases of this kind (obviously not the environmental ones, which are specific to contemporary times). Western states had to intervene to prevent the emergence of civil wars or communist political revolutions or uncontrolled forms of crime.

However, if there are no such particular cases, Western capitalism, relying on the exploitation of its colonies, tends to remain the same, that is, based on private entrepreneurship, which benefits from the protection of a classist state.

In Western Europe, the USA, Canada etc. there is no point in harking back to pre-bourgeois rural traditions: they have disappeared for centuries. The sense of "collectivism" has been lost in our country in the mists of time. It is something that must be built from scratch, continually smoothing out the harshness of unbridled individualism, made possible by the aforementioned colonialism, which allows for high rates of well-being.

These are concerns that Russia and China with their Asianism do not have to face, precisely because on a political level they are solid, they can make long-term plans, without having many problems in realizing them. Their standard of living, on the whole, has always been modest, having not been able to benefit from the exploitation of human and natural resources outside their nation.

If anything, the collective West has other problems, grappling with a Global South that wants to emancipate itself from all points of view. For this area of the planet, half a millennium of labor exploitation, theft of natural resources, and environmental devastation are considered more than enough.

It's me, take me

On the occasion of this Easter I asked myself: if Christ had the power to disappear after his death, why didn't he do so immediately after his arrest on the Mount of Olives? How much unnecessary suffering would he have saved himself?

Naturally a believer would have the answer ready, which would equally naturally be wrong: "Jesus had to die to redeem sinful humanity in the eyes of God". He would say this thinking of a purely moral or religious redemption, as the social one sends him back to the afterlife.

But what is the secular answer to that question? If Jesus had mysteriously disappeared while he was still alive, he would have proven that he was not exactly a human being, but some kind of extraterrestrial with extraordinary powers. Which would have fueled the bizarre idea of not resisting evil and of entrusting the resolution of humanity's crucial problems to an external entity, of a divine nature, which naturally would have occurred at the end of time.

Now it is evident (to common sense) that Jesus had not entered Jerusalem to be killed: he would have been a masochistic madman. That he wasn't, I don't know if it's enough to say that he went there with a large crowd of followers, since all of them could have been plagiarized by absurd ideas, as were the followers of Jim Jones' sect in Guyana. But it must be admitted that if he really wanted to be executed, he could have gone alone: he didn't need to involve a multitude.

It is therefore easier to believe that he was realistically afraid of being eliminated, having been a wanted man with an arrest warrant for some time. Hence the need for a certain popular consensus that would allow him to feel sufficiently protected. Among other things, if he really wanted to be arrested, he would not have taken refuge in Gethsemane after leaving the Cenacle with the apostles.

But then what did he go to Jerusalem to do? Couldn't he have died of old age, as a refugee, in any other part of the Middle East or in an Asian or African country? He certainly would not have been the first Jew to preach some saving doctrine. No one could have reproached him for anything, since you cannot ask someone to have the courage to die for another or for their own people. Who doesn't remember the famous phrase that Don Abbondio said to Cardinal Borromeo in The Betrothed? "Courage, if one doesn't have it, he cannot give it."

So it is clear that he had chosen him and not to provoke the powers that be on purpose. His intention, and that of his movement of Judaeo-Galilaic followers, necessarily had to be subversive, destabilizing. Taking advantage of the period of greatest influx in the Jewish capital, due to the solemn Easter celebration, the Nazarenes wanted to overthrow, with a popular insurrection, the two fundamental established powers: that of the Sadducees and high priests in the Temple and that of the Romans in the Antonia Fortress.

At the very moment in which he had decided to enter Jerusalem, he must have been convinced that there was a good possibility of defeating both powers, of which the first was completely collaborator of the second. A revolutionary not convinced of this possibility is just an adventurer, an irresponsible person.

Therefore, if things are in these terms, Jesus, in Gethsemane, did not at all give himself up to his tormentors to fulfill a phantom paternal will, but simply because in that way he was able to avoid the decimation of his disciples, who would not have been able to cope against the Roman garrison of 600 soldiers placed on alert by the tribune. In fact, Judas' betrayal had compromised the surprise effect.

In the fourth gospel it is easy to imagine that dramatic scene, which took place in pitch darkness, illuminated only by the torches of the Temple guards.

- Who are you looking for?
- Jesus of Nazareth?

- It's me, take me and let my disciples go, otherwise they will defend themselves and many of you will die.

- We're here, come forward.

March 31

Resurrected or disappeared?

For Christians, the empty tomb must be interpreted as "resurrection". But it's a stretch. It would be so even if the theft of the body to make people believe in a miracle or, on the contrary, to prevent the religious cult (perhaps of a political nature) in that place were excluded. Che Guevara was also buried in a secret place, found only in 1997, 30 years after his death, when it was now believed that his icon would no longer have anything subversive about it.

In reality, no one saw the moment when Jesus' body disappeared from the tomb. When the women went to warn the disciples, the door of the tomb was already open and there was no one inside.

If Jesus really wanted to demonstrate that he was an alien, endowed with superpowers, he would have had to transform himself in the presence of some witnesses, that is, he would have had to make people believe that on the cross he had only apparently died. Which, however, the apostle John excludes, since he wrote that he saw the centurion who stuck the tip of a spear in his side to break his heart and verify if he was really dead.

In fact, in the tomb they found only the sheet in which they had wrapped the corpse, which many identify with the Shroud of Turin (stolen from Constantinople during the Fourth Latin Crusade): a very particular find, which many clues lead us to assume is actually 2000 years ancient.

In any case, if that finding were authentic, all the gospels would need to be revised: when in fact did the Jews or the Romans ever treat in such an inhuman way an absolutely peaceful therapist, one who pays tribute to Caesar and who asks to pray to God in spirit and truth? Some at most stoned the blasphemers; the others crucified rebellious slaves, but without needing to torture them so severely.

Then naturally the evangelical editors took care to make some of the apostles believe that Jesus had reappeared. But they did it because evidently not everyone believed in the "resurrection" thesis. Except that when the gospels were approved by the primitive Church, the generation contemporary with Jesus had already disappeared, so any pious legend could be embroidered on them.

The moral of the story was actually different. If we give more importance to what a man does when he is dead than when he is alive, not only do we not take on the task of continuing his message of liberation, but we also deceive those who were not fortunate enough to be an eyewitness to him.

April

April 1th

The limits of Stalinism

What did Stalinism do wrong? Surely in a rush to get everything right away. Where did this need arise from? From the mistaken belief that if this objective had not been achieved, Western capitalism would have declared war on Russia and win.

Hence the need to maximize state coercion, without which forced collectivization in the countryside and the construction of large industrial, civil and military works would have been impossible.

The price that the populations of the USSR paid was very high, also because any opposition to this unfounded fear and this paroxysmal haste led to millions of deaths, caused by ruthless terror.

Stalinism, in a nutshell, eliminated the generation that had brought about the Bolshevik revolution. And replaced it with another totally devoid of critical spirit, used only to obey.

Germany decided to declare war on the USSR after realizing that Stalinism had lost real popular consensus with state terrorism. Hitler was convinced that the war would last only a few months, that is, that the Russians would welcome the Nazis as liberators.

From this aspect it must be said that it was not exactly Stalinism that defeated Nazism, but it was the heroism, the indomitable resistance of the Russian people, or in any case of the entire Federation. If anything, Stalinism took the credit for it, and continued with its authoritarianism until Stalin's death. Indeed, if we exclude Khrushchev's brief interlude, it continued throughout the period of stagnation.

The idea of state socialism did not fail with Gorbachev, but it had already failed when Stalinism wanted to put an end to the New Economic Policy inaugurated by Lenin. The NEP was nothing other than a sort of "merchant socialism", that is, a socialism that tolerated within certain limits the presence of private capitalism.

The idea of planning everything from above proved to be a failure already in the first half of the 1930s. In the second half, state terror was unleashed for not wanting to admit this defeat.

Today any revival of nationalized socialism is doomed to fail. The idea of socialism must be totally rethought. Without democracy, socialism dies. But democracy, to be effective, authentic, must be direct. Direct democracy on a political level necessarily implies local management of the territory in which the main resources belong to the entire population that lives there. Ultimately it is also the relationship with nature that must be completely revised.

April 2

In what sense global and local?

Only very specialized theologians know that the word "Catholic" is also used by the Orthodox confession. The latter defines as "Roman Catholic" (or Latin) the theology professed by the papacy and by Catholics in the broadest sense, also called "papists", due to that sort of "cult of personality" that they reserve for a person deemed "infallible", capable of issuing valid judgments ex-sese, that is, in itself, or ex-cathedra, or ex consensu ecclesiae, that is, regardless of a conciliar decision.

Well the word "Catholic" is understood by the Orthodox in the opposite way to that of the Catholics. Originally the primitive Church used it to indicate something "complete", that is, a whole that does not need anything else.

One was Catholic if there was a local community that could officiate its sacraments around the figure of a bishop recognized by an ecclesiastical tradition and therefore by other local bishops. Below the bishop were the presbyter and the deacon, but above there was no one.

This interpretation of the word "Catholic" has been preserved in the Orthodox confession, even if the ranks of the hierarchy have grown (archbishop, primate, metropolitan). However, everyone had to consider themselves primus inter pares.

In other words, the Orthodox feel "Catholic" starting from a "completeness" experienced at the local community level. It is by virtue of this local "fullness" that it is possible to recognize oneself on the "universal" level.

Among Catholics, however, the universality of their Church is given by the fact that the pontiff is recognized throughout the world as the leading person.

This means that Catholics are in communion with each other only if they obey everything the pontiff says. It is no coincidence that Catholicism presents itself as a universal and absolute monarchy.

It is not a constitutional monarchy, since the Pope's actions are not subject to the limits of a Fundamental Law approved by a collective body.

Even the Catholic "Creed" differs from the Orthodox one, as it contains an aspect introduced arbitrarily by the papacy: the Filioque.

Roman Catholicism is not even a parliamentary monarchy, since synods are convened to ratify (at a local-regional level) decisions already taken by the Pope and the Cardinals (chosen by him exclusively and without appeal). Councils are used to do the same thing at a national or international level, or to elect a new pope.

Why all this talk? Because today if we replace the word "Catholic" with the word "globalism" we get the same result.

Capital wants to be global in the sense that it wants to impose itself with the power of money throughout the world. Once upon a time, when we spoke of "capital", we were referring to a specific entrepreneur or even a merchant or banker. Today, however, everything is depersonalized. The "god" who commands does not have a specific face. You never know who to fight. We only know that globalism for capital means that local communities must not have any autonomy, that is, they must depend on something that is foreign to their ability to control.

These communities must feel part of a "global village" not because they experience similar productive autonomy, but because they are all subjected to the same conditioning by the strong powers.

April 3

Sankara, a pragmatic visionary

There are alternative models to the capitalist system, but you have to be willing to die to achieve them. Unfortunately. And courage isn't something you can buy or sell.

Thomas Sankara, president of Burkina Faso, the African country known as the ("Land of the upright"), knew something about this, and for having revolutionized everything, ended up being killed in 1987 at the age of 37 by a military commando, after only four years of government. Even his body was hidden.

Sankara was the president of the peasants, very poor, ruined by feudal traditions, by the destruction of nature, by colonialist practices, by the absurd import-export laws that impose monocultures, fertilizers, etc.

He thought it scandalous to be a rich president in a poor country. He couldn't stand corruption and abuse. He sought well-being for everyone based on the principle that one must rely on one's own strength, without depending on external entities, such as for example. the World Bank or the IMF.

He was a supporter of direct democracy: he trusted mass organizations (peasants, workers, women, students...) more than small urban and elitist parties. Indeed, for him the city/countryside relationship had to be reversed: the latter should not be at the service of the former, but the opposite.

He promoted an important water policy with which to stop the desert, prevented the cutting of firewood, demanded the reforestation of all villages, asked to look for simple forms of alternative energy with small dams...

The food program was overturned with respect to the capitalist parameters imposed from outside: after placing agriculture at the center of attention, the objective became that of self-consumption, obligatory for everyone. Indeed, taking example from Gandhi's battle for khadi (hand-woven raw cotton tunic), Sankara asked the country's top leaders to wear a local artisan fabric to set a good example.

Preferring to rely on the work of thousands of volunteers, he built a 100 km long railway, rejecting funds from the World Bank, which wanted a highway instead. That was the opportunity to also enhance the importance of manual work.

In just four years the goal of two daily meals and ten liters of water a day for everyone was achieved. No meat, no coffee, tobacco, or multi-national products.

The country went to war against superfluous expenses, waste of energy, ministerial blue cars, luxuries of representation, and so on. Private ownership of fundamental means of production were abolished, as were private schools for wealthy children and even air conditioning in public offices.

All salaries had to have a maximum ceiling, and a share of them had to help farmers make the country completely self-sufficient in food. The state budget broke even in four years.

What was it that killed Sankara? His speeches against foreign debt and financial and economic subservience to the globalist West. According to him, one should only accept help that helps one quickly do without help. He asked the countries of the South to help each other, rather than go to war to please the strategies of the West.

He was eliminated, along with 12 of his officials, perhaps because he had asked for too much in too short a time. The order even came from his most trusted party comrade and Minister of Justice, Blaise Compaoré, who, with a coup, replaced him from 1987 to 2014, initiating a dictatorial and neoliberal policy. He was also accused of fomenting conflicts of various kinds in Sierra Leone, Liberia and Angola.

Naturally he brought the country back into the fold of the IMF and the World Bank, becoming a safe ally of the USA, as well as of France.

The uprising of the popular masses against him occurred only in 2014, and only in 2021 did a military court accuse him of the murder of Sankara, sentencing him to life imprisonment the following year. However, Campaoré had taken refuge in Ivory Coast, from where he asked to be "forgiven".

April 4

Does environmentalism still have a future?

Even if some say that, without class struggle, ecology is just gardening, I have always respected the Greens. I attributed their lack of relevance in Italy to the immaturity of politics. In the sense that if you want to be an environmentalist to the core, you cannot help but be anti-capitalist.

Unfortunately, the system does not offer many alternatives: if you want comfort, you have to accept pollution. In other words: you can fight against pollution as much as you want, but you can only do so up to a certain point.

In fact, the problem is not only that of how to dispose of waste, but also that of how not to produce it, or at least not to do so in such a way that nature is not able to recycle it in a reasonable time.

This is because an industrialized society is inevitably toxic. It is regardless of the fact that renewable energies are better than fossil ones. It is in the four fundamental elements that constitute the essence of our life, already identified by the ancient Greeks: air, water, products of the Earth and products of fire.

I remember that at the beginning of the 1990s many of the Italian radical left decided to start a political movement with the Greens. We wanted to go beyond the pure and simple workers' protest (the struggle between capital and labour); we wanted to make a criticism of the system as a whole.

The German Greens were the model to imitate. (Speaking of these people: what a disappointment to see them so staunchly anti-Putin in the Russo-Ukrainian war!).

I liked the idea of condemning en bloc the Promethean actions of bourgeois man, who used science and technology to exploit, without restraint, human beings and natural resources.

The supporters of modern socialism (utopian and scientific) judged with pity the attempts, in the phase of proto-capitalism, to block the development of the system by physically destroying the factory machines. It was said that progress could not be stopped, and that industry could provide well-being for everyone, obviously provided that its products were equally distributed: something possible only by socializing the ownership of the means of production.

Not even the so-called "real socialism" ever had second thoughts in this scientistic conception.

Today, however, if you don't question your entire lifestyle, you won't get anywhere. That is, it is the enterprise itself, whatever political system it belongs to, that must be questioned; it is its industrialised, mass-produced products, aimed at selling in the markets, that need to be rethought; it is the storage, wholesale and individual packaging of goods, transport, unsold inventories, the destination of obsolete products, the consequences on human and environmental health, not to mention the suffocating advertising, which leave us disarmed, since they seem to be unsolvable problems, indeed, destined to become increasingly macroscopic.

Should we perhaps be satisfied with a superficial environmentalism? Should we perhaps resign ourselves to the fact that, in order to talk about ecology, we must resign ourselves to the risk that it itself becomes a business opportunity for the powers that be?

It seems that in the West the only thing left for us to do is to wait for a protest with a final tone from the global South: "If you want well-being, use your resources, not ours".

Today, in the various global forums on environmental protection, others are added to this protest: "Don't make us pay for the consequences of your industrialization; don't ask us to be environmentalists, when the first ones who aren't are you." In short, it is now clear that there is no truly "human" economy without truly "natural" ecology.

April 5

Listen to other people's reasons

Despite what Kant said, if something can be thought of but cannot be known, we certainly think of it badly, or in any case we have no certainty that we are thinking about it adequately or at least in a sufficiently correct manner.

If we stuck to this empirical observation, which in its essence has a certain logic, we would have to avoid any mystical, religious or metaphysical discourse. What is not knowable is of no use to us, at least not in our present time, even if we can abstractly, in a completely hypothetical way, assume its existence.

If philosophy talks about the "noumenon", it does not deserve to be studied. The same theology, which takes for granted the existence of something or someone, which should instead be demonstrated, leaves the time it finds. At a minimum we should say that theological themes can be used if they are translated into a philosophical sense, but philosophical themes make sense if they are translated into a key political term (or at least legal or economic).

The presuppositions of any knowledge must be concretely verifiable, also because they must contain operational aspects. That is, if there is a "thing in itself", some objectivity that helps to understand certain phenomena, this thing must be able to be known, and to the point where a true interpretation can be distinguished from a false one, or a sufficiently exhaustive interpretation from one that is incomplete, superficial or, worse, tendentious.

If all interpretations were equivalent, there would be no progress or science, but only opinions. Naturally, this does not mean that an objective interpretation should not undergo further clarifications over time. However, it is one thing to make the truth false, it is another to attribute new elements to the truth that make it even more convincing (or in any case that do not undermine the objectivity it had when it was formulated).

Is there an absolute truth? We can also answer in the affirmative, but since we live in an evolutionary path called "history of the human race", the absoluteness of this truth will only be evident to us when this process is completed (concluded). Naturally, while waiting for this to happen, it is absurd to think that all interpretations of the phenomena are equivalent.

Already now we can easily distinguish between objective and subjective interpretations of reality, that is, between relevant or congruent interpretations of a certain phenomenon, and ambiguous, fallacious, mystifying interpretations. Anyone who thinks that everything is relative should at least ask themselves whether their belief is also relative.

Therefore the most important thing we must do is to seek objectivity in the interpretation of phenomena, avoiding taking absolutist positions, which cannot compete with us, as we are immersed in a flow of historical events which prevent us from having a clear whole-encompassing vision.

If we all thought in these terms, we would be more willing to listen to other people's reasons. Of course we would be much less fanatical, much less ideological.

April 6

Let's not beat around the bush about surplus value

In state-controlled socialism, the exploitation of paid labor (industrialised or rural or employed in services) took place by the State, the sole owner of the main means of production. What should instead be studied is the self-management variant of the Yugoslav state.

In mercantile socialism (like the current Chinese one, which still draws on the ideology of scientific socialism), the economy is mixed: the land belongs to the State, as do many companies; another part is managed by private individuals (foreign and national), who are however kept under control by the government.

Mercantile socialism resembles Russian state capitalism, with the difference that in the latter the ideology of scientific socialism is not officially present, so certain concessions are made to nationalistic ideas, even of a religious nature.

In all three cases the surplus value exists, that is, that unpaid part of the work. However, the State is concerned with transforming a part of this surplus value into social services, offered at low or even negligible costs.

The remaining part of the surplus value is managed on the basis of the power projection of the State, i.e. in military spending, in intelligence, in propaganda, in diplomacy, in maintaining a political, administrative ruling class, etc.

Therefore, as can easily be understood, the State does not stand on its feet on the basis of simple taxation, also because if you work for a State it is likely that the salaries and wages are not particularly high. The State has to bear expenses that are incomparable to all privately managed companies. Even large financial institutions, which have capital equivalent to the GDP of many advanced capitalist nations, ask states to be able to pay as few taxes as possible.

However, if surplus value is theft under private capitalism, it is also theft in the three cases above. It is impossible to talk about authentically democratic socialism as long as surplus value exists. And today, unfortunately, no one is asking this problem. There are no solutions on the horizon on how to resolve it. The new multipolar ideology says nothing about it.

Yet the classics of scientific socialism had spoken clearly. Communism means self-management, cooperation, primacy of use value over exchange value, progressive extinction of the State to the advantage of civil society which self-organizes and self-administers. We cannot prevaricate on these objectives, if we do not want the problems of social antagonism to recur in other forms and ways.

At most we can talk about minimum and maximum objectives, medium and long-term strategies, but we cannot pretend that the problem does not exist. Nor can we continue to maintain – as Stalinism did – that, as long as capitalism exists, communism is unachievable, and that indeed, the more aggressive capitalism becomes, the more the State must be centralized.

April 7

Between saying and doing there is a deep sea

Let's imagine for a moment what could happen in a highly individualistic society if an atomic war broke out. The survival instinct would make us irreducible enemies. The worst feelings we experience regardless of this exceptional case would suddenly and dramatically multiply. We already see them increasing with the progressive impoverishment of certain social classes. Imagine what the presence of a nuclear conflict could do to human misery.

Those who have the means will want to protect themselves in every way, saving their assets and relatives as much as possible. We would no longer trust anyone. Everyone would go around armed. We would kill ourselves for nothing. The life of someone who is a stranger to us would have no value. *Mors tua vita mea*, this would be the dominant thought.

The strong powers know that we would behave like this, and they would pay the police forces (public and/or private) handsomely to instill even more fear in us, to keep us even more subjugated, and to expropriate us, if necessary, of all our assets.

They would probably do it even in the presence of a very contagious pandemic, which they themselves perhaps caused to greatly reduce the population, in the absurd belief that the fewer we are, the better off we are. The strong powers would behave in a violent, arrogant manner, even if an apocalyptic environmental disaster occurred.

And we, remaining divided, armed against each other, would be even weaker. We would not be able to understand that those are the most favorable moments to overthrow the system, that is, to join forces, to show human solidarity towards those who suffer the most and to direct all our subversive potential towards those who are responsible for these deliberately created disasters on purpose, or against whom nothing has been done to prevent them.

Didn't the last two world wars break out for this reason? The (political and economic) power did not know how to resolve the ever more acute and ever wider social contradictions, and thought that the best method was to exterminate part of its own population, convincing them that salvation lay in fighting an external enemy, of another nation, source of all social evil.

When Lenin said that the imperialist war should be transformed into a civil war, even his party comrades thought he was crazy. In fact, everyone was convinced that Russia would have to win the war first and only then should the revolution take place. In fact, if the country had lost the war, it would have found an even stronger enemy at home. Lenin risked being seen as a traitor, as a Prussian agent.

Instead he thought that if the revolution had taken place while the country was at war, it would have been easier to obtain a strong popular consensus against his government, which was sending an incalculable number of soldiers to their deaths. When coming to terms with the victorious enemy (at that time Germany), they would have granted themselves large portions of their territory (Treaty of Brest-Litovsk).

In the meantime, the inevitable internal counter-revolution (that of the Whites, paid by private entrepreneurs, landowners and above all by capitalist countries) would have been harshly repressed.

Once things were settled, we would organize ourselves to go and recover the territories previously ceded to the enemy. It seemed like the crazy project of an unrepentant dreamer. Instead, as luck would have it, Germany lost the war, and it was quite easy for the Russians to break the peace treaty, even though in the early 1920s they had to face armed interventionism from many foreign nations, whose statesmen and capitalists were terrified at the idea that communist revolutions could take place in their own countries. In that case, however, the Soviets conceded nothing to anyone and all the armed contingents that entered their territory were soundly defeated.

Indeed, for a moment the Russians themselves hoped that other revolutions of this kind would also take place in Western Europe, but they were soon to be disappointed. Desiring a revolution and knowing how to organize it are two completely different things.

April 8

Manifesto against war

In Italy, we need a public manifesto to share, to discuss, to propose against the strong powers, as a platform for a political battle for civilization. A long-term anti-war manifesto, capable of creating the conditions for a lasting, sufficiently guaranteed peace. This could be the starting draft.

1- Italy is committed to becoming a nuclear-free country not only in civil aspects but also in military ones. It has no intention of resorting, either now or in the future, to any nuclear source, as it considers all of them, especially in the event of war, to be particularly dangerous. Indeed, it declares that it feels very worried if other countries (near or far) do not make a similar commitment.

2- Italy ensures that in the event of war it will never resort to weapons of extermination of any kind, as it declares from now on that it wants to dismantle any such weapon in any military base, and is firmly intent on prohibiting any scientific research it can do in the future to produce them. This is because it deeply fears that the use of such weapons could have unpredictable or imponderable effects on the population. Not only that, but it categorically refuses that the consequences of such a war could fall on generations that did not wage it. It also declares itself open to forms of control by those who accept reciprocity.

3- Italy assures all the countries of the world that it will forever renounce any offensive weapon capable of hitting any neighboring or non-bordering country. The weapons will only be useful for defensive purposes and, as such, will never be used first.

4- Italy will never host foreign military bases on its territory, unless it has to do so for reasons of force majeure. In this case, however, the decision will have to be taken by national political bodies, not military ones. This decision will have a clearly pre-established duration and will not be automatically renewed, nor will the military leaders ever be able to claim any type of exclusive (or extraterritorial) sovereignty.

5- The defense of the entire national territory will be entrusted to the population as a whole, not to specialized bodies. Everyone (except for documented exceptions) must feel responsible for the defense of their homeland, in whatever capacity this occurs, in compliance with current legislation. Therefore everyone will have to undergo periodic military or paramilitary exercises or civil support for a defensive war. In conditions of peace, citizens will be prohibited from circulating armed, unless expressly authorized for security reasons or to guarantee the safety of certain people, at the times and places decided if necessary.

6- Italy undertakes not to sell weapons to any country for any reason and not to purchase them from anyone. That is, it will limit itself to self-producing them. This is because weapons and détente are considered incompatible. We want to discourage the idea, at an international level, that any conflict can be resolved with weapons in hand.

7- If Italy were nevertheless forced, for some objective reason, to go to war, it would strictly respect all the conventions already approved at an international level. In particular, it will approve the request to establish a tribunal to judge those who wanted to start the war or instigate it with various provocations. It declares its willingness to do so also for previous situations, if the testimonies and documentation are considered sufficient.

8- Italy believes that the best way to resolve interstate, regional or international conflicts is omnilateral diplomacy, all-out negotiation, and the use of international peace bodies that perform mediation functions. The principles of non-violence and mutual security must be placed as the basis of any plea bargaining. In this sense, Italy believes it is profoundly wrong to maintain that war is the instrument for conducting politics by other means. It will never assume a resigned attitude towards those who maintain that to want peace one must prepare for war or that peace can only be achieved in the name of deterrence.

9- Italy declares itself a neutral country by definition. It does not join any military alliance between states: at most it accepts peaceful alliances between the respective populations. Refuses to place military bases on the borders with other states. It also refuses to use the weapon of retaliation in the event that it is struck by mistake by a foreign country: it will only demand compensation for damages. It reserves the right to use its secret services and its diplomacy to avoid the start of a war anywhere in the world, that is, to prevent any hostile or provocative attitude.

10- Italy does not claim any territory outside its current borders and is willing to discuss the claims that neighboring states can make towards historically disputed territories.

11- Italy cannot adopt principles in foreign policy that differ from those adopted in domestic policy.

12- This Manifesto must be taken in its entirety. It is excluded a priori that any part of it is more or less binding than any other part.

April 9

We like to dream

Perhaps one day, in a who knows distant future, the enemies to be fought, which involve an incalculable number of deaths, will be the subject of a type of narrative that today we only see in science fiction films.

Some states, to have the pretext with which to dominate the world, will speak of an "alien invasion"; and, to simulate their presence, it will begin to attack populations using cosmic weapons (satellites, space-ships...). In fact, in today's reality we are killing ourselves to overcome neoliberal globalism and Western unipolarism.

At the beginning of 2000, the USA, by allowing the attack on the Twin Towers, invented the abstraction of international Islamic terrorism, with which they were able to unleash various regional wars of no small importance (Iraq, Syria, Afghanistan, Libya, etc.).

With past European colonialism and imperialism, the abstraction was the people to be civilised, devoid of science and technology, incapable of exploiting their natural resources, lacking adequate industry.

Donatella Di Cesare is convinced, in her book "Terrore e moder-nità" (2017), that only with the abstraction of terrorism has war become truly global. This is because the enemy has become omnipresent and in-visible, ready to exploit any place and means to cause death and destruc-tion. Americans specialize in seeing enemies everywhere: hence the need to invent superheroes, fairy-tale narratives, commercials that make you dream...

If she had written it today, she would have said that for the collec-tive West the enemy is those who oppose international law, representative democracy, common rules, that is, first and foremost Russia and China, but also quite a few Middle Eastern countries of the global South.

The more abstract and generic the enemy becomes, the less in-clined we are to make a difference between military and civilians, between the use of legitimate and illicit means of war, between strategic and terror-ist objectives, between attack and defense. We are all involved, we all risk dying. And ultimately it must be said that, if we do nothing to stop our statesmen, we are all responsible, in different forms and ways, for the fate that awaits us. No one can declare themselves innocent, unaware of the events that occurred.

It is therefore useless to wonder, like Job, sitting on a mountain of manure, what we have done that was so serious to deserve such a great punishment. We have certainly done one thing: we have not reacted with the necessary courage in the face of the injustices that happen before our eyes. We have transferred to others their solution. We have blamefully underestimated them. We have naively believed in the restorative power of institutions, of those institutions that live a life of their own, completely escaping our control.

They tell us fairy tales from the cradle to the grave, because they know that we like to dream.

April 10

You can be different

Strange as it may seem, even in the Greco-Roman world there was talk of a universally valid natural law, which allowed human beings to coexist peacefully, regardless of ethnic, political, cultural, etc. diversity. This right was based on reason and therefore on speech, humans being rational and dialoguing beings.

For example. the Stoics of the Hellenistic era were the main defenders of pacifism and cosmopolitanism. The great jurists of the Roman Empire thought the same way. Cicero, Ulpian, Gaius... spoke of "natural law" as something very different from civil law, something capable of creating a "natural society".

They used the same concepts, more or less, that the Christian bourgeoisie would use at the end of the Middle Ages to justify the birth of capitalism. They were, exactly as they still are today, absolutely abstract concepts, devoid of actual evidence. In fact, in reality the right of the strongest was in force: si vis pacem, para bellum. "Imperial" needs had to prevail over everything. At most, it was added not to rage against the defeated, as war should only be used as an extreme remedy, after having asked for submission through the tools of diplomacy (but also threats or intimidation, blackmail, etc.).

This strangeness of knowing how to live in peace, but of practically implementing a warmongering policy, can make us think that the human race, among all animal species, was born with some congenital defect, which makes it too dangerous to be tolerated beyond a certain point. Nature, for its own survival, should get rid of as soon as possible such a dangerously unreliable subject, who says one thing and does another.

Please note that this duplicity is also found in all religions born in the slave, feudal or bourgeois era. Only the most primitive ones, of an animistic-totemic type, saved themselves. In fact, religions generally behave in two ways when faced with the demands of world domination: either they justify them, thinking themselves that they can expand more easily; or they tolerate them passively, adopting indifferent attitudes. At best they oppose it, but using purely moralistic statements.

When the native North Americans met the Europeans, they described them, after a short time, as people with forked tongues, that is, hypocrites. They had easily understood us precisely because the word given between them was sacred and did not have to hide an ulterior motive. They were humanely better than us, and we, in order not to feel judged by populations considered "primitive", were forced to carry out a great ethnic cleansing. And in order to do so we invented the most vile and bestial things about them, we devised the most perfidious deceptions.

On the other hand, according to our life criteria, we had no choice: the indigenous people absolutely did not accept becoming our slaves. They were born free and wanted to remain free. We were forced to import millions of Africans from Africa to replace them. The so-called "Indians" were not like the Indians of the three Mesoamerican and Andean civilizations, fundamentally slave-based, which the Spaniards however reduced to nothing.

It's easy to say why the Red Indians were better than us: they rejected the idea of being able to privatize natural resources and were satisfied with what the Earth could offer. They were the most eloquent demonstration that one could be different.

Christopher Columbus also wrote it during his first voyage, when he landed in the Bahamas. Meeting the Lucayans, he said of them: "They are an affectionate people, free from greed and flexible. There are no people or land better than these in the world. They love their neighbor as themselves and have the sweetest and most delicate voices in the world, and are always smiling... In contact with others they have excellent morals."

But then he began to exterminate them, because they resisted submission and did not help him fulfill the reason why he had organized his travels: to find gold.

April 11

We were not born wrong

For at least 3000 years, that is, since the time of the Etruscans, Italy has known peace only as a moment between two periods of war. It is a nightmare from which we must escape: at the very least we must lay solid foundations for future generations.

We cannot take for granted that the human species, among all the animal species, has fared very poorly. After all, the freedom of choice, which we pride ourselves on, is unknown to animals, and we cannot do without it, even if it would be very convenient for the powers that be.

I do not believe (like Erasmus of Rotterdam) that the origin of violence was the practice of hunting and the sacrifice of animals for religious purposes. I don't think we have started killing ourselves due to the constant shortage of game (especially large mammals).

I am not even convinced that war is an inevitable product of agriculture and livestock. As long as social and gender equality exists, violence does not exist, even if it emerges immediately as soon as someone starts talking about private property.

When military activities arise to defend this anomalous property, and economic, political or religious motivations to justify it, we could say that the ancestor of our civilization is born, which is classist and inevitably chauvinist.

All ancient Greek thinkers (with exceptions) agreed in considering war an innate element of man, precisely because - according to them - the love of glory, fear and profit are our three main instincts. But such a vision was false: it only served to justify the interest of those who wanted to command. How false are those solutions that see the sovereign or the State as the remedy for social antagonism.

When Plato said that in his ideal state only essential needs are satisfied to avoid the desire for wealth, he was simply favoring the construction of a dictatorship. In itself it was not a wrong concern, but it immediately became one if it was left to be managed by an external entity, the State, which ordinary citizens could not control.

To live more peacefully, citizens do not need more state and less market or less freedom of decision. They don't need a father and master state to prevent themselves from making bad choices. It makes no sense to make people believe that the socialism of poverty must become a generalized lifestyle to guarantee everyone a minimum personal freedom: in fact we know very well that whoever wants to impose such a system would live in a privileged condition (such as Soviet-era nomenklatura).

It is no coincidence that Plato himself saw war against other states as a very effective tool for avoiding civil wars and class and class conflicts within his ideal state.

It is simply monstrous to think that war is something natural, as it implements the right of the strongest to command the weakest. We should ban all literary works that glorify war as a solution to conflicts.

It is private ownership of the fundamental means of production that must be abolished. Utopian socialism said this well before scientific socialism. Indeed, if we go back in time, we find this idea in all utopian works, from that of Campanella to that of Thomas More. But we also find it in the heretical pauperistic movements of the Middle Ages and even in the monastic movements that arose with the crisis of the pagan slave world of the classical era.

Marx's genius had invented nothing. He had only taken up an idea from the past, placing it in a new context. Only today, however, have we understood that it is illusory to think of achieving social equality and therefore personal freedom by simply nationalizing production tools.

A state socialism is a contradiction in terms: it confuses "social" property with "state" property. And a mercantile socialism will also be able to aspire to better efficiency compared to Western-style private capitalism. But it cannot offer greater guarantees of freedom just because it allows easier enrichment. Also because those who savor the smell of money will sooner or later ask the State to step aside or place themselves at their service.

April 12

First of all, change your lifestyle

The other evening I listened with great interest to the presentation that Andrea Zhok gave of his latest book, "The profane inquisition and the kingdom of anomie" (On the historical meaning of "political correctness" and woke culture).

A truly intelligent person, who led me to reflect above all on the following aspect. When difference is feared in a society, because it is thought that it can be used to discriminate, then it means that social conflicts are very acute. What is it that makes us live in constant mutual suspicion if not extreme individualism?

But if this is the case, thinking that we can reduce or even eliminate discrimination by fighting all possible differences is the most illusory thing there could be. It would be like saying that, to prevent the abuse of freedom, its use must be prevented.

Woke culture, cancel culture, political correctness, gender ideology and other such phenomena do the powers that be a huge favor just as they say they want to fight them. In fact, they want to overcome the mystifications of chauvinistic, patriarchal, colonialist, racist, sexist ideologies... by eliminating any difference, that is, reducing the population to a faceless herd, easily manageable by those who have the levers of power.

Those who think they can respect differences by first affirming their own identity are undoubtedly wrong. Anyone who behaves like this respects the difference only in a formal, conventional way, so much so that at the first critical point, he reveals himself for what he is, that is, an intolerant person.

In fact, for a truly democratic person the opposite principle applies, that according to which identity is given precisely by difference. Who you are, as an individual, social class, ethnic group, national people, you can only know by relating to other individuals, social classes, etc. And in this relationship you understand that difference and discrimination are two very different things.

It is true that any difference can be the object of discrimination, but it is also true that when this happens, it is because there is something wrong with the identity, that is, with the values of this identity.

This is why we must first of all rethink our lifestyle, that is, those behaviors that the dominant powers want to impose on populations. We Westerners live in societies where seemingly insurmountable hierarchies exist. For example, nature must be dominated by science and technology, capital imposes itself on work, man on woman, the strong on the weak... Such beliefs allow or tolerate the use of privileges that have no justification.

Processes and tendencies are taken for granted which are not "natural", but simply the result of historical evolution. It is not written in the Tables of the Law that exchange value should prevail over use value, or industry over craftsmanship, or the market over self-consumption, or delegated democracy over direct democracy... Examples like these could be given everywhere 'infinite. Just think about the fact that we take for granted that writing is more important than speech, when for millions of years we have at most painted images on rock.

We are slaves to an institutional narrative that prevents us from thinking differently. This is why we say that anyone who wants to abolish differences, for fear that they may be used in a discriminatory way, inevitably, even against his intentions, is serving the interests of the dominant system, which is anything but democratic.

April 13

Understanding the Chinese is not easy

The modern Chinese Communist Party is based on an ancient philosophical saying: "Only when the granary is full, people learn etiquette; only when people are well fed and clothed will they know honor and shame."

Economic growth is therefore the basis for peace/security and for civilization (cultural, scientific...). However, without security there is no prosperity/growth, and without both there is no civilization (spiritual strength of the nation).

In particular, the Chinese government thinks it must address the development of the Global South, to overcome the unequal exchange imposed by Western capitalism.

China does not want to impose its civilization on any state, it does not interfere in the internal affairs of states and expects there to be reciprocity in this regard. A striking example of this strategy, of which it was the architect, is the rapprochement between two long-standing enemies: Iran and Saudi Arabia. You can find common ground by respecting diversity, you can seek harmony without uniformity.

Therefore, if traditional Western theories on international relations tend to see the world from the perspective of force and geopolitics (theories such as that of "hegemonic stability" and the "clash of civilisations" are imbued with exclusionary ideas), vice versa peaceful coexistence, win-win cooperation, inclusiveness and shared growth have always been part of Chinese civilization.

Historical-dialectical materialism is grafted onto a philosophy of life that is already democratic and socialist in its own right. That is, Chinese collectivism is not a consequence of the adoption of Marxism-Leninism, but the opposite: this ideology was adopted precisely because China has thousand-year-old collectivist traditions.

Honestly speaking, however, I still haven't understood whether socialism with Chinese characteristics is more familiar with the aforementioned ideology and not rather with its own collectivist tradition, which can be found in many cultural traditions, such as Confucian, Buddhist, Taoist...

Having said this, it remains quite curious how, on the one hand, we want to remain tied to a specific ideology (Marxism-Leninism), while, on the other, we hope for collaboration between states that totally ignores any ideological aspect.

It seems that for the Chinese Communist Party the objective of guaranteeing every population the minimum subsistence, up to economic well-being, is a priority above all else. Without achieving this goal, it is useless to talk about everything else.

But how can we be sure of this automation? Who said that a population, after having achieved material well-being, wants to delve deeper into the immaterial aspects of its culture and civilization? When in the West has it ever been possible to combine personal enrichment with the pursuit of common interest?

What secret do the Chinese have for managing to keep two such opposing practices together? To truly want to be socialist, one would have to maintain the opposite, that is, one must first seek common property as a shared ideal, and only then, within this presupposition, should one seek personal well-being.

In fact, the Chinese experiment consists of this: promoting social capitalism (within civil society), safeguarding the socialism of the party/state and its Marxist-Leninist ideology. But in doing so we fail to realize that if capitalism develops too much, a social class tends to form that does not want a collectivist tradition and much less an ideology that does not place itself at the service of private interests.

April 14

Appetite comes with eating

We all know what the so-called "carnation revolution" was in Portugal in the mid-1970s. A 40-year fascist dictatorship was eliminated, in which 40 families dominated the entire private sector of the country. A socialist state was built, master of all the means of production. We went from one extreme to the other.

The turning point lasted about a decade. Then, as often happens in these cases, a revisionist current within the dominant socialism managed to make the country become capitalist again, with the pretext that it could not remain isolated from the rest of Europe. However, we had to wait until the beginning of the 1990s to completely abolish the principle of state ownership of the means of production, land, natural resources, etc.

Portugal, once a great colonialist country, became a land of conquest by the world's large capitalist companies, attracted by very low labor costs and very favorable taxation.

Naturally the state did not benefit from it. Indeed, since the public debt was constantly growing, Brussels asked the population for great sacrifices.

However, perhaps few people know that it was China above all that conquered Portugal. The Chinese decidedly focused on the energy sector, without which there is no capitalism that can survive.

They made offers that it would have been foolish to refuse. On the other hand, the Chinese are among the most advanced in the world in the energy sector. They couldn't miss the opportunity to enter the European market.

At the beginning they were content to purchase 25% of the shares of the entire Portuguese energy network, but you can bet that even in their country there is a saying similar to ours: appetite comes with eating. It is no coincidence that they also began to buy insurance, banks, private clinics, etc.

It is curious, however, that the multinational China Three Gorges corporation (CTG), at the head of all energy operations, is not private at all but state-owned. So can we understand the difference between private capitalism and mercantile socialism?

April 15

Why did Portuguese socialism fail?

In 1974, a revolutionary movement led by military forces removed the leaders of a fascist government that had lasted over 40 years in a coup, also ending the colonialist relationship with some African countries (Angola, Mozambique, Guinea-Bissau, etc.).

The so-called "Carnation Revolution" made one mistake after another, and in fact in little more than a decade it was dismantled. The main one was to nationalize all private companies, making them managed by the State.

Why was this decision wrong?

1) It is not certain that there were officials in the State with adequate skills to make them work;

2) it is not certain that the previous managers, once ownership had changed, agreed to continue carrying out the same tasks on the basis of ideological reasons;

3) it is not certain that the new state officials, despite having the same skills as private managers, had the same motivations, given that they received much lower salaries;

4) it is not certain that, despite having similar skills and adequate salaries, continuing to produce for a market, that is, continuing to be part of a global capitalist system, is the best solution for achieving truly democratic socialism.

Haste is a bad advisor. We need a gradual transition, which the entire population is able to assimilate.

The State cannot impose on civil society the forms and ways to create an alternative. The State must put citizens in a position to decide which choices to make regarding the industrial goods and natural resources that they can finally freely dispose of.

The land, for example, was rightly taken away from the landowners and redistributed to the farmers, but everything else was nationalized, including the production of cement, paper, fertilizer, tobacco, beer, glass and fishing companies... You could understand such an attitude towards banks, insurance companies, financial institutions, ports and airports, railways, oil companies, etc. That is, towards nerve centers for any modern state.

In fact, it is one thing to socialize the ownership of the "main" means of production, those essential for the survival of a civil society; another is to nationalize everything.

When in the name of a political revolution you want to radically change the economic management of society, you cannot think that it is enough to change the owner of the means of production. You need to ask yourself one, a hundred, a thousand questions about what lifestyle you want to aim for.

Aristotle already said that it is the objective we set ourselves that decides how the available tools should be used. With a political revolution carried out from above, the State must limit itself to creating the conditions for society to learn to manage itself. Self-management and cooperation are the key words to promote local autonomy.

Citizens must learn to take responsibility for themselves. Political revolutions only serve to put them in a position to do so freely, without the heavy constraints of private management of common goods.

The other mistake was no less serious: maintaining close relations with Western Europe. To not feel isolated? Fearful of not being able to bear the inevitable sanctions, embargoes, boycotts? But you cannot expect preferential treatment from an enemy.

In fact, that very relationship entailed the progressive dismantling of state socialism and the reintroduction of private capitalism, within the context of a formally democratic political management of the State.

April 16

One president is as good as another

I have the impression that now the real problem is not whether to choose capitalism or socialism, but precisely in which type of socialism we want to place our trust.

In fact, it is clear that private capitalism of the Western brand is destined to lose the comparison (economic, financial and military) with state capitalism or mercantile socialism of the Asian brand. Whatever war we Westerners wage, we are destined to lose it, since we no longer have to deal with naive nations.

Asia is very quickly overtaking both the USA and the EU. It does not need to retrace our entire technical-scientific process: it can start from the latest acquisitions and look much further than us, like a dwarf on the shoulders of a giant. And China, with its population and its surface area, is already a giant of its own.

For half a millennium the world has been in our hands, but we will not yet be the protagonists in the coming centuries. Like in the athletics relay; the baton must be passed on, and we have to give it to them, either by hook or by crook.

Which does not mean, in itself, that the after will be better than the before. The idea of progress does not have a magical content: it can also involve involutionary processes, or in any case characterized by new antagonisms of a different nature.

Certainly we Westerners, if we want to survive, must demonstrate that it is possible to build a truly democratic socialism. And to do this, we must first wipe out the entire ruling class (politically, administratively, militarily, industrially and financially). A task absolutely beyond our strength.

So at the moment we better prepare for the worst. In fact, it is not possible that a large country like the USA can continue to get into debt in such a monstrous manner, without suffering significant consequences.

It makes no sense for the American people to continue to live beyond their productive capacity, relying solely on the power of the dollar. Imposing certain commercial and financial transactions in this currency or attracting capital from all over the world by virtue of its high interest rates, are not factors that today can avert another 1929 or 2008 (which affected private finance) or a state bankruptcy. The public debt is so astronomical that it cannot be saved by anything, not even by war, much less by the devaluation of the currency. It is absurd to even think that you can stop ongoing inflation with ever-higher interest rates.

When matters come to a head, there will be civil wars in the USA, secessions of federal states, military dictatorships, new regional wars in the world, or even global wars against China, Russia, Iran, North Korea and who knows who. Eventually the dollar will be replaced by precious metals or even barter.

If Trump manages to win with the consensus of the apparatus, he will have to convince Americans that, without him, the country is lost. And he will probably use the "subversive" card, the one he used against Biden, organizing the occupation of the Capitol in January 2021, when he was prevented from holding a second term with electoral tricks. That time Trump was ousted because he was not sufficiently warmongering in foreign policy.

Now, however, he must guarantee the war against China 100%.

And, to have the power that he will use to take revenge on the democrats, we can be sure that he will do what the apparatus asks of him. After all, already in his first term he had said that the greatest danger for the Americans is not the Russians but the Chinese.

April 17

A film already seen

That Western statesmen have a weakness for Nazi-fascism was seen in 1938, in that shameful Munich Conference, in which Hitler was allowed to occupy the Sudetenland (Czechoslovakia, although allied with France and the United Kingdom, was not even invited to discuss).

To tell the truth, Czechoslovakia itself, as it was wanted by the victorious countries of the First World War, made no sense: it only served to annoy the Germans. So much so that in 1993 industrial and Protestant Bohemia separated amicably from rural and Catholic Slovakia. Not a single shot was fired. The EU and the UN accepted the fact without question. Ultimately, nothing changed for the interests of capitalism.

It was not like recognizing the separation of Transnistria from Moldova or the two republics of Donetsk and Luhansk from Ukraine, and the two mini-republics of Abkhazia and South Ossetia from Georgia. Those will never be recognized either by the UN or by the collective West, because they are pro-Russian: a fine example of double standards!

1938 was a true watershed in 20th century European history. It was demonstrated to the whole world that the great Western democracies were incapable of opposing dictatorships. Indeed, they boasted of having averted a world war. Hitler's promise that he would be satisfied with the German-speaking Sudetenland was trusted.

In reality, Germany wanted to return to the borders of 19th century Prussia, so it considered the reappropriation of the Gdańsk corridor to be a given. Except that for France and England the Sudetenland was one thing (all in all rather insignificant), while the Danzig corridor had a very different importance. They felt terrified at the thought that Germany might once again have great imperial ambitions.

Poland was also created to annoy the Germans: it was granted an enormous territory, despite being a power of the lowest rank. When Hitler occupied Poland, war throughout Europe was inevitable: the French and English once again felt threatened.

Then naturally Western historians placed all the blame on the USSR for having signed, on the heads of the Poles, a non-belligerence pact with the Germans (Molotov-Ribbentrop). Who knows why they always forget to add that no European country wanted to sign a military agreement with the Russians against the Nazis. All statesmen were more afraid of the Communists than of the Nazis. Indeed, they hoped that Hitler's imperial aims would only turn eastward.

The basic idea that European statesmen had was to wait for Germany to attack Russia (Poland and Czechoslovakia could have allowed the transit of troops under the surveillance of the Anglo-French). After that, one would passively observe the unfolding of events. If it really would have been so easy for Hitler to conquer the USSR in a few months, they would have offered him, in exchange for non-belligerence, to have a piece of the Federation, whose territory was too large to be occupied by a single capitalist nation. The USA and Japan would have done the same thing in the east. The entire world capitalism was coveted by the exterminated natural resources of the USSR.

However, events unfolded in the opposite way to that desired. The 27 million deaths suffered by the Federation had no impact on its fate. Indeed, it was Western Europe and Japan that felt crushed under the weight of American hegemony.

Today, a film already seen is being repeated. NATO neo-Nazism, which started a proxy war against Russia in Ukraine, aims to take over the territories of the Federation. Anti-communism, obviously, cannot be the main motivation. It is simply being said, in the most idiotic way possible, that Putin intends to take back the territories acquired by Stalin at the end of the Second World War.

This time, however, we must be careful: a third world war against Russia could be the last one that the West is capable of unleashing.

April 18

We should disappear, not them

Why are the Inuit destined to disappear? Because with climate change the ice will tend to melt, and the lands where they live will be exploited for energy purposes. It's already like this now.

They will end up like the North American natives, with whom they are also closely related, as well as with the Mongols.

They have lived in the Great North, between Alaska, Canada, Siberia (Chukotka) and Norway, perhaps for 30-35,000 years. At the beginning of the current third millennium there were approximately 180,000 left, spread over a total of 15,000 km of coastline.

They were once called Eskimos, coming from southern Asia. They have already undergone Euro-American and Russian colonization.

They are animists, that is, they think that everything is alive, even stones. A religion that is actually a philosophy of life.

The basis of their diet is reindeer and any fish species. But once upon a time they also ate the mammoth and the bison.

The environmental conditions in which they live are obviously very harsh. However, those who really threaten their existence are the companies that search for hydrocarbons and precious metals (gold, uranium, zinc, etc.).

They once had to deal with other forms of colonization, from hunters in search of valuable furs, whalers, merchants, even missionaries from all over Europe.

"Globalization" has always been an absolute tragedy for this and other Arctic populations. In half a century they forced them to live in urban centers, to "civilize", to move from the Stone Age to advanced technologies, but the consequences were catastrophic, as always happens in these cases.

A small example is enough to understand it. Westerners have introduced the use of alcohol and tobacco to this population. However, when you don't have the enzymes to dispose of them, their toxicity is much more dangerous: it can lead to psychological alterations.

We Europeans have even gone as far as to ban the trade in seal skins, to protect this animal from extinction, thus contributing to the starvation of the Inuit themselves, who use them to feed themselves.

In order not to disappear completely, they started to claim their rights. They have joined together in various organizations, with which they defend their culture, traditional means of subsistence, and the protection of the natural and animal environment.

The Inuit Circumpolar Conference, founded in 1977, was recognized by the UN in 1983. But we know the importance of the UN well. That is certainly not an organism capable of averting the deviant and alienated forms of the daily existence of these populations, acquired after coming into contact with our "civilization".

Furthermore, in the Arctic Council, established in 1996, those who decide everything are not the Inuit but the eight Arctic states: Canada, the United States, Norway, Finland, Sweden, Russia, Iceland and Denmark.

The fate of the Inuit seems to be sealed. Of course, someone will integrate into our lifestyle, to become "like us". But most of them will live on subsidies and, like animals in a zoo, they will stop reproducing.

April 19

The first Russian ecologist

Leo Tolstoy, perhaps the greatest novelist in Europe, was ostracized by all the pro-tsarists (because he could not tolerate autocracies), by the industrial capitalists (because in his opinion they devastated the environment), by the Orthodox Church (because he wanted a of separation between Church and State), by the Bolsheviks (because he could not tolerate the concept of "revolutionary violence" nor the subordination of the peasant to the worker), by the populists (because they judged him to be a troglodyte in terms of agricultural management).

Certainly, however, many had understood that he was not only a great novelist, but he also had a philosophy of life to propose to humanity, undoubtedly not without the defects of patriarchy and utopianism.

Despite being noble by origin, he lived like a farmer with a spade and hoe. He didn't even care about the royalties on his literary production. When he saw that his masterpiece, War and Peace, did not meet with any success in Russia, he preferred to devote himself exclusively to his agricultural activities.

He asked Americans to abolish slavery, just as serfdom had been done in Russia.

He was clearly against national borders, since, according to him, people, in order to respect each other, must associate with each other without impediments of any kind.

He asked for omnilateral education in schools but not ethical education, and education, in order not to be abstract, had to be linked to the cooperation to be experienced in society.

When he fought against the birth of the big cities, the railways and the telegraph, he was considered a reactionary.

Yet he was the first Russian ecologist able to understand that industrial development would be lethal for the environment.

By the mid-1960s, when it seemed that Khrushchev's de-Stalinization would create a democratic future in Russia, the environmental damage caused by state-socialist industrialization had already been enormous. The indiscriminate use of virgin lands, forests, rivers, lakes, in the name of the inexhaustibility of natural resources, had caused damage that is still considered irreversible today (think of the Aral Sea disaster). Even Tolstoy's property fell into disrepair due to pollution.

However, his message did not fall on deaf ears. It was inherited by

Gandhi, who freed himself from English colonialism with Tolstoyan principles.

It was certainly no coincidence that one of the first documents signed by Gorbachev and Rajiv Gandhi was the New Delhi Declaration (1986), an eloquent example of what it means to establish friendly relations between two States on the basis of universal human values.

However, Lenin said (quite rightly) that the revolution of 1905 failed precisely because he was unable to overcome the limits of the ideology of the great Russian novelist.

April 20

Empires are not all the same

After all, if we think about it, today the countries in favor of multipolarism are fighting against Western globalism to assert a national sovereignty not very different from that which the satellite countries of the former USSR have claimed.

At the time of the Cold War, the collective West argued that these satellite countries had a democracy with limited sovereignty. As if all Western countries, compared to the USA, enjoyed full independence!

There were two dominant blocs, which were ultimately two empires, although the USA has around 800 military bases in 80 nations, while current Russia has no more than a dozen (the only country to have them, outside of space post-Soviet, is Syria).

The difference between the two empires lay in the fact that one was of an ideological-political type (state socialism), while the other was of an economic-financial type (private capitalism). In the Western world, if we exclude the era of the great bourgeois revolutions (Dutch, English, American and French), ideology has always had a secondary weight, aimed at satisfying economic needs.

Dominant Western values exclude public ownership of the means of production or, in any case, consider it subordinate to private ownership. The bourgeoisie has never had a particular interest in the economic rights of all social classes: at most it recognized rights to the aristocratic class, but on the condition that on a political level it left the state to be governed by the bourgeoisie itself. All other social classes must earn their rights with tears and blood.

The aforementioned bourgeois revolutions were not only not fully democratic, but they did not even know topics today considered fundamental such as environmental protection and gender equality; indeed, they were quite racist towards non-European or non-American populations.

In all Western Constitutions, the bourgeoisie judges freedom to be unthinkable without private ownership of the means of production, without a free international market, without a national state that defends it militarily, without a currency that acts as a universal parameter for the exchange of equivalents, and without a legislation that acts as a binding support for economic-financial transactions.

Before the law everyone is formally equal, but in reality true equality lies only between the few owners of the means of production. Which, often, in the furious struggle to grab increasingly significant market shares, tend to transform themselves into real monopolists. Today the collective West is made up of a few gigantic monopolies (of economics and finance), which make many countries with limited sovereignty.

There is no explicit ideology to follow in the West, other than the abstract one of universal human rights and parliamentary representative democracy. What is substantial and generalized is only the lifestyle based on consumerism, which creates our "addiction": the consumer must work to purchase substances that are in a certain sense "doping", since he does not have to do without them.

In state socialist countries this form of consumerism was interpreted by many not as a sign of slavery but of freedom. And it was never linked to the exploitation of the Third World.

Having weakened enormously after its own implosion, Russia accepted not only the autonomous affirmation of the former Soviet republics, but also their longed-for entry into the EU and NATO. Probably if Putin had not replaced Yeltsin, Russia would not have been able to do anything even towards Ukraine and Belarus, and would have resigned itself to losing Kaliningrad too.

However, let's ask ourselves how the USA would have behaved if Western Europe, Japan, South Korea, the Philippines, etc. had behaved in a mirror-image manner, that is, if they had detached themselves from the hegemonic country in order to embrace socialism. Certainly the trial would not have been accepted without disproportionate reactions (Vietnam *docet*). So here we are dealing with two different concepts of "empire".

The Western one is extremely aggressive, since it continually tends to expand at the expense of others and does not at all like international stability and mutual security between states, since when faced with the weaknesses of others it immediately tends to take advantage of them. This is an empire that must be demolished as soon as possible, especially given the fact that it is equipped with nuclear weapons, and all of humanity must take on the burden of doing so.

Nationalisms to be abolished

I have never been able to tolerate nationalism. I have always considered it a rhetorical and potentially warmongering (at the very least aggressive) ideology.

We need to get used to living with those who are different, not with attitudes of paternalistic tolerance, but precisely to learn something different. After all, we live in such a complex and varied world that there is always something to learn.

For me, the nation is the place where someone finds himself living for reasons beyond his control, a place that could change at any moment, for more or less serious reasons.

I feel more nomadic, more cosmopolitan or more internationalist. If right now I had to go and live in another place, I would strive to adapt to the new living conditions, without feeling nostalgic for what I left behind.

Of course cosmopolitan and internationalist have different meanings. The bourgeois, wanting to do business with the whole world, cannot show that he has preferences for a particular nation, that is, for a particular language, religion, diet, habits and customs. If anything, he seeks protection from his own State if he is unable to earn as much as he would like.

Instead, the proletariat must be internationalist, since it must learn to help itself regardless of the nation in which it lives. That is, it must above all avoid the trap of fighting the foreign proletariat in the name of war in favor of his own nation, according to the wishes of its own bourgeoisie.

In fact, the bourgeoisie has specialized in sending its national proletariat to die in war when it is unable to resolve certain serious crisis situations, and fears that the contradictions, if they continue to worsen, could cause a civil war to break out.

Not only that, but also in normal, non-belligerent situations, the proletariat, who work as wage slaves in the factories of capital, becomes, whether they want it or not, co-responsible for the bourgeois colonialism made to suffer by the global South. It takes a certain mystifying art to achieve such an astonishing result.

Here, from this point of view the bourgeoisie is cosmopolitan precisely when it thinks of defending its own class interests. Except that for the same reason it can suddenly become nationalistic: this happens when, for example, it wants to declare war on another bourgeois nation, or on another nation that has embraced socialist or anti-colonialist ideologies.

The two world wars were disastrous for the proletariat class in all nations, since, except in Russia, in no nation were the left-wing leaders capable of transforming the imperialist war into a civil war. The concept of nationalism was so strong that socialists feared being seen as traitors to their homeland, as unscrupulous profiteers.

The civil war was at most postponed until the end of the world war, and only if the nation had lost, or obtained a "mutilated victory", which denounced the lack of certain planned territorial compensations. But it certainly cannot be said that the occupation of factories in Italy in the post-war period, or the partisan resistance against the Nazi-Fascists, or the Weimar Republic in Germany achieved truly convincing results.

Generally, when the nation won, statesmen simply said that their motives had been right; and the populations, in exchange for their enormous sacrifices, expected concrete results, based on the promises that had initially been made to convince them to enlist.

For many centuries Westerners have tried to impose their nationalism on the whole world, always achieving more or less horrible results. The pre-bourgeois populations were mercilessly crushed, and their natural environment was plundered and devastated.

The consequence of this is the massive migratory flows from the colonized South towards the Western metropolises. In this way, however, Western nationalism has inevitably lost its original identity, its native cultural physiognomy.

Fighting against this process of depersonalization is absolutely useless. We created it by demanding exaggerated well-being in a short time, and now we are paying the consequences.

When the collegiate bodies of an Italian state school decide to keep it closed for a day, in order to favor an Islamic holiday, we see that students of that religion constitute a numerically very significant presence in the classes. Opposing this measure, saying that our culture or tradition is different or that there is no reciprocity in an Islamic country, means living outside of reality. In these cases we have in mind a concept of nation comparable to that of "ethnicity".

In short, we live in such an interconnected world that talking about nationalism is simply ridiculous. We have created such global problems that only by uniting together will we be able to solve them.

April 22

The GDP deception

We should stop using sectoral and merely quantitative indices of gross domestic product.

This senseless, indeed fraudulent, measurement of material well-being was devised by the US Department of Commerce in 1933, therefore a few years after the stock market crisis of 1929.

In practice the formula added consumption, investments, public spending and net exports. Unpaid but socially useful human activities were absurdly excluded. It is still like this today.

In the USA themselves they came to understand in 1995 that it was a completely abstract index, incapable for example. to explain why, despite a 55% increase in GDP, the country had recorded a 14% decrease in wage levels in the period 1973-95.

They literally discovered hot water when they realized that GDP did not distinguish between activities that produce well-being and activities that reduce it, and that it did not even distinguish between the quantity and quality of economic growth.

A country can suffer all the pollution and natural disasters it wants, it can also be subject to large-scale organized crime and can even be continuously at war, but its GDP will always remain something else. For example. currently, due to the fact that many soldiers are, from civilians, professional experts, the GDP in Israel has dropped by 20%, but we can bet that, once the war is over, the reconstruction of Gaza by the Israelis will bring the index back up in a very short time. Also because the increase will be related to 1-2 years earlier, not to previous decades.

Today we are faced with the paradox that Eurostat would also like to include some illicit activities in the calculation of GDP, such as drug trafficking, prostitution and smuggling. It would be a truly reckless decision, as criminal activity itself discourages foreign capital from entering a country.

On the other hand, the same GDP per capita makes no sense, as it does not put the general data of the wealth produced in relation to the actual criteria for the distribution of the same wealth. The classic example is famous: if you eat two chickens and I eat nothing, statistically we eat one each. Just look at the situation in India: the GDP is far higher than that of the USA and China, but 50% of the population benefits from a paltry 3% of the overall wealth.

This is without considering that not all our needs can be precisely quantified. For example, a social relationship is a primary need, but it is certainly not economically measurable. Social and ecological factors are far more important than the economy in establishing the quality of life. However, under capitalism existential needs are not counted (at most food needs are due to market prices), even less so are non-solvent ones, i.e. those who do not have monetary resources or do not use them for the tasks they carry out. Therefore, voluntary activity (almost 5 million in Italy) is excluded from the GDP, but also domestic work.

We talked about food needs, which can easily be counted if the consumer supplies himself at a shopping center (self-production is irrelevant). Other essential services such as water, electricity, heat, housing, etc. are regulated by the dynamics of supply and demand. However, none of these services is an absolute right, that is, unconditional by disparities due to economic conditions. This means that they can only be included in GDP calculations at the discretion of the dominant powers.

It is no mystery to anyone that Italian economic growth over the last 20-30 years has disproportionately benefited the richest segment of the population, leaving the rest of the country behind. This trend was not highlighted by the GDP.

Perhaps Fair and Sustainable Wellbeing (an index developed by ISTAT and CNEL in 2016) could be a better tool for evaluating the progress of a nation, but it must be simplified, to make the calculation mechanism less complex.

April 23

Is it all Serbia's fault?

The figure of the Serbian Slobodan Milošević has been re-evaluated for some time. Indeed, it is now clear that the reasons for the disintegration of Yugoslavia must be sought in Western Europe, which used NATO to implement them.

In the name of the self-determination of peoples we have allowed the end of a socialist state, where workers' self-management of companies existed (a more unique than rare case, as companies in socialist countries are generally state-owned). It should be noted that we deny the same self-determination to the inhabitants of Donbass, as we would like them all to be pro-Western, not pro-Russian.

Even today there are analysts who attribute the origin of all the European evils of the 20th century to the Balkans. People with short memories. In fact, it is enough to see that the conflict between the French and the Germans lasted for more than a thousand years, without forgetting the Spanish civil war, the war between the English and the Irish, and so on.

If anything, in fact, it was Serbia that played a driving role in the 19th century, when the decline of the Ottoman Empire was evident, for the creation of a great federal nation, in which the Islamic element (which in the past was imposed by the Turks) would cease to prevail over the Catholic and Orthodox ones.

Those who opposed this plan (for political reasons) were the Austro-Hungarian empire, which, after German unification in 1871, felt induced to expand towards the south-east, in the hope of even hegemonizing Greece. In fact, the late-feudal Habsburgs did not want to be incorporated into the new capitalist nation born thanks to the Prussians. On the other hand, not even the Serbs wanted to be swallowed up by Austro-Hungarian expansionism.

That was one of the triggering causes of the First World War, which even today, very superficially, school textbooks attribute to the Sarajevo massacre of Crown Prince Franz Ferdinand.

After the end of the Habsburg empire, the nations that were formed on its ashes had Constitutions clearly influenced by France. After all, continental Europe, after the victory over the English in the Hundred Years' War, has always been considered by the French as their own "hunting territory". The English, to have colonies, had to look elsewhere, as did the Dutch, the Belgians, the Italians and the Germans themselves.

Even today, Macron's demented grandeur aspires to militarily resolve the confrontation between Europeans and Russians in Ukraine, as at the time of the Crimean War of the 19th century. The French forgot that if the Russians had not defeated the Nazis in the Second World War, half of France, even today, would be under the heel of the Germans.

However, returning to the former Yugoslavia, today it appears clear that its disintegration was wanted above all by the Germans, precisely to minimize the influence of Serbia, historically close to Russia's interests. The USA was content to install its own powerful military base in Kosovo, just to show that NATO is not to be trifled with.

April 24

Yugoslavia had to die

The grayzone.com website has revealed that, according to declassified British Ministry of Defense documents, several officials in London plotted to involve US troops in a secret plan to occupy Yugoslavia and overthrow President Milošević during the 1999 NATO war against the country.

Even today that war is defined by the Western mainstream as a humanitarian intervention aimed at preventing an imminent genocide of the Albanian population of Kosovo. In reality the war was an illegal and destructive aggression, based on lies and atrocious propaganda, against a sovereign and multi-ethnic country. Belgrade was in fact engaged in a battle against the Kosovo Liberation Army (KLA), an extremist group linked to Al Qaeda, supported by the Anglo-American secret services (CIA and MI6).

The KLA – funded by drug trafficking and organ trafficking – explicitly sought to maximize civilian casualties, in order to convince Westerners to intervene. Only in May 2000 did a British parliamentary commission conclude that all the alleged abuses against Albanian citizens by the Yugoslav authorities had occurred after the start of the NATO bombing. And only in September 2001 did a UN court in Pristina establish that Belgrade's actions in Kosovo were not of any genocidal nature.

NATO fighters bombed Serbian civil, government and 372 industrial facilities for 78 days, killing over a thousand innocent people, including children, and violently destroying the daily lives of millions of people (hundreds of thousands were left without work). Beijing's embassy in Belgrade was also bombed, killing three journalists and injuring dozens of people taking refuge inside.

The deliberate destruction of chemical plants has polluted soil, air and water in the Balkans with over 100 toxic substances. It is no coincidence that Serbia today leads the world in cancer rates.

It should be noted that the International Criminal Tribunal for the former Yugoslavia, when it investigated the bombing of the Yugoslav television network RTS in Belgrade (in which 16 journalists died and 16 others were injured), justified the crime by claiming that the action served to interrupt the network of Belgrade. An absurd justification, as RTS returned to the air after just three hours.

Tony Blair and Bill Clinton were mainly responsible for this massacre. The declassified documents say so. In Italy there was the D'Alema government, of which Mattarella was defense minister.

It was with that war that Russia had a clear perception that NATO had the intention of expanding into Eastern Europe and imposing the will of the USA on all of Europe.

When the Serbian army withdrew from Kosovo, the fascist fighters of the KLA proceeded to harass if not eliminate the Roma and Serbian population of that region (the inhabitants of Pristina went from 40,000 to just 400 inhabitants), under the "watchful eyes" of NATO and UN peacekeepers.

Even today, US politicians continue to praise the KLA's brutal leaders. In 2010, then-Vice President Joe Biden called war crimes suspect Hashim Thaci the "George Washington of Pristina."

April 25

What do we celebrate today?

We all know that if Mussolini had not entered the war, we would have had fascism for at least 40 years, like in Spain, and also the monarchy. And the transition from fascism to democracy would have been painless, as in Spain.

Why wasn't the half century of Christian Democracy a fascism sweetened by Catholic moralism and American consumerism?

And wasn't Berlusconi's twenty years an oligarchic fascism, which made use of a territorial fascism like that of the Northern League?

Do we want to understand that Italy has been a "fascist" country since the times of the papal theocracy? Those times when the popes organized crusades against Muslims, Byzantines and Slavs, and practiced the inquisition against internal dissidents?

Italy was "fascist" even in the times of the bourgeoisie of the Municipalities, Lordships and Principalities. In fact, a social class was in command that lived by exploiting the work of others (exactly like the feudal aristocrats), a profoundly racist class, which had given itself a "democratic" guise only on a formal level and which claimed to officially profess Catholicism.

Even today we are fascists. The government is this in all its three components.

Fascism, when we see it transversal to parties, ideologies, ethical or philosophical conceptions that we have had in Italy, means nothing more than dictatorship, obedience, hierarchy, militarism, gender discrimination, social exploitation, colonialist tendencies, purely formal law, judicial coverage of excellent crimes, powers parallel to official ones, shameful compromises, exclusive interests, unspeakable truths, media censorship...

Then everyone can insert all the relative differences they want: from the welfare state to neoliberal privatisations, from a united Europe to national sovereignty, from NATO to the European army... The substance does not change, so much so that we are still here telling ourselves that Russia is threatening us, as we did in the time of the tsars. And the clearly right-wing parties and the so-called left-wing parties say this.

The great thing is that when someone says they can't stand this hypocrisy anymore, they have in mind a general clean-up that is so similar to fascist methods!

Aboriginal people are still feared

In October 2023, Australians voted in a referendum called for by the Labor government which asked the question: "Do you approve a bill to amend the Constitution to recognize Australia's first peoples, establishing an Aboriginal and Torres Strait Islander Voice?" . The answer was negative.

But what is so dangerous about the body called the "Voice of Aboriginal and Torres Strait Islanders"?

In essence, the majority of Australians do not want the Torres Strait, with its islands, to be controlled by Aboriginal people.

The Voice would have been a purely consultative body. It would provide advice to the Australian Parliament and Government on matters affecting the lives of Aboriginal and Torres Strait Islander peoples (education, health, housing, justice etc.).

The Voice would not handle money, provide services, or have the power to block or veto government policies and parliamentary laws.

Members would be selected from various Aboriginal and Torres Strait Islander communities and serve for a fixed period of time.

The Voice would be subject to standard governance and reporting requirements to ensure transparency and accountability. It also would not have given rights to anyone and would not have changed or taken away the rights of non-Indigenous people.

The government agency National Indigenous Australians would continue to exist with different functions, those that serve to implement the policies and programs of the government in office.

Well, despite all this, the fact that the Voice is – as has been said – "a movement that goes beyond politics", Aboriginal people are still scary to conservative white Australians, especially when they do not limit themselves to demanding something at the level of "community local".

And to think that the Voice is considered very moderate even by the aborigines of the Blak sovereignist movement (BSM), for whom racist colonialism has never ended and the Constitution must be defined as "illegal".

Source: niaa.gov.au

April 26

Will the EU become like Yugoslavia?

Yugoslavia became an independent national state only in the 20th century, after having fought against the Ottoman Turks, Austro-Hungarians, German-Prussians and Nazi-fascists. Patriotism was confused with nationalism, trying to overcome ethnic differences due to languages, religions (Christian-Orthodox, Roman Catholic, Islamic), habits and customs.

Yugoslavia was also born for another reason: France and Great Britain wanted to exclude the German bloc (Germany and Austria) and Russia from the geopolitics of the Adriatic Sea. If it had depended exclusively on ethnic-national realities, a single national state would hardly have been born, especially if configured in a centralist way.

The trigger for the country's disintegration was the end of the Cold War, which led Western Europe to eliminate a socialist state, considered anomalous on the continent. Tito, who was a Croatian-Slovenian by birth, had been able to keep all the ethnic groups together, but after his death in 1980, things began to degenerate.

Was Yugoslavia under Tito a dictatorship? Perhaps. Certainly, starting from 1948, it had stopped being pro-Soviet, opting for non-alignment. Culture circulated more freely than in other socialist states. Bookshops quietly displayed works by foreign authors. Theaters were open to aesthetic experimentation and social criticism. The so-called "black wave" of Yugoslav cinema offered decisive resistance to political monolithism. But above all, an unprecedented self-management of the means of production was promoted, arguing that the State had to progressively step aside, in order to avoid the bureaucratism typical of Soviet-style five-year plans.

All this ended due to the fault of four states: Germany, USA, United Kingdom and France, which immediately recognized the illegal and unilateral secession of Slovenia, Croatia and, later, Bosnia (which could have obtained their independence in Parliament, as happened with Czechoslovakia, instead of with a war). They wanted the introduction of capitalism, and therefore the privatization of all means of production.

Then the Western press did everything to paint the Serbs as an inhuman people. So much so that among the ethnic Serb victims there were many civilians, including children, elderly people and women, in considerably higher quantities than Croats and Muslims.

Now the question is: what happened to Yugoslavia could happen to the European Union, deprived as it is of a real political government, of a parliament that counts for something, of a shared Constitution, of a common fiscal policy and above all of a foreign independent from the American one?

April 27

What does the experience of the former Yugoslavia teach us?

When the new republican Yugoslavia was created after World War II, the model was that of Soviet-style state socialism.

Tito, the charismatic leader who, with his strong army of partisans, had managed to free himself from the Nazi-fascists, seemed to be Stalin's man.

Ethnicities and nationalities were clearly subordinated to the needs of a centralist state; the multi-party system was liquidated; ecclesiastical properties (especially Catholic ones) were confiscated; Private ownership of most of the means of production was nationalized. Yugoslavia was considered a victorious power, whose territorial claims had to be satisfied.

However, already in 1948 the break between Moscow and Belgrade occurred. Tito immediately realized that Yugoslavia was too economically weak a country to function like the USSR; it was also too characterized on an ethnic-regional level for the socialist system to be imposed from above. The objectives set were too ambitious.

The federalism affirmed in the constitution reflected the historical nationalistic divisions, which enjoyed a certain administrative autonomy, complete with the right to secession. The Serbian and Croatian identities clearly prevailed (also on a linguistic level), but Tito, to prevent the emergence of ethnic tensions, tried to valorise the Slovenian, Macedonian and Montenegrin minorities.

After Stalin's death, Khrushchev mended the rift with Belgrade, admitting that there could be various ways to achieve a socialist society. In particular, he agreed on the idea of experimenting with workers' consultative councils, aimed at a self-managed form of the means of production, in the context of a mercantile socialism, which would also provide for a certain liberalization of prices and wages.

In essence, we wanted to make a significant difference between the terms "state" and "social" (or "public"). Economic decentralization in the corporate governance of companies implied the progressive dismantling of the managerial role of the State (except, obviously, for military functions). Inevitably, the role of the various republics increased and, within these, that of the various Municipalities. Regional federalism seemed to be able to replace state centralism. Such a thing had never been seen in the context of socialism.

Unfortunately, fundamental errors began to be made. Since self-management allowed a well-being unknown to the countries of the Soviet bloc, the desire to increase it even further did the rest.

The various republics began to move closer to the West. Commercial and military agreements were signed, financial loans were requested, relations were established with the non-communist left. Perhaps it was not a mistake to form the non-aligned movement, but it was certainly illusory to think that there could be a "third way" between socialism and capitalism.

The unity of the various populations began to crumble. The last three centralized structures (Communist League, army and secret police) managed to maintain a forced unity only until Tito died (1980). But in the face of growing social and economic problems, extremist forms of power developed, especially among Serbs and Croats.

So what does the experience of the former Yugoslavia teach us?

1) The union of multiple ethnic groups, divided by language, religion and various traditions, cannot be something artificial imposed from above or from outside. Either they all contribute freely, seeking above all what unites, or it is better to remain divided.

2) A nation cannot be held together by an exceptional leader (such as Tito). If this happens it is because democracy does not work. Any cult of personality should be wisely prevented.

3) If to create an ethnic-nationalist separation we rely on external forces (e.g. Western ones), we can be sure that, once the separation is achieved, these same forces will have a prevailing power over everything.

4) A federalist state is always preferable to a centralist state, as it facilitates the process of democratization of the popular masses, but it is clear that this requires a greater commitment to respecting the diversity and needs of all the actors involved.

April 28

War is horrible

War is a horrible thing, that only horrible people could want or love.

I can understand a defensive war, but against those who launch an offensive war or against those who plot to make it inevitable, the whole world should rise up.

I can understand those who enlist in some armed forces for a personal passion, for a family tradition, or because they are convinced that they are performing a patriotic service, or because they come from a marginal, deprived background, and need to redeem themselves, having no viable alternatives, sufficiently credible. But the mercenary, who fights individually only for money, without any specific ideal, disgusts me, especially if he has other chances to live. Nor can I tolerate those who enlist just to make a career, to have easy money and privileges of all sorts and to retire as soon as possible.

The soldier considers himself untouchable by definition, he exalts himself in the name of his presumed inviolability. He doesn't have many scruples when he has to carry out terrorist actions or when he has to torture someone for whatever reason. He knows that he will always be protected, he knows that he will never suffer consequences as if he were a civilian.

When war is waged, ethics are reduced to a minimum: either you die or I die. The enemies of my enemies are my friends. You never fraternize with the enemy. Nature can be devastated as we want. In the name of nationalism everything is permissible. The mass media will always be on our side.

Politicians, journalists and statesmen who send entire populations to their deaths, both their own and those of others, are criminals who should be judged by international tribunals and severely punished. They should be completely deprived of their assets and functions.

States that launch wars without any UN mandate should be expelled from this body, even if they are part of the Security Council. Indeed this same Council should be completely replaced by the General Assembly of all the people of the world. The Council should only have an executive function of resolutions decided by the aforementioned Assembly.

War is a monstrosity, since with today's means of warfare it is no longer possible to make a difference between civilian and military, adult and child, between man and woman. Deadly shots are fired at a distance of hundreds or thousands of kilometres, without seeing the enemy's face, in the vague hope of being as precise as possible, so as not to incur public criticism.

But perhaps even more dangerous than war is social injustice, peaceful treaties that are not respected, coups d'état, civil wars that occur in the face of the world's indifference, murders of excellent people, which we want to prevent to govern... All these things are smaller than a real war, yet on an ethical level they are equivalent. Instigating murder or being a killer, giving an infamous order or carrying it out are not differences that human conscience is required to consider as abysmal.

April 29

Gorbachev's undeserved end

In 2021 Rossano Pancaldi gave an impeccable summary of post-Stalinist Russia in the magazine "Slavia" (no. 3).

He confirmed that the real innovation, after the period of stagnation of Brezhnev, Andropov and Chernenko, was Gorbachev's leadership. It was he who understood that the disconnect between institutions and society was leading the country to the abyss and that Stalinist methods, in essence, had never been overcome.

Gorbachev had to face enormous problems, which the political power hid in the name of its own authoritarianism. He was the first to initiate a true democratization of the political system, allowing free elections and multi-party politics, decoupling the functions of the CPSU from those of the state and the economy. He favored what the Russians had known only in Lenin's short period: the freedom of dissent and the New Economic Policy, which Stalinism had eliminated in a hurry.

Gorbachev did not want to restore capitalism at all, but to give socialism a clearly democratic guise, self-managed by society, capable of making the system efficient and transparent.

He wanted a mixed economic structure, in which management planned from above was measured against private management of certain means of production. The free market was not to be completely abolished.

To keep this social project of his in the right direction, he had to fight both the old conservatism (and he later regretted not having done so with the necessary authority) and the new ultra-liberal radicalism. The Stalinists considered it too democratic; the others too little.

He ended the nuclear threat and the Cold War, leaving Americans disconcerted, accustomed to having enemies to fight. He withdrew soldiers from Afghanistan, Africa and Cuba. He unilaterally reduced Russia's armaments, the armed forces of Eastern European countries. He eliminated chemical weapons. He closed the ideological disputes with China and Yugoslavia. He allowed the reunification of the two Germanys, asking only that NATO not expand to the east (a promise that was not kept in Yeltsin's time).

He trusted external enemies more than internal ones. He even dissolved the Warsaw Pact, hoping that NATO would do the same. He was a very naive idealist, but the whole world saw him as a powerful beacon of high brightness. Those who did not understand the historical importance of perestroika and glasnost understood nothing about democracy.

He allowed the return of dissidents, opened historical archives and encouraged the publication of once banned works. He granted the first free elections by universal suffrage for the office of the Presidency of the USSR, which were won by the radical Yeltsin, who since then became his fiercest rival.

At this point it was the neo-Stalinists who organized the coup in order to get rid of him. The pretext was that the USSR had ceased to be a great power. Eight collaborators very close to him betrayed him.

The military coup was foiled by the resistance of the democrats and radicals led by Yeltsin, who, however, from that moment on, began to take away all of Gorbachev's powers. Not only that, but he declared the CPSU illegal and banned funding for all communist parties around the world.

Yeltsin began a process of detachment of the Republics from the central power. More than 20 million Russians suddenly found themselves outside the borders of the new Russian Federation. And today we know what this can mean when the countries that host them begin to persecute them.

The USSR was dead precisely because of those who wanted to preserve it by force. And the free-market radicals took advantage of this collapse, that is, the worst elements in the country, those closest to the new "bourgeois dictatorship" of Yeltsin, those who allowed the West to take advantage of an unexpected manna that rained from heaven. After all, it often happens like this: when it is not possible to obtain something in a democratic way, extremists exploit popular requests to turn them in favor of groups that aspire to have all the privileges and that are not at all concerned about sending millions of people into poverty.

The ex-Soviet people, however, made a sensational mistake: they began to blame not only Yeltsin but also Gorbachev for the failure of the USSR. And it hasn't stopped doing it since.

April 30

A strong democracy is decided by the population

In the collective imagination of the Russian people, a narrative still dominates today which, in certain respects, is mythological.

1) Before Gorbachev there was a stable, developed and powerful country;

2) the oligarchs, supported by foreign secret service agents, began

a path of economic and political reforms that led the country to catastrophe;

3) in 1999-2000, people came to power (the first of which was Putin) who brought things back to normal.

When you are used to obeying, ideas see only part of the problems. For example. agriculture has always been inefficient in the Stalinist and post-Stalinist USSR. The rapid urbanization demanded by a Stalinism that wanted to compete on an industrial level with the advanced capitalist countries, to demonstrate that it was not afraid of anyone, could not be satisfied by an agriculture where millions of farmers, opposed to forced collectivization, had been exterminated (not to mention those who had abandoned the land, preferring to become workers).

At the beginning of the 1960s the USSR was economically isolated from the world, without light industry and with the population waiting for hours in front of food shops.

In 1965 and 1973, with the Kosygin reforms, attempts were made to give greater economic independence to businesses, favoring material incentives, and greater autonomy to local and regional authorities, but, ultimately, the regime preferred stagnation.

When Gorbachev came to power, the economic situation was already desperate. However, the real problem is that he didn't give himself time to launch any real economic reform. Unlike Yeltsin, Gorbachev never had the idea of overturning the collectivist foundations of socialism.

Only after 1991, with the implosion of the USSR, did an accelerated process of neoliberal privatization begin which led the country to bankruptcy: a few ultra-rich oligarchs with millions of starving people.

When Putin arrived to put things right, the population ended up considering Yeltsin an inevitable consequence of Gorbachev.

Russians are not used to democracy. They always need an authoritarian leader, also because, having never had traditions of private enterprise, they cannot do without a certain state protection. Something that Yeltsin was absolutely unable to guarantee.

The uncontrolled liberalization of prices, the wild privatization of the entire industrial sector, sold off at ridiculous prices, the corruption of the governors of the various regions, the growing organized crime, the collapse of the federal financial system, the concentration of economic power in the hands of a few entrepreneurs and the financial crisis that hit the country in 1998 were not a consequence of perestroika, but of the reforms of the wretched Yeltsin and his entourage, hostages in the hands of the nascent oligarchy of the energy sector.

The Russian Federation should ask itself now what its fate will be after the end of Putinism. After all, the pragmatic Putin has managed to masterfully reconcile state needs with private ones, and in foreign policy he has shown a lot of common sense and foresight.

However, the economy of a large state like Russia cannot depend on the subjective qualities of its President. Nor can it rely on the enormous abundance of energy resources. Sooner or later the inhabitants of this gigantic country will have to understand again that there is no future without socialism, and that true socialism, the democratic one, certainly cannot be imposed from above.

Was Gorbachev weak? Perhaps, but it was also the population that was not ready for a strong democracy.

May

May 1st

The Heart of Uluru

The "Uluru Statement from the Heart", drawn up by the Aboriginal and island tribes of Australia in 2017, has something poignant, which should make it clear not only to the racist and colonialist West, but to the entire planet how relative the progress of 'humanity. (Uluru is the name of the large stone that the whites call Ayers Rock, now managed by Aboriginal people).

In fact, these tribes still feel united with their ancestors, who according to science are more than 60,000 years old. The bond is so strong that they cannot give up the mandate they have received to preserve the sovereignty of that continent.

For them, sovereignty is a spiritual concept, which cannot be extinguished or surrendered, as it excludes private property. The earth is "mother nature", which gave birth to all the aborigines. The link between land and population is eternal, even if British colonialism has been trying for 200 years to make it futile and irrelevant.

In fact, if it is true that colonialism was based until 1992 on the absurd principle of "terra nullius" (according to which Australia for the English was a no man's land, legitimately colonized), it is also true that after that date it little has been returned to the indigenous people, who today represent 3.8% of the Australian population, for a total of approximately 984,000 people, of which 33% are under 15 years of age.

More than half of this population lives in cities, often in terrible conditions in the most degraded suburbs (this is demonstrated by the suicide and infant mortality rates which are much higher than those of the rest of the population).

One of the worst tragedies for young aborigines continues to be the issue of Deaths in Custody. Just in 2022–23, there were 110 deaths: seventy in prison custody and forty in police custody or custody-related operations. Aboriginal deaths in custody is a political and social issue in Australia. The issue rose in prominence in the early 1980s, with Aboriginal activists campaigning following the death of 16-year-old John Peter Pat in 1983. Subsequent deaths in custody, considered suspicious by fam-

ilies of the deceased, culminated in the 1987 Royal Commission into Aboriginal Deaths in Custody (RCIADIC).

Experts estimate that the number of Aboriginal and Torres Strait
Islander people was more than 770,000 at the time of the invasion of the
English First Fleet in 1788 (it was Captain James Cook who claimed the
Australian land in 1770). By 1900 Aboriginal people had already fallen to
an all-time low of around 117,000 people, a decline of 84%.

Indigenous people claim to be, all things considered, the most in-
carcerated people on the planet, as if they were criminals by birth. Their
children are being removed from their families at an unprecedented rate,
to be placed with white families or missionary boarding schools. And their
young people languish in prisons in obscene numbers.

They feel helpless and fear that if things continue like this, there
will be no future for them.

They are calling for constitutional reforms that can guarantee justice and self-determination, but Australian conservatives won't hear of it.
And Aboriginal people have no use for government laws that can be overturned by a change of government.

The first apologies from the government for having robbed Aboriginal people of their resources date back to 2008. But the end of racism,
formally, only occurred in 2013.

May 2

I regret the past

In a world in which the collective West is not resigned to leaving
history in a peaceful manner, I strongly regret the Gorbachev period, when
we spoke of universal values, of a common European home, of common
interests, different from class or national ones, which are no less objective.

He was very clear that in the conditions of a nuclear threat, lethal
for all humanity, or an environmental catastrophe of planetary proportions,
the main objective had to be to safeguard the life of mankind, seeking
agreements or compromises that were advantageous for all.

I remember well when he said that a policy that does not take into
account reflections on the destinies of humanity is a policy devoid of ethics.

Was he perhaps naive? An idealist? A utopian? Perhaps. But anyone who does not understand the historical importance of his message, by
virtue of which millions of people could finally feel free, or at least confi-
dent in a better world, understands nothing about democracy.

In his autobiography, Everything in Its Time, Gorbachev said that perestroika (restructuring) and glasnost (transparency) not only brought the countries of the Soviet bloc out of the isolation they had found themselves in, but also stimulated progressive movements throughout the world. He understood the importance of freedom of conscience and speech, as well as the need for a mixed economic system.

In Russia the monopoly of the single party and ideology came to an end. Hundreds of thousands of people, unjustly convicted under Stalinism, were rehabilitated. The policy of opposing blocs and the division of the world into "us" and "them" was rejected. It was demonstrated that it was a contradiction in terms to speak of a "State of the whole people", since a people, when they are masters of their own means of production, do not need any State, being able to manage themselves.

I wonder what sense there is in blaming Gorbachev if the collective West interpreted this democratic turning point as a defeat for the USSR, that is, as a good opportunity to take advantage of its weakness.

The implosion of state socialism did not make the capitalist countries pay: there were no world or even regional wars. The West thought that that revolution of thought and values should only concern socialist countries and not itself.

I remember well when we said that "we" already felt free; if anything, it was "they" who had to change. And since we thought we had "won" the Cold War, we felt authorized to impose our lifestyle on Russia, finding our privileged partners in the wretched Yeltsin and in the oligarchs who had become masters of energy resources. It didn't seem true to us that we could expand the number of NATO bases towards the east.

For us, it was not so much a matter of "democratizing socialism" but rather of transforming it into full-fledged private capitalism, and in the most accelerated time possible. From 1991 (collapse of the USSR) to today we have believed we were invincible, immortal, like certain mythological figures of ancient Greece.

Now, however, after not having understood that that message of peace, democracy and pluralism did not only concern "them" but also "us", we suddenly discover that our daydreams have been shattered. The Russian Federation does not accept being colonized by the West, on the contrary, it is ready to support any war conflict with NATO.

China (but it would be better to say Asia in general) has proven to be more productive than the entire West. World capitalism is less and less American-led; and fewer and fewer countries are willing to tolerate it.

Power centers are forcefully emerging which we Westerners perceive as a threat to our global hegemony. And we accuse them of wanting to violate our "values", those values that we have imposed on the whole world, making people believe they are "universal".

The collapse of the West is ultimately the collapse of a gigantic illusion, fueled by half a millennium of abuses. What amazes me most about us Westerners is that when we enter a perverse tunnel, we are no longer able to get out.

May 3

A politics that serves ideology

When you read the analyzes that some Trotskyist movements (heirs of the Fourth International) make of the current situation in Ukraine, you are quite disconcerted. In the name of scientific socialism they do something that the classics of Marxism would never have done: subordinate politics to ideology. They lose their sense of reality, like certain religious sects or the fanatics of neoliberal globalism.

Let's see the main oversights:

1) They give very little importance to the 2014 Maidan coup, which overthrew a democratically elected government. Nor do they see that the coup was led and financed by the USA, with the active commitment of the neo-Nazi forces in Kiev, who have Stepan Bandera as their "idol". The Azov and Aidar regiments were armed and trained by American and Canadian servicemen. Indeed, the entire NATO exercised Ukrainian forces to go to war against Russia.

2) They ignore the killing of over 60 trade unionists in Odessa. Arseniy Yatsenyuk, the prime minister appointed by Victoria Nuland after the coup, not only supported the attack on the union building, but blocked any attempt to launch an investigation into the massacre.

3) They give no weight to the discrimination and civil war that the populations of Donbass suffered from 2014 until the start of the Russian armed intervention. Nor do they mention the two Minsk Agreements, much less the shock declarations of Merkel and Hollande, which they signed only to give the Ukrainians time to arm themselves.

4) They claim that Ukraine has the right to self-determination, without understanding that if Moscow could accept the country's entry into the EU, it absolutely could not accept it also joining NATO. The USA's own Monroe Doctrine holds that any intervention or placement of weapons by foreign powers near its borders is judged to be a potentially hostile act.

5) They seem not to know, just like European statesmen, that Russia has been seeking a national security pact with the United States and NATO for years, without ever having obtained it.

6) They pretend not to know that Zelensky's government is clearly anti-worker, being completely in favor of the oligarchs. The EU itself, before the war, considered him particularly corrupt.

7) They absurdly equate Russia and the USA on an imperialistic level, when if there is a country surrounded by American military bases it is Russia (now they are also found in Sweden and Finland).

8) Incredibly, they did not understand that this is not a war between Russia and Ukraine, but between the collective West and Russia, and therefore it is a proxy war, which can even turn into a nuclear war, in case there is a defeat of the Ukrainian army. This is not a war of aggression on the part of Russia, but of protection of a persecuted Russian-speaking minority and of defense of its territory from NATO missiles.

9) They demand that Russia stop the war and leave Ukraine even without a negotiated settlement. In this way, however, the war would never end. It wouldn't end even if Russia kept Donbass and the rest of the country went under NATO.

10) They are convinced, in the most ridiculous way possible, that if Ukraine wins the war, the working class will drive the oligarchs and fascists and NATO out of the country. In fact, we have seen what the Ukrainian working class has done from 2014 to today... Who is stopping them from overthrowing the fascist junta that rules Kiev? It does not make a revolution because it fears that Russia will take advantage of it or is it because it is blinded by an absurd Russophobic nationalism? It took Putin 8 years before intervening to help the two tiny republics of Donetsk and Luhansk, and sometimes he regrets having taken so long.

May 4

Truth and evidence

That the truth does not lie in the evidence is well known to scholars. Marx himself said that if the laws of capital were easily understandable, he would not have spent half his life trying to decipher them.

When he wrote the three volumes of Capital (two of which were published by his friend Engels), Marx was convinced that he had understood not only the essence of capitalism, but so many of its particular laws that he was able to anticipate the evolution of the system.

Yet right before his eyes the transformation of capitalism from competitive to monopolistic was taking place, and within the latter the financial aspects were becoming more important than the industrial ones. It will take other eminent economists to fill the gap.

Marx himself, after publishing the first volume of Capital, realized, in the face of criticism coming from Russian populists, that it was wrong to consider the transition from feudalism to capitalism as inevitable. In Russia, in the name of the agricultural commune emancipated from serfdom, one could move directly to socialism. That's what the populists said. He agreed, however, specifying one condition, that in Western Europe the industrial proletariat had managed to carry out a victorious revolution.

However, the facts proved him wrong: in Russia there was a transition to socialism despite the presence of European capitalism. And this revolution was not carried out first and foremost by the peasants, but by an industrial proletariat, led by an urbanized party, willing to meet the demands of the most marginal rural strata (those strata that Western Marxism never took into serious consideration).

Only at the end of his life, when he dedicated himself to ethnographic studies, did Marx understand something completely ignored by subsequent Marxism, namely that use value was to be considered clearly more important than exchange value. The use value made the economic aspects much more easily understandable and manageable. But at that point he would have had to rewrite *Capital* and by then it was too late.

He pondered another thing about him for many years, without coming to terms with it with crystal clarity. Why was capitalism born in Western Europe when in Byzantine Europe the riches were disproportionate (remaining so even for a thousand years)? The Islamic and Indo-Buddhist civilizations themselves experienced levels of trade higher than those of feudal Europe. Evidently these cultures lacked that something that the Roman Catholic one had and that the Protestant one will have to the nth degree (especially in the Calvinistic variant).

Marx understood only that European capitalism had found the most favorable ideological support in Protestantism. But since he considered culture a mere superstructure of the economy, two things escaped him: 1) that capitalism (as a concept of life) was actually born in the communal Italy of the year 1000, which was Catholic; 2) that culture is able to significantly influence economic processes, albeit with a certain slowness.

It is no coincidence that after the year 1000 it was Latin or Catholic Europe that unleashed continuous crusades against Islam and Eastern, Byzantine and Slavic Europe. This *ante-litteram* colonialism, preceding that inaugurated by Columbus' voyages, enormously favored the development of capitalism in Western Europe.

However, only towards the middle of the 20th century. Marxist scholars of the Third World (in the wake of Luxemburg) went so far as to say that without modern bourgeois colonialism, Euro-Western industrialization would hardly have developed in such a short time and in such an impressive manner.

In *Capital*, however, Marx considered colonialism as a collateral, even secondary, effect of capitalism, as all the fundamental laws of capital were independent of any colonialist practice.

I remember that in the 1970s eminent Marxist economists, such as Samir Amin, André Gunder Frank and Hosea Jaffe, got very angry when Western Marxists argued that the Third World, before moving to socialism, had to carry out the industrial revolution, by virtue of which a revolutionary proletariat could have been born. Engels himself was responsible for this very deterministic and artificial mental scheme in the last period of his life.

In short, the importance of Marxism was undoubtedly that of having made it clear that in the context of capitalism there is nothing "natural", and that the politics of statesmen must respond to directives coming from the industrial and financial world, which ethical and democratic only has the words with which to deceive public opinion.

It therefore appears clear that the road to human emancipation is still very long. And without understanding things, there is no evidence that matters. Suffice it to say that today 1% of the planet's population holds 50% of the world's wealth. This would be enough to start a world war. However, the topic is not even on the agenda.

May 5

The African way to socialism

It is probable that the African path to socialism will not have to face the limits of state socialism, which weighed so heavily on the destinies of the countries of the former Soviet bloc. To understand things, there is no need to repeat the mistakes that others have already made.

However, it would be a mistake to think that Africa will not have to deal with state socialism because it is currently less equipped on an industrial level. It no longer makes sense to think that where industry is highly developed and a socialist transition is to be inaugurated, the dirigiste role of the State will inevitably have to take priority over everything.

Honestly speaking, I hope that when states embrace socialism, politicians will have enough intelligence to promote collective self-management of the means of production, regardless of their technological level. Whether the industry is very, little or not at all developed, this should not have any impact on the decisions to be made regarding the social management of common goods, those fundamental to the survival of a society.

For me a civil society or a nation is simply a collection of local or regional communities. The State should not be above a nation. At most, alongside one nation there may be others, with different uses and consumption. But it would be good to also fight to overcome the borders that separate one nation from another.

When local or regional communities have common problems to solve or conflict situations to resolve, they should not need to establish a permanent, bureaucratic state, with its own parliament and army, and with a capital on which everything depends.

If there are common problems, of an economic, environmental or military nature, ad hoc institutions can be created, representative of all local or regional communities, and having a limited time, precisely the time necessary to solve the problem.

In this sense I think that Africa, once it has completely freed itself from the yoke of colonialism, will have less difficulty achieving the socialist transition. This is because they are more used to living the experience of the local community. This is also demonstrated by the fact that when they come to live with us, they are very surprised by our individualism and the coldness of our relationships.

Africa has nothing to learn from the capitalist West. Indeed, it must hurry to unlearn what it has already learned, otherwise its collectivist traditions will die forever.

Let's take the example of Tanzania. When it got rid of English colonialism (which had replaced German colonialism) in 1961, the first thing President Nyerere did was to distribute the land to the entire population.

Since he realized that if he asked for financial aid from the West, the country would be easily blackmailed, he decidedly opted for autarky. The villages had to manage all local resources in an equitable and shared manner. The State would have intervened only to eliminate inequalities between the various villages.

Nyerere said that the State was socialist not because it had imported communist ideology from abroad, but because village communities, long before European colonialism, had always been "socialist". They had been so in a "natural" way.

Here we should still have some hope towards this pre-capitalism.

May 6

Two mantras compared

When Western economists criticize the traditional subsistence economies present in the global South, it makes one nervous. They know very well that it is precisely thanks to those structures that massive migratory flows towards Western countries do not occur, those flows that we try to hinder in every way.

Yet they cannot help but judge those ancestral structures with the most derogatory terms: crude, primitive, prehistoric, etc. They must necessarily make the interests of capital, the owner who pays them to tell falsehoods.

We have seen it with our own eyes: already in the 1990s the indebtedness process of the Global South had begun to take on a monstrous dimension, demonstrating that, without economic independence, political independence is worth very little.

It was already a clearly uncollectable debt, which capitalist countries, through the World Bank and the IMF, used to keep the global South subjugated. Conditions were imposed which, to say the least, were usurious.

The great thing is that, on the one hand, the West is asking to be increasingly dependent on the needs of international markets; on the other hand, however, due to the interest that must be paid on loans, it slows down the processes of transformation towards the market economy, except for a privileged few. It imposes monocultures, but then those who manage them are the multinationals.

Capital destroys the management autonomy of self-consumption, which is a collective phenomenon, and allows countries that are up to their necks in debt to enter international markets, transforming traditional communities into places of chronic poverty, from which people try to escape, individually, as soon as possible.

The global South is a paradise for our multinationals, who pay very few taxes (compared to their income), and beautifully appropriate natural resources and labor below cost. And if some enlightened statesman threatens to nationalize industries or resources, he must watch his back, since those are unscrupulous companies, which do not take long to sponsor excellent assassinations or coups d'état, possibly using the inevitable foreign military base of the country from which they come.

The mantra that capital wants to achieve on a global level is "less state, more market". The countries that have managed to remove the noose around their necks, in the best of cases, manage to replace it with this: "more State in the market". Which means that the slipknot marks on the skin no longer go away.

In fact, the markets remain, since without them there are no comforts, material well-being, etc. etc. The collective ownership and management of all means of production is yet to come. Self-consumption is pure utopia.

One can only hope that the State will be able to control the economic powers, forcing them to keep the public interest in mind. This (relative) primacy of politics over the economy is clearly visible in the BRICS countries. It is the most one could wish for today, if one wants a minimum of democracy.

May 7

Enough with nostalgia for what needs to be overcome

I don't understand Rita di Leo, a historian and economist who is still nostalgic for the old USSR. She has written about it in myriad publications.

She does not exclude Gorbachev's good faith, but she considered him totally incapable. He delegitimized the power of the CPSU she says, but in my opinion this is a mistake.

The USSR was a state managed by a one-party system, with the single thought of the Marx-Leninist ideology (used according to Stalinist criteria) and with institutions so intertwined between the CPSU and the state that the weakening of one automatically caused that of the other.

There can be no democracy without pluralism. The truth can never be imposed. And then it is absolutely not true that without an official truth we end up in the relativism of values, and we do capitalism a favour.

Here we need to be convinced of something of fundamental importance, which Leo did not understand: the people are more important than the State. Concepts such as national state, political state, territorial integrity managed by the state should count for nothing compared to the right to self-determination that the various populations (ethnicities, nationalities, regional realities...) that constitute the nation as a whole can claim.

If it were clear throughout the world, and in the UN itself, that people are superior to states, wars like those in Ukraine, Chechnya, Georgia and so on would never have broken out. When a certain segment of the population demands, in a reasoned manner, its own autonomy, it must be granted to them without much discussion.

The State is a powerful but faceless instrument. Whoever takes over its institutions can commit exceptional abuses and get away with it. It is officially responsible for everything, but it is never guilty of anything.

The classics of Marxism were very clear on this: the State can serve against the inevitable internal counter-revolution and the belligerent interventionism of foreign States, but, once the situation is consolidated, it has the task of progressively extinguishing itself, allowing civil society to self-administer.

The controversy that the communists have waged on several occasions with anarchism was true: a society cannot aspire to self-management if the revolution has not first taken place, and this is not possible without a centralized direction of operations and without occupying the vital nerves of the State. However, once the objective has been successfully achieved, we must begin to dismantle that which removes responsibility from the population, that which makes it dependent on decisions that fall from above.

A democratic state is a contradiction in terms, as is the rule of law or the state of all the people. Any form of state (monarchic or republican, hereditary or constitutional, presidential or parliamentary) must be considered as a historical product of the last half millennium. There is nothing "natural" about it.

Human beings were not made to submit to the power of the great Molochs or Leviathans. It is only funny that an imperialist country like the USA, founded on the genocide of natives, accuses Russia of wanting to expand into Europe. This is because, since it was born (a thousand years ago), Russia never intended to do so. Which does not mean that it is not an "imperial" state, but simply that no Western country is capable of giving lessons in democracy.

This imperial mania is part of a "history of civilizations" that must definitely be overcome. The very concept of "civilization" is an opprobrium. In fact, with it historians refer to the first slave empires, branding everything that preceded it as "primitivism".

On this I want to be sincere but categorical: democracy (the social one, not just the political one) does not lie in multipolarism in itself, nor in multipartyism. Democracy lies in the possibility that a local community has to manage the resources of the territory in which it lives in a shared and integral manner. Which does not exclude delegated democracy, but clearly subordinates it to direct democracy.

If the State favors this decentralization of functions, it deserves to be respected, otherwise it is useless to have illusions: we will move from one form of dictatorship to another.

May 8

History repeats itself

Today we find ourselves living in a geopolitical situation which, in some ways, resembles that of the 1960s. A lot of time has passed, but it seems that the fundamental problems are still the same.

Indeed, when some fifty countries gathered in New Delhi in 1961, the World Peace Council made it clear that general and complete disarmament and the liquidation of colonialism were not separable issues. At a certain point, a third topic was added that was inseparable from the other two: security for all European peoples, Eastern and Western.

The same thing was repeated in numerous subsequent international meetings in other cities around the world. There was a fear of the proliferation of nuclear weapons, also because Japan and West Germany were about to receive them from the USA for an anti-Soviet purpose.

Furthermore, it was impossible not to listen to the anti-colonialist voices against Portugal, coming from Angola, Mozambique, Guinea-Bissau, etc. Not to mention those who called for national liberation from British, Spanish, French colonialism...

At that time American imperialism dominated to a large extent (as demonstrated for example by the war in Vietnam), and nuclear tests were countless. Many African and Asian countries firmly rejected the lie that the struggle for general disarmament would lead to the disarmament of the peoples fighting for their political independence. It was the first time that such countries expressed themselves collectively, with a unanimous feeling in favor of peace and decolonization.

Indeed, there was a call for the immediate formation of completely nuclear-free zones in various regions of the planet. The closure of military bases in foreign territories was also called for (today, just to give an example, the USA has more than 800 located in 80 countries!).

The USA was accused of genocide in Vietnam, because it used chemical weapons, and it was deeply despised that it supported the Zionists of Israel, who were completely averse to the idea of recognizing the Palestinians as having their own autonomous state.

In 1968, world public opinion persuaded people to sign the treaty on the non-proliferation of nuclear weapons, and blocked the American bombing of Vietnam for a few years (which was resumed in 1972, leading to the definitive defeat of the USA in 1975).

The main difference compared to those distant years is that today Western provocations and tensions in favor of a world war are very high, while international demonstrations in favor of peace are reduced to a minimum.

It seems like we are witnessing an aged West, whose populations, too accustomed to seeing their democratic ideals defeated, have taken on a resigned attitude towards their warmongering statesmen, who, in an irrational manner, want to bring the whole of humanity to catastrophe. We need a new generation...

May 9

Sleep peacefully

In 1988, at the UN, Gorbachev made it clear that the idea of the disconnection between developed and underdeveloped countries was an illusion: at most, debt policy had to be completely revised.

The USSR was ready for a moratorium of up to 100 years on interest, and in some cases even limited to writing off the debt altogether. He said this, of course, not because he was in favor of neocolonial dependency, but because he saw world processes as closely interconnected.

The fact is that the great Marxist economists, who represented the interests of the Third World (such as Samir Amin, Andre Gunder Frank and Hosea Jaffe), were disappointed, although they were aware that even if some Third World countries managed to disengage from completely from Western imperialism, no Marxist was clear on how to build a socialist alternative.

Ultimately, Marxism was a Western ideology, which had benefited from various additions and clarifications by Leninism, another ideology that we could define as semi-Western, as Russia presents many elements of Asianism that modern Western Europe has long ago removed.

We were very far from understanding that in the pre-capitalist structures of the Third World there was more "socialism" than in the "real" one of the Soviet bloc or in the rural one of Maoism. We were still dazzled by the idea that without strong technical-scientific progress, only a "socialism of poverty" would be achieved.

Today, fortunately, this Marxism no longer exists, and where the countries of the global South send home the old and new colonizers, they do not go looking outside their countries for solutions to the new problems they face.

Even if this is only true up to a certain point. In fact, a lot depends on how far-sighted the new politicians who come to power are. It is not a rare case that the countries of the global South, which carry out popular revolutions or coups d'état against the government councils colluding with the Westerners, go to look for military support in Russia, while they ask China for economic support that does not fall back into the dependence of the past.

However, the global South must be very careful. Multipolarism, taken in and of itself, cannot be considered the panacea for all its ills. In the 1970s not even the so-called "real socialism" constituted a great economic advantage for the Third World. It was certainly a significant counterpart to Western imperialism, but it would be hypocritical to say that, in the Third World countries that had embraced the ideas of industrialized socialism, it was able to lay the foundations for a truly democratic change in the economic structure.

The ideas may be the most progressive in the world, but if they do not take into account the real situation, that is, if one tries to impose them from above, at a certain point they reveal themselves for what they are: a form of unjustified prevarication.

In the 1970s it was the USSR that acted as the economic model of reference for the Third World. Today it is China. Which does not imply that the Global South really stands to gain. When you do business with superpowers, you can never be sure of anything.

No one doubts that the Chinese attitude towards the global South is a step forward compared to Western-style private capitalism and Soviet-style state socialism, but it would be illusory to think that, with its enormous financial investments for productive purposes, China does not expect a significant return for its projection of power in the world.

Let's be honest: we must admit that China has all the strengths (even on an ideological level) to progressively replace the entire collective West in the management of the planet. But such a transition cannot make us sleep peacefully.

May 10

From private to state

By now this has been sufficiently understood. With these wars in Ukraine, Gaza and tomorrow in Taiwan we are not witnessing the collapse of capitalism, as a productive economic system, but only its transformation, from private to state.

This is a global transition, which cannot be led by the collective

West, since the power that we have exercised for half a millennium is based on more or less unbridled individualism.

The impetuous technical-scientific development, applied to economic processes, which in the West has required exceptional changes in mentality, values and lifestyles, can no longer be carried forward by countries where social antagonism, class conflicts, the obsessive competition and mutual hatred give us no respite, they exhaust us like boxers in the corner of a ring.

We Westerners have given everything we could give. Only instead of handing over the inheritance calmly, hoping for better use of our assets, we expect them to take it from us by force. "If you want to inherit our heritage, you have to earn it on the battlefields, with the sound of bombs, with dead people (whatever their age, sex, function...), and naturally at the price of environmental pollution that will leave its mark for centuries to come.

The death knell is sounding its final tolls, but, strange as it may seem, the religious man who pulls the rope does not represent socialism. In fact, even state socialism is dead. Perhaps the last one to resist is North Korea, which however would have already imploded without the help of Russia and China.

Today no sane person is nostalgic for those oppressive regimes of the past, which were more brutal towards their citizens than towards the outside world.

However, it must be said, breaking a spear in favor of those regimes, that the constant presence of the State nevertheless constitutes a guarantee for the protection of social rights (housing, work, education, healthcare...).

Today we have moved from state socialism (whether Soviet or Maoist) to state capitalism and/or mercantile socialism, but who would have the courage to argue that, as part of this transition, human rights are being violated more than before? Only a person in bad faith or profoundly ignorant could fail to admit that rights (especially social ones) are much more trampled upon in those capitalist countries that have reduced the functions of the State to a minimum or have completely subordinated them to the needs of capital.

The West did everything to win the Cold War, but after the end of that war, enemy countries emerged unexpectedly that wanted to surpass it on its own terrain, that of industrial, commercial, financial and military development, based on a solid techno-scientific base.

We already know how this competition will end. There is no need to bet on it.

May 11

The evolution of the times

What good the colonialist West has not done in Africa in half a millennium, China has been doing for a few years.

Since the war broke out in Ukraine, Putin and Lavrov's Russia has certainly enhanced the entire African continent on a political level as never before, inviting it to free itself, once and for all, from Western neocolonialism, to join the BRICS, to abandon the use of the dollar, to accept the idea of multipolarity and above all not to be afraid of the arrogance of Europeans and Americans.

We are very far from traditional Western approaches, based on relationships of subordination, on political interference (which goes as far as the imposition of certain collaborationist elites), on unequal economic exchanges, on financial blackmail, on the ad libitum exploitation of natural resources and labor force below cost, and so on.

However, it is also China that since the time of Ciu En Lai (1960s) has avoided behaving like a colonialist master on the African continent. It was precisely that statesman who said that Chinese aid would never violate the sovereignty of the beneficiary countries, nor ask for privileges or impose conditions. If it had granted financial aid, it would have done so at very low interest rates, and in any case the aid should have promoted the economic self-sufficiency of the recipient country.

In fact, Ciu En Lai assured that Chinese technology allowed projects to be carried out with low investments and rapid results. Not only that, but the secrets of this technology could easily be learned by the technicians of the beneficiary countries, whose technicians would have seen with their own eyes that the Chinese experts, their colleagues, would never have had a higher standard of living.

It was difficult for African statesmen, even if linked to Western colonialism, not to accept such favorable conditions, which were confirmed in the following decades. When President Jiang Zemin visited Africa in 1996, he reiterated non-interference in internal affairs, and indeed expanded in supporting the struggle of African nations for independence, sovereignty and territorial integrity. He even promised that there would be no interest whatsoever on the financial loans, indeed some outstanding debts were cancelled.

This is to say that China has not been helping Africa to develop economically since the current president Xi Jinping. There is an impressive line of continuity that seems to reflect an underlying philosophy.

Furthermore, in China itself, statesmen immediately understood, once they had embraced capitalist ideas (i.e. after the end of Maoism), that no planned economy would be successful without guaranteeing the decentralization of functions and regional self-sufficiency.

When Chinese managers identified those industrial centers to be purchased at convenient prices from advanced Western countries, they transferred them, reassembling them with the necessary variants, close not only to the sources of production of raw materials, but also to consumers. The workers' apartments themselves and the related service centers had to be built around the workplaces.

Above all, the State had to worry about connecting the most productive coastal strip to the hinterland with efficient roads. This is how 800 million people were able to escape poverty in 40 years.

Anyone who does not understand that market socialism has an edge over our private capitalism does not understand the evolution of the times. Which of course doesn't mean that China's presence in Africa isn't creating new problems. But this is another matter.

May 12

Chinese presence in Africa

Reading "Nigrizia" one must admit that the Chinese presence in Africa is not all sunshine and roses.

For example. in Senegal, Chinese (20%) and European (29%) shipowners control the fish sector through their trawlers, ruining the native artisanal fishermen, who are forced to abandon their profession and attempt the crossing in the Atlantic Ocean towards the Canary Islands. Not only that, but the nets of fishing boats scrape the seabed, lifting the carbon stored in natural ocean sinks and transforming it into carbon dioxide. And, what's worse, tons of small fish, which used to be part of the average diet of the Senegalese, are now caught to be transformed into feed to be sold especially in Europe to feed livestock or farmed fish, or to be used in the cosmetics industry.

Another example, Akinwumi Adesina, president of the African Development Bank, argued that it is too disadvantageous for Africa to guarantee, with its own natural resources, the repayment of the financial loans it receives as development aid. This is because it is impossible to adequately define the real value of subsoil resources not yet marketed.

This value could be much higher than the lenders' credits. Not only that, but the lenders (including China), being governments, multinationals or large commercial banks, have bargaining power incomparable to that of the governments receiving the loans, especially if these governments are short of liquidity. Not to mention the fact that some African nations, having at their disposal large quantities of rare materials (think lithium), now considered strategic for the ecological transition, are even more induced to accept credits of this kind.

Yet another example. The increase in Chinese security companies and contractors to protect their country's investments in Africa is recent, especially due to problems caused by terrorism, political instability and piracy. Their main customers are government agencies, state-owned enterprises, transportation companies, logistics companies, oil and gas related companies.

Naturally, Western countries immediately took advantage of this to accuse China of violating one of its fundamental political principles in foreign trade relations: that of non-interference in the internal affairs of other countries. A principle that in half a millennium of colonialism the West has never, ever respected.

Last but not least. China has been Africa's main trading partner for 15 years. However, China exports to the continent much more than it imports: 173 billion dollars compared to 64 billion dollars. Analysts predict that it will take time and long-term effort to find a trade balance.

May 13

Gertler, the irresponsible capitalist

I like the africa-express.info site because it doesn't mince its words. In fact, it explains in detail why Israel sought very close commercial relations with the most corrupt African country on the continent, the Democratic Republic of Congo.

The two respective presidents, Netanyahu and Tshisekedi, have decided to open each other's embassies.

Congo needs military security (including cyber security), agriculture and infrastructure.

Security is related to the elimination of the pro-ISIS armed group of Ugandan origin, called Allied Democratic Forces, which has operated mostly in the eastern part of the country since 1995. To obtain it, Tshisekedi, in power since 2019, had no qualms about fully supporting the Zionists against the Palestinians.

But what does Israel want in return? Oil. To get it it used the multi-billionaire Dan Gertler, on whose behalf Yossi Cohen, former director of the Mossad, had personally interceded, who had wanted to meet Tshisekedi and ex-president Laurent Désiré Kabila three times in 2001, to whom Gertler had lent 20 million dollars to take political power.

In fact, Gertler is under sanction from the US Treasury for high-level corruption in Congo, involving not only oil but also gold, diamonds, copper and cobalt. Congo lost more than $1.36 billion due to Gertler's "opaque and corrupt dealings." "Forbes" magazine had defined him as "The emerging face of irresponsible capitalism in Africa".

Nonetheless, Gertler managed to find his staunchest protector in Tshisekedi, even in Biden's eyes. Naturally he has always denied any involvement in corruption, so much so that he boasts of never having been criminally prosecuted. Indeed, it was he who took several legal actions against anti-corruption activists, whistleblowers, journalists and civil society groups, especially in relation to the case of the Swiss company Glencore, condemned to pay 180 million dollars to the Kinshasa government for acts of corruption from 2008 to 2017, the period in which he worked with Gertler.

Not only that, but when two informants, Gradi Koko Lobanga and Navy Malela, employed at Afriland First Bank in Kinshasa, revealed acts of money laundering for Gertler's benefit, they were sentenced to death in absentia at the ensuing trial!

May 14

The infantile disease of Eurocentrism

Under Putin, relations between the EU and Russia have always been difficult. It is not true that before the war in Ukraine things went smoothly.

Of course, on an energy level the Europeans only had to gain: the gas was of excellent quality and inexpensive. But Europeans are hypocritical and selfish, so they preferred Gorbachev on the military and geopolitical level, and Yeltsin on the economic-financial level so they could downsize and pulp Russia.

Putin's idea of creating a state capitalism was not liked at all in Brussels, which preferred a private capitalism like in the time of Yeltsin, who had reduced the power of the institutions and the CPSU to nothing.

Putin was not against the idea of the market, but he wanted it regulated by the state, especially in the key energy sector, but also in that of armaments.

Russia did not want to be incorporated into the EU, as the other countries of the former Soviet bloc had done, which were practically starting to be plundered by Western capitalism and subjugated by NATO.

In fact, in order to keep Russia sub-conditional, they accused it of not respecting human rights and of not allowing the energy sector to be managed by private individuals.

Russia did not have all these problems either with China (or India) or with Africa. Putin felt that he had no debt of gratitude towards the EU, precisely because the Russians had freed themselves from the burden of an oppressive regime such as the socialist-state one.

The Russians could not understand why European statesmen, despite receiving all possible favors from Russia, respecting different traditions and cultures, continued to have such a haughty, so arrogant attitude.

Fortunately, Russia's relations with other Asian and African states were excellent. In exchange for the purchase of Russian products, Putin was even willing to completely cancel the debt of some African countries and eliminate customs tariffs on all goods coming from the continent. Scholarships were also offered for African students who wanted to graduate or specialize in Russia. High-tech weapons were being sold, surpassing Western competition.

Indeed, the technical and commercial relations with Algeria for the valorisation of the energy sector were so close that Russia did not disdain the idea of creating a "gas OPEC", if any other producing country in Africa or the Middle East was associated.

The last two Italian governments, after having sanctioned Russia in every way due to the war in Ukraine, went to look for an alternative to Russian gas in Algeria, without knowing that all of this country's energy technology depends on Russia. Can you be more clueless and incompetent than that?

European statesmen are still convinced that "Putin's reign" constitutes a kind of "parenthesis" in trade relations between the EU and Russia. We are so Eurocentric that we still haven't understood that we need Russia more than the other way around.

Now, to avoid a military catastrophe in Ukraine, how do we intend to act? Are we willing to wage a nuclear war to prevent the myth of a united Europe from being shattered in the name of private capital? Do we really want to grant full powers to European statesmen, who until now (with exceptions) have behaved in the most absurd way possible?

In order not to see NATO collapse in its anti-Russian proxy war, are we perhaps willing to accept the apocalyptic idea that European capitals will be razed to the ground by Russia's atomic bombings? Do we know that Belarus already has dozens of nuclear missiles aimed at our heads?

We have understood that Putin's military strategy is no longer that of the "second strike", formulated during Brezhnev's stagnation, but is that of the immediate nuclear response, in the event that Russia perceives that it is suffering an "existential threat" to its security? Above all, has Finland, which has 1,300 km of border with Russia, understood this now that it is part of NATO?

Can we convince ourselves that the Russians are not used to using aggressive or threatening tones in diplomatic relations to make their case? And that when they say they are worried about the development of certain events that are very unfavorable to them, independent of their control, they then know how to take adequate countermeasures?

May 15

A paradoxical existence

If it were possible to choose between democracy without a state or state without democracy, it would be an easy choice. In fact, any state presence is always a form of dictatorship, more or less violent, depending on the level of existing contradictions.

The problem, however, is that if we try to reduce the functions of the State to a minimum, such as in Russia in the 1990s, democracy becomes very weak.

The reason lies in the fact that, given that a capitalist system exists in the world which, thanks to the markets, makes relatively rapid and abnormal enrichment possible for those who have capital and means of production, the inevitable tendency is to transform democracy into a 'oligarchy. The government is no longer that of party officials and state employees, but that of private entrepreneurs, of unscrupulous businessmen.

From the time of the ancient slave civilizations, which then transformed into feudal civilizations, and these into bourgeois civilizations, ideas and experiences of a communist or collectivistic type have always existed. But everything that has opposed the dominant antagonistic systems has inexorably failed.

Didn't socialism exist in those community experiences of Qumran frequented by the Baptist and Jesus Christ? Yet it was wiped out by the Roman legions.

And what about the monastic experiences of early Christianity?

Wasn't self-consumption practiced? Yet the temptation to transform themselves into feudal potentates, capable of exploiting the work of the peasants, was at a certain point irresistible.

Experiences of this kind continued until the forced collectivization of the peasants under Stalinism and Maoism, with catastrophic results from every point of view.

Only the forms changed compared to previous experiences: in fact the presence of a strong State guaranteed these experiments a vast territorial extension, which entailed an enormous involvement of people. In this respect it seems that the ideas of communism are destined to fail regardless of any territorial or demographic factor.

We began to abandon primordial communism starting from the birth of slavery, 6,000 years ago (but some historians say starting from the birth of agriculture, 10,000 years ago), and since then we have not been able to go back. We have only changed the methods of exploitation and social injustice, but the substance has remained the same.

The last primitive communities, hidden in remote places on the planet, do not constitute a model to imitate for anyone, also because the planet's population has become so numerous and commercial exchanges so intense that it is considered impossible to satisfy all needs without the help of 'industry.

However, the great limits of machinery are before our eyes. Without a social intent, industry only enriches its owner and leaves the worker in poverty. Not only that, but even when the owner and worker coincide in the same person, the one who loses out is still nature, which tends to become deserted.

Nature returns to feel at ease only when the human presence disappears. Something like this is not normal, also because it takes a very long time to restore one's functions (indeed, the deserts we see growing on the planet often appear irreversible).

This means that we have a completely wrong attitude towards it, which needs to be reviewed at its root.

May 16

Ready to create the United States of Europe?

We Europeans are unable to understand Russia: too superficial, too ignorant of its history, which is incredibly complex. A country this large is not a state or even a nation: it is an empire.

We too have had empires: Roman, Carolingian, Hispanic, Lusitanian, English, French, Prussian, Austro-Hungarian. But we Europeans have exhausted ourselves managing all these empires. The continuous internal wars between empires or to destroy these empires from the outside (think for example of the claims of colonized peoples) have enormously weakened us, especially after the last world wars, which saw the progressive, unstoppable rise of the United States, a European product that has escaped our control, like many other products.

The Russian Empire undoubtedly lost many territories gained during the Second World War, but overall it remained what it was at the time of the tsars, after the liberation from the Tatar-Mongol yoke.

It is impossible for us Europeans, so individualistic, to understand the reasons for this longevity, this compactness. Since the time of Napoleon (but also before, with the Teutons, the Poles, the Swedes...) we have tried to subjugate the Slavic populations, but all our failed attempts have led, by virtue of the Russian counterattack, to the end of those who had had the dare to try.

This leads us to think that even if NATO dropped atomic bombs on large Russian cities, all our capitals would disappear from the face of the Earth, including large American cities. It's not a risk we can take.

We don't know what holds Russia together. Ordinary citizens only know that it makes no sense to declare war on it. At this moment even our statesmen are convinced that at most we can wage a proxy war, which lasts as long as possible, in the hope that that empire will destabilize internally.

If we were the least bit careful, we would have to say: Russia is half European, it has many characteristics in which we can recognize ourselves; since it is full of natural resources, it would be better for us Europeans to try to obtain them under the most advantageous conditions.

Why don't we do it? The reason is very simple: we are dominated by an American narrative according to which our main enemies are Russia and China (as we thought the Islamists were until a few years ago). Anyone who opposes this scam ends up giving in to threats and blackmail, and indeed risks being eliminated, or, at the very least, their country is no longer financed.

We Westerners not only pride ourselves on being democratic, but, in order to define Putin's regime as autocratic, we are willing to greatly reduce our well-being and our development prospects. Naturally always to the advantage of the bully and cunning American, who also knows very well how devastating a nuclear war is for everyone, even for itself.

For these reasons, one has the clear impression that both the EU and the USA are exploiting the propaganda that sees Russia as an implacable enemy only for the usual, banal reason: to solve problems of internal credibility.

Western private capitalism finds itself in very serious economic difficulties vis-à-vis Chinese mercantile socialism. The competition from Chinese products is too strong: it is ruining all our industrial and commercial businesses, even the most technologically advanced ones.

We taught the Chinese to become capitalists like us, and now we don't know how to scale back their planetary ambitions. We need something to wage war against them. Our statesmen need a population that is convinced of this necessity.

Russia represents only the first piece of a much more complex operation. We can also leave Ukraine alone, but only on condition that we find an alternative that replaces it more or less immediately (such as Taiwan or North Korea). After all, when we suddenly left Afghanistan, we did so only to concentrate our forces in Ukraine.

The proxy war against Russia must only give us time to arm ourselves properly, to reinstate compulsory military service, to transform a large part of the nations into war economies, and above all to impose authoritarian political regimes. The populations must do nothing but remain submissive and believe that these transformations are being made for their good and for the construction of the United States of Europe.

May 17

Democracy is something else

It is very naive to think that after the collapse of a dictatorial regime, democracy can triumph quickly. It is even illusory to believe that those who support a regime whose common good is managed by the State can boast a higher level of morality than those who are used to living in so-called neoliberal societies, in which private interest is the parameter for all human values.

That is, when you are used to living in a dictatorship, more or less an explicit one, it is normal to see ethics completely subjugated to politics. So it makes no sense to think that, once the dictatorship is over, we can immediately move on to a phase in which human values play a leading role. We are inevitably influenced by a collective past, which has involved the entire civil society. And the longer the dictatorship lasts, the worse it will be.

Let's look at the Italian example. Fascism lasted for twenty years, twice as long as the Nazi one and half as long as the Spanish-Portuguese one. These are not short periods. And they were not facade dictatorial regimes, but effective ones.

When the Italian one was eliminated, the population stopped being fascist only because the USA had introduced the idea of mass consumerism into the country (starting with household appliances), which also included every form of leisure and entertainment. Economic activity in the 1950s was based on careerism, corruption and unscrupulous competition.

Those who held the reins of politics were a Christian Democracy colluding with the Church, prone to American diktats and in favor of a centralized state as in Mussolini's time, a state that only apparently showed a politics independent of the economy.

To undermine the power of the Christian Democrats it took the worker-student protest that began in 1968 and lasted a decade. Only in the 1970s did a strong criticism of the capitalist system and its (Christian) bourgeois values begin. What could not be done in the time of fascist state capitalism was done in the time of Christian Democrat private capitalism (which initially retained some aspects of the welfare state to satisfy the too numerous militants of the social-communist area). With the aforementioned protest, social, civil and political rights were significantly expanded, even if the system, in fact, remained capitalist, but, in the 1980s (those of the ebb) the Welfare State began to be demolished.

Please note that a similar process also occurred in the countries of the former Soviet bloc. The fact that in those countries the dictatorship was more favorable to the proletariat changes nothing. Those were countries without solid bourgeois traditions. Dictatorships could not be closely linked to large private monopolies. The communists could easily nationalize everything because there was nothing so strong, on an economic and financial level, to be able to oppose this expropriation.

However, when state socialism collapsed, corruption reigned supreme in all sectors of society. The oligarchs were formed in the 1990s, and so was organized crime. Paradoxically, all this happened in the name of a presumed democracy. That is, the power wanted to make people believe that the transition from communist dictatorship to bourgeois liberalism was a step forward in the direction of all democratic values.

If Russia had not had Putin, it would have been another Ukraine. But it is absurd to think that democracy was achieved with Putin. The immoral private capitalism promoted by the wretched Yeltsin has simply been transformed into a sort of state-controlled capitalism, therefore into something that has greatly reduced the power of the oligarchs and organized crime.

It is right that Putin is considered a sort of "savior of the homeland", but democracy is something else.

May 18

The conditions of the collapse

Since we all live in more or less conflictual societies, where individualism, alienation and social antagonism are the rule, there is really no point in becoming purists when examining the facts.

We must necessarily give ourselves some margin of tolerance towards certain attitudes that we judge to be equivocal, ambiguous or amoral. Even Pope Bergoglio, who certainly does not represent the most democratic Church in the world, scandalized moralistic believers when he said: "Who am I to judge homosexuals?".

With this we do not mean to say that, when engaging in geopolitics, one must necessarily be cynical, indifferent to values. We know well that in these societies, which are so difficult to live in, demanding the maximum of ethics or democracy is naive, or rather hypocritical.

Let's take for example the proxy war that the collective West wages against Russia in Ukraine. It's ridiculous to take Putin's side as if we were in a football match. The current political regime that the Russians have is certainly not the best one could wish for. It already showed profound contradictions at the time of state socialism, let alone today, in which the state manages its form of capitalism.

Have words perhaps come out of Putin's mouth in favor of democratic socialism? No, yet anyone who thinks that the reasons of the oligarchic and neo-Nazi regime in Kiev deserve to be considered better than those of the inhabitants of Donbass is simply a person who is obtuse or in bad faith, or completely unaware of historical facts.

In Donbass or Transnistria there are still many who are nostalgic for the old USSR. Putin could have let them stew in their ideological broth, but faced with the persecution that those populations have suffered since the so-called "Euromaidan" coup, widely supported by the Americans, he believed that indifference would be a form of shameful complicity.

Quite a few texts on Putin describe him as a person who, in some ways, would be better not to have as a friend, but in this war, comparing him with Zelensky and the Western statesmen who support the Kiev dictatorship, one cannot have many doubts about which side to be on.

Of course, we are not convinced that the fate of humanity would be better if unpresentable figures such as Biden, Blinken, Macron, Scholz, von der Leyen, Borrell, Trudeau, Draghi, Meloni and many others stepped aside. We know well that they are just puppets managed by much less visible powers, which could replace them with others at any time.

However, the air would be less heavy, and we would be more willing to listen to the sound of words that no longer exist today, such as negotiation, deal, agreement, diplomacy, good neighbourhood, ceasefire, peace…

Convinced of being the best of all possible worlds, Western private capitalism, rather than adopting a relativistic attitude, prefers to create the conditions for its ruinous collapse.

May 19

Europeanist temptations

Russian culture is perhaps the most contradictory in the world. I am also referring to the mentality, the lifestyle, the ways they react to critical situations. They easily go from one extreme to the other.

Westerners are more consistent. Since the rise of the medieval municipalities in Italy they have opted for a bourgeois-type civilization, and since then they have never gone back. If they have sometimes had doubts (for example following catastrophic war situations), it must be said that, on the whole, the second thoughts have never led to an overthrow of the dominant system, which on the contrary has always been reconfirmed with more conviction, using and ever new methods.

Western civilization has been evolving for a millennium. It inherited many things from Greco-Roman slavery: consider that the first modern civil code dates back to Napoleon! But, starting from the year 1000, it added two unprecedented aspects of its own: the Christian-bourgeois ideology in its two fundamental variants: Catholicism and Protestantism, and capitalism as an economic system (first commercial, then manufacturing, finally industrial).

As is known, capitalism is closely related to the technical-scientific revolution and formal law. With the latter we have invented a paradoxical condition of existence: one can be legally free and socially slave. The "Christian" children of God are free by nature: at most they suffer for some fault they have committed or because they have to overcome tests. However, those who are not "Christian" must be subjugated until they convert.

With seventeenth-century scientism (primarily astronomical), we even dethroned God and placed man at the center of the universe, absolute master of nature too.

Russians are partly fascinated by secularism and Euro-Western well-being, but in another place of their conscience they reject our individualistic, so amoral attitude. Only oligarchs appreciate it.

Why can't they be "coherent" like us? If we take Stalinism, it is impossible not to admit that there were elements in common with Nazi-fascism. Yet it had something "collectivist" (to be found in the feelings, in the habits of the population), which has not been found in Western Europe for a while.

The 1990s were disastrous for Russia, but precisely because they wanted to imitate, with as much haste as possible, the Western lifestyle: something which inevitably entailed a lot of cynicism, if not downright ruthlessness.

Then with Putin there was a sudden backtrack. And not because Putin was a political visionary like the democrat Gorbachev, but only because he understood that without a strong government, society goes haywire and weakens in the face of its foreign enemies.

Having full awareness of its natural resources, Russia does not want to be robbed at home; it cannot tolerate impositions from the outside (at least not beyond a certain limit); it started with Putin, to become very annoyed at the constant threats from NATO; it does not like internal dissent, since it prefers security and stability to freedom; always looking with admiration at the strong man who directs it.

Such a country can be as patient as it wants, but if it wanted to overthrow the Kiev regime, using its military might at much higher levels, no one could stop it. This is why it would be good for Zelensky's government to ask for peace negotiations as soon as possible. Indeed, we can be certain that the Russians would win the war even if NATO directly engaged with all its troops.

So what's wrong with this gigantic country? Its destiny seems to be sealed: to win all the wars and lose peace every time.

Russians must not become like us, but they must be more consistent with the best of their traditions. They must acquire a real democracy, which in our country is only fictitious. In this sense, Putin is not the right man. The very fact that he has been in power for a quarter of a century does not speak in his favour.

On the other hand, it is not possible to aspire to a post-Putinism that is even more authoritarian than the current one, even if the threats coming from the collective West do not leave much choice for a country that has always suffered from the problem of encirclement from 1917 to today. However, Russians must break the chains that force them not to be what they should be. It is their Asianism that must overcome Europeanist temptations.

May 20

Destined in a common vortex

One thing must be said clearly: if the dollar holds up, despite the monstrous American public debt, it is because many countries in the world feel attracted by the high interest rates set by the FED.

In fact, there would be no reason to support an increasingly war-mongering country which, due to its very high levels of social criticality, could risk an economic default every day, if not even a civil war. A country that issues banknotes without worrying in the slightest about whether they have an underlying basis in economic production, and which has been mainly responsible for the most serious financial, speculative and stock market crises in the world, starting from that of 1929 (which was also totally unexpected by investors), it should not should be considered a reliable country.

Yet the evidence belies this simple observation. In this sense it is right to talk about the "collective West". If the US ends up bankrupt, the entire West will be swept up in the vortex. The savings of millions of people will be burned, since today there is no bank, insurance company or financial institution that does not invest a significant part of citizens' savings in the USA, and without them even knowing it.

All countries that believe in the power of finance, in the absurd dream of easy money, will suffer deadly repercussions. It will not be possible to attribute all the responsibility for the Western financial collapse to a single state, no matter how much it claims to be the locomotive of all the others. They will necessarily have to be "collective", since in a globalized world it cannot be otherwise.

Just as today it appears historically clear that we cannot attribute the triggering of the Second World War to Germany alone: it is in fact established that Nazism was supported by US finance in an anti-Soviet (and also anti-European) function. The USA never perceived the victorious countries of the First World War as "partners", but only as dangerous economic competitors. The USSR was obviously feared for other reasons.

Anyone who thinks that a united Europe is an "American creation" is completely off the mark. There was no need to wait for the Nordstream sabotage to understand this. A united continent, with a strong currency, is much more frightening than various autonomous nations, which march separately from each other and who actually feel like rivals among themselves.

Let's remember that the USA strongly supported BREXIT and uses NATO to keep the entire EU subjugated. In this sense they absolutely needed the EU's economic ties with Russia and China to be seriously compromised, since the well-being of Europeans was closely linked, for different reasons, to these two large markets.

It was not acceptable for the USA (the greatest military and financial power in the world) to deal with a European economy more stable than theirs, with many fewer social problems, with a larger population than theirs, with sophisticated industrial production... To Europe it was necessary to make her understand that we cannot be equal partners with the USA. The proxy war in Ukraine served its purpose.

Now, to return to the pre-war situation, it is difficult to say how long it will take. All European statesmen seem to be on the Americans' payroll. They do and say things against the interests of Europeans. They make us feel like subjects of an empire that hates us and blackmails us with the fear of completely invented enemies: Islamic terrorism, the threat of a Russian invasion, China's commercial expansion.

The Europeans themselves, who rightly ask themselves what sense it makes to remain within an EU with such a servile attitude, do not realize that by encouraging division, they will be even weaker.

May 21

Truths and lies about ARMIR

In n. 4/2018 of "Slavia", the historian Giorgio Scotoni wrote an essay on Italian, German and Russian historiography dedicated to the defeat of the ARMIR (Italian Army in Russia) in 1942-43.

Unfortunately, even today only Russian historians are interested in reconstructing the objectivity of the facts; the Italian-German ones tend to make things up or to valorise the memoirs of the survivors. Of the diaries of the latter, the German ones, in general, were not able to metabolize the military defeat, while in those of the Italians there is very rarely an apology for the fascist dictatorship.

However, our post-war General Staff continued to view the anti-fascist memories of war veterans in a bad light for a long time, e.g. demonstrated by the cases of Captain Giuseppe Lamberti (multi-decorated) and Major Giusto Tolloy, convicted, respectively, in 1948 and 1958 for anti-patriotic propaganda, contempt and defamation of the armed forces (of the latter they had a horror of the book, With the Italian Army in Russia).

Examining the Russian archives some stereotypes are easily dismantled.

1) The Wehrmacht did not lose the battle of Stalingrad due to the inefficiency of the Italian Army - as German historians maintain - but, on the contrary, the ARMIR was easily defeated by the Red Army because it was completely abandoned to itself by the Hitlerite command, whose tactic in Russia was always to spare its own troops at the expense of the allies.

2) It is not true - as German historians maintain - that the Italian soldiers entered Russia with the aim of carrying out a war of extermination against civilians, exactly as the Nazis did. At most they plundered occupied Russian cities. If anything, wars of extermination were waged in Ethiopia, Libya and Yugoslavia.

3) It is not enough to say - as fascist historiography and that of our General Staff has always supported until the 1970s - that the 10 divisions of the ARMIR were overwhelmed by the attack of the Soviet tanks because the extension of the front assigned by the German command was too broad; and because the German divisions retreated to the flanks, allowing the Russians to surround the Italians. The real reason for the defeat lay in the total underestimation of the enemy forces. This is a mistake which, if we think about it, NATO and the entire West repeated again today in the proxy war waged in Ukraine.

4) Only in the 1970s was Italian historiography able to argue that the Russian campaign was not wanted by Mussolini alone, but also by the entire fascist leadership and the General Staff. It was because of this campaign that the needs of the Italian troops in Africa went unheeded.

5) On one point, Soviet historiography confirmed the findings of our General Staff: the Italian dead and missing were almost 85,000. It would be interesting to ask ourselves how many soldiers we would be willing to lose today to go directly to war against Putin's Russia.

May 22

Willing to do anything

There was a certain difference between the English revolution of the 17th century. and the American one of the following century.

In Cromwell's time, a significant democracy could have developed more easily if the requests of those groups of soldiers (Levellers and Diggers) coming from the more marginal classes had been listened to.

But Cromwell wanted to impose his own dictatorship, and after his death the revolutionary bourgeoisie had to come to terms with the backward aristocracy. An artificial symbol of this agreement was Anglicanism, a mix of Catholicism on the level of rites and Calvinism on that of ethics.

In the USA, however, democracy expressed itself as a national liberation struggle against British colonialism. Everyone participated in this struggle, bourgeois and proletarians. And when they managed to write down the principles of this revolution (Declaration of Independence), democracy was more advanced than the English one, even if it did not foresee either social equality or the end of slavery (at most the equality was political and only for Anglo-Saxons). The revolutionary leaders themselves used Negroes on their plantations. And the settlers generally had little qualms about eliminating the natives.

It would take a century before, by virtue of a civil war, the industrialized north (in need of paid labor in its industries) eliminated southern slavery. But it would take the two world wars and the subsequent anti-communist wars in Korea and Vietnam before we understood that if African Americans conformed 100% to the white lifestyle, it would have been stupid not to exploit their intellectual resources and above all their labor. in the armed forces.

This is obviously not to say that the USA was free from racist ideologies. If anything, it can be said that, while in the United Kingdom racism was a product of the feudal aristocracy, transmitted to the bourgeois class, which practiced it above all in the conquered colonies; in the USA, however, racism was used to hide the fact that social antagonism had economic roots, i.e. a class nature. Hence the clear aversion towards any socialistic idea that supported the opposite.

Furthermore, it must be said that the Americans did not worry about imposing a particular ideology on the colonies they occupied. Their strict Calvinism led them to accentuate the commercial, financial and consumerist aspects more. Profit, interest and income: these are the three main criteria of social life of Americanism.

Then there is the question of individualism, which is unbridled in the USA. It is no coincidence that all citizens are armed. Which is unthinkable in the United Kingdom, where even officers have at most a small truncheon.

We see the fundamental values of American society in their cinematography: making money at all costs, deceiving the State in some way and taking revenge for the offenses suffered, without waiting for the delays of justice. The citizen is, as in all Western countries, formally free, but if he goes against the strong powers, he must have a mountain of money to defend himself.

The collective instances are few: the lobbies (where, to be part of it, blue blood certainly doesn't count, but only the bank account); organized crime (where kinship has a certain weight); the trade union (which protects the strongest social categories); military environments (where, in exchange for the license to kill and lavish benefits, the leaders ask for absolute silence); religious communities (who fanaticize their followers, deprive them of their resources and use them to make money); charitable institutions (always looking for private funding with which to support themselves first and foremost); the school system (where the public sector is reserved for marginal classes and where teaching anything is a titanic undertaking). We are not talking about political parties, since neither of the two dominant parties is independent from the economic, financial and military world. The citizens know this and half don't even go to vote.

Until the 1950s it was thought that the various religions (mostly Protestant) could have been a brake on this shameful oligarchy. Today, rather than give up their world domination, the Deep State elites are willing to do anything.

May 23

Siberian homo novus

Anyone who thinks that Russia has never been a colonialist country is greatly mistaken.

The first armed expedition from Tsarist Muscovy towards Siberia, then occupied by the Tatars, was in 1581: the precious furs of Arctic animals were coveted. The absolute protagonists were the Cossacks, with their firearms. From then on, exploiting the weakness of the native nomadic populations, there would be no stopping.

After having occupied the entire northern band of Asia, they even reached Alaska, which was then sold in 1867 to the Americans for an amount that did not correspond at all to its real value and which barely covered the costs of colonization (it is no coincidence that it still today it is claimed by some Russian politicians).

Explorers, missionaries, traders and soldiers carried out the same tasks as their Western colleagues, trying to avoid brutal methods and without imposing serfdom.

Indeed, let's say that until the mid-19th century. Siberia was seen more than anything as a punitive colony for common criminals and politicians, as well as a refuge for dissident groups or for peasants who wanted to escape serfdom or for bandits who wanted to escape the law. In a century and a half, over a million people were deported there by the tsars.

Only populist and Slavophile intellectuals, opposed to Westernist ones, believed that, due to Siberian culture, Russia was a set of Euro-Asianism that Western Europe could not understand.

The North Siberian populations, unlike the Islamic ones of Central Asia, were of animistic faith, did not know writing and were poor in myths. They lived mainly by hunting, fishing and gathering. Agriculture was a secondary resource and only south of the permafrost frontier. They much preferred reindeer herding.

The tsarist government wanted many peasants, facilitated by the Trans-Siberian Railway (1892-1904), to move there to exploit the enormous virgin lands (which they initially did according to the natives' methods of cultivation). In this way they would also have been able to pay the State the balance for their redemption from serfdom, abolished in 1861. Even today the Trans-Siberian is the longest railway on Earth (9,288.2 km): in nine days it crosses 14 regions and 100 different peoples.

In the same period the Americans committed genocide against the Native American tribes. It must be said, however, that while in the USA the lands taken from the natives were privatized by the "conquerors", in Siberia they remained state property and were granted in usufruct only to rural communities. Furthermore, the distances and the practically unlimited wealth in Russia made the extermination of the local populations completely useless, who indeed, being many experts at surviving with nothing, were convenient for the colonizers. There was no extermination of the natives even when precious metals were discovered.

Only in the period 1905-11 did the State begin to grant agricultural privatizations, with the aim of obtaining greater tax revenues and political consensus. But in order not to ruin the farmers of the European area from the competition of Siberian products, tsarism was forced to impose severe duties on wheat. However, by now the Romanov autocracy was about to be replaced by bourgeois democracy.

Obviously not everyone liked these Siberian migrations: not the agrarian nobles, who saw themselves being deprived of abundant cheap labor; nor to the agricultural communes, which found themselves paying the State a greater tax burden on the land obtained through usufruct (the quota was in fact related to the extension, not to the number of workers).

In the period 1898-1913 migrations involved around 5 million people. In 1914 Siberia had a total of 10 million inhabitants, compared to less than a million indigenous people. It had therefore become something else.

Siberia offered not only economic but also strategic advantages: the government in fact did not want to be caught unprepared in the race for the Pacific that the USA, China and Japan were undertaking (the latter had even defeated Russia in 1905, offering the opportunity for the first anti-tsarist Russian revolution).

However, it was Stalinism that used Siberia as an internal colony to be developed in an exclusively industrial manner.

The 30 indigenous ethnic groups had become a tiny minority compared to the Russians, Ukrainians, Belarusians, Germans, Poles, Estonians and Lithuanians who came here to work. In 1937 the Cyrillic alphabet was imposed on all languages of the USSR. From 1957 any teacher could be arrested if he continued to speak the indigenous language outside of school. The government forced many nomads to become sedentary.

When World War II broke out, the Nazis completely underestimated the importance of Siberia, of which as many as 10 divisions arrived in Berlin. Even the Japanese were taken aback: seeing that the Soviet forces were twice as strong as theirs, all they had to do was negotiate. Perhaps this is also why the USA rushed to carpet bomb Tokyo, Hiroshima and Nagasaki.

May 24

We cannot do without socialism

If we think about it, since modern socialism was born (utopian and scientific, then state and now mercantile), all wars have had to deal with this ideology.

There is some form of "socialism" even in Western dictatorships. What was Italian fascism if not a right-wing socialism, that of the lower middle class, in favor of the nationalization of various aspects of the social economy? This is of course regardless of the fact that fascism was also the protector of the interests of large industrial and agricultural capital.

And wasn't Nazism perhaps a nationalistic socialism as opposed to the internationalist one of the classics of Marxism? Didn't it have many aspects typical of state capitalism? That capitalism which today, in its Asian specificity, is contrasting itself with Western private capitalism...

And how many Iberian and South American dictatorships had socialist components derived from Roman Catholicism? Hasn't the Church always boasted (and illusorily so) of possessing a "third way" between state socialism and private capitalism?

Haven't the socialist-state dictatorships themselves (Soviet, Chinese, etc.) exploited, distorting the collectivist conceptions that existed in Asia in the past? And what about the African continent? Before being colonized by Europeans, didn't it perhaps have typical characteristics of primordial communism, the one that existed in the great forests? Even when slavery was imposed in certain African empires (first and foremost the Egyptian one), was it not true that this slavery was imposed in its nationalized form? Exactly like in the three Andean or Assyrian-Babylonian civilizations. A form very different from the private one of the Greco-Roman world.

Let's look at the genocide carried out by Europeans in North America: didn't the natives live a socialistic life experience? What about Aboriginal people in Australia? It has long been established that all slave civilizations in history, whether state or private, were born in opposition to primitive communism.

But let's also look at capitalist-type Americanism. Stretching things a little, we could say that it is a form of social democracy based on mass consumerism, on national parliamentary representation, on formally equal rights for all. The American Revolution granted nothing to the blood aristocracy, the late feudal one typical of the English, Germans, etc.

The whole world seems to wander in the void, looking for a lifestyle that must necessarily deal with the needs of socialism. No matter how much effort we make, we cannot find the right model, capable of lasting over time.

We invented an industrial, state, mercantile, authoritarian socialism..., but all attempts have failed. Supporters of capitalism (and also of any religion) have always taken advantage of this to say that on this Earth it is not possible to go back to being natural, that is, truly human. They delight in wanting us to believe that socialism is not a democratic economic system. They claim to present capitalism as more suited to human nature, as equality is given by the market, by universal human values expressed in international law. They do not know that the last bell is about to ring for Western private capitalism.

The real problem, however, is that many think they can resolve the great limitations of this system with other forms of capitalism, more collectivistic, more state-controlled. We are about to enter a new great illusion. Who knows how long the planet will allow us to experience all these precarious, or rather fictitious, transitions towards the true common good.

May 25

What is Stalinism?

I am reproached for not knowing what Stalinism is. I am told that Stalin never developed his own political ideology. This forces me to reiterate what should not be done to build democratic socialism. I say this in three points.

1) Nationalizing everything is a huge mistake. The State must ensure that civil society is able to manage itself, otherwise the authoritarianism of the single party identified with the dirigiste State, the bureaucratism of five-year plans imposed from above, the inevitable productive inefficiency caused by the absence of a market, the artificial voluntarism to overcome the lack of responsibility of those who are used to obeying to respect the hierarchy, paternalism as a weapon of mass distraction, the endemic corruption of the upper classes (selected with the method of co-optation and not of merit), the ideologization of all political decisions, the subordination of law to politics, the imposition of single thought and therefore the absence of freedom of conscience, inquisitorial methods based on suspicion and the presumption of guilt, the cult of personality (consequent to the fact that loyalty was preferred to ability), the physical elimination of the political or ideological opponent, the conception of the union as a "transmission belt" of the dominant system, the deportation of entire populations from one place in the State to another, the imposition of "Great Russian" nationalism on all other nationalities or regions, the inaccessibility of archives and other "pearls" typical of Stalinism will never end.

2) It is a mistake to argue that the more capitalism develops, the more socialism must become authoritarian, so the idea of the classics relating to the progressive extinction of the State can only be achieved in the absence of capitalism.

3) Forced industrialization, the choice to opt for heavy industry to the detriment of light industry, but also the forced collectivization of the countryside, eliminating the wealthy peasant class, were mistakes that caused epochal disasters in terms of human losses and environmental devastation.

4) It was not Stalinism that defeated Nazism. Stalin was by no means a great military strategist; indeed, because of him the USSR had a disproportionate number of victims, from which it never recovered. It was the Soviet people who won the war. They were the generals of the General Staff who survived the terrible purges of the 1930s.

May 26

What do I mean by democratic socialism?

When I speak of democratic socialism I do not at all mean to refer to bourgeois social democracy. Once it has been clarified that there is no socialism without democracy, and vice versa, we need to think about the meaning of the individual terms.

I never intend to question whether a market should exist. I simply deny that the market determines what is or is not democratic. On the other hand, I deny that it is the State that establishes when one can or cannot speak of socialism.

State and market, as they developed in state socialism and mercantile capitalism, are two entities that must be abolished. How much more or less quickly is not up to me to say: I can only say that they are two sources of alienation, as well as environmental devastation.

The democracy I don't believe in is national parliamentary representative democracy. For me there is only one true democracy: direct and local democracy. It is direct precisely because it is local; and can only be representative on condition that the person elected is voted for by individual local voters.

This is the only democracy that should be permanent, the one in which either there is no difference between elected and voter, or the voter always controls the elected. In this second case the number of mandates is not important. The important thing is control and therefore the possibility of revoking the mandate at any time.

The elected person is always responsible for the will of the voter, so he must periodically report what he does. He must always justify his decisions.

If for some reason you are forced to convene an assembly that goes beyond the local level, it must be made clear in advance that this is something temporary. In this case the elected person must directly represent, as a whole, the will of the local community that gave him the mandate, i.e. he cannot take any initiative of a personal nature.

When there is no longer a need for representative democracy, and we will only rely on direct democracy, then it will mean that the local community will be so small that everyone will feel like they are protagonists in the first person.

As far as socialism is concerned, the common management of the fundamental means of production that guarantee the existence of a local community is mandatory. Private ownership of such means makes no sense. At most, there can be private or personal ownership of accessory, integrative and non-fundamental means.

Therefore socialism means self-management or co-management of common activities. If we do not want to depend on the market for what substantially ensures the survival of the local community, the resort to self-consumption, that is, the self-production of what is consumed, is inevitable. The market can be used to exchange surpluses, or to purchase products considered important but not essential. And the exchange would be best if it took place through barter. This is because money favors indefinite, unlimited accumulation.

Has such socialism ever existed? Yes and for millions of years. We began to destroy it about 6,000 years ago, when we gave birth to slave societies, which, over time, became real "civilizations". Since then we have only configured slavery in various forms, be it private or state, but, in essence, we have always reconfirmed it.

May 27

How to interpret reality?

When I have to try to understand an event or a historical fact I prefer a thousand times a fundamentally correct methodological analysis, which presents various errors even in the details, compared to that analysis which, although saying many true things in the details, is vitiated by an approach with a completely wrong method.

In this sense, just to give an example, I calmly recommend throwing away all that confessional exegesis of the gospels, which prefers to talk about "redeemer" instead of "liberator" or "resurrection" instead of "insurrection", and a thousand other rubbish.

However, finding a methodologically correct analysis is not so easy. We are always incredibly conditioned by the environment in which we live, by the needs or interests that we develop in these environments.

Take, for example, the current conflict between Russia and Ukraine. If one has studied the historical background, which goes from at least 2014 to today, it should not be difficult to understand that the responsibilities of the coup by the Kiev junta are infinitely superior to Russia's decision to carry out a special military operation.

If it is clear that no historical event or fact can be interpreted only from an ethical perspective, as there are other economic, political etc. factors which must be taken into careful consideration, everything becomes much simpler to understand.

Only a very naive or naive person would be able not to see that behind this conflict there is an imperialistic intent on the part of the Euro-

Americans to the detriment of Russia. NATO bases around this country have multiplied since 1999.

Western private capitalism has been experiencing a phase of profound contradictions for at least 25-30 years. The way it deals with them is irrational, since it makes the weakest social classes pay the consequences, internally, and externally to the States that cannot compete on a military level.

Now, however, it is encountering unexpected resistance worldwide. Naturally I am referring to the Russian, Chinese and Iranian ones, but also to those of some countries in the Global South. The capitalist West suffers more from these geographically external resistances than those socially within its borders. The world is changing rather quickly, and those who, until yesterday, were used to dominating it, are unable to downsize.

However, it would be good not to get caught up in easy enthusiasm. Russian state capitalism, Chinese mercantile socialism, the Iranian Islamic Republic cannot be considered true "alternatives" to the drama we are experiencing.

For 70 years we believed that state socialism (industrial, like the Soviet one, or agricultural, like the Chinese one) was an alternative to Western capitalism. We were wrong. We are always wrong when we look for solutions outside of our experience and do not personally commit to changing it.

May 28

The kinship between Russians and Ukrainians

Who has not read Gogol's *Taras Bul'ba* (1809-52)? The book is certainly known in the West also because, starting from 1909, it inspired various films (the latest is from 2009). The most famous of which is that of director John L. Thompson, with the legendary Yul Brinner (1962).

Gogol was a Ukrainian writer who, in that book, narrated in Russian the epic of the Cossacks, of which Ukrainians are still proud today, although already at the time of Tsarina Catherine II (1729-96) they were co-opted within the Tsarist State, obtaining in exchange for their loyalty, the same benefits due to the Russian nobility.

The Cossack knights, courageous, reckless, not subject to feudal obligations, at first nomadic, then organized into military communities, in the 16th century. they had to face the Polish-Lithuanian occupation of Ukraine and that of the Tatar-Mongols in the east.

At the time of the tsars, the Ukrainians, if they did not speak Russian, did not provide elites to the central state, so much so that for the bureaucracy of "Little Russia", dedicated almost exclusively to agriculture and with little culture, tsarism relied on Russians, Polish or Germans.

Gogol came from an aristocratic family of Cossack origin. To learn Russian writing well, he moved to Petersburg, where he became a "classic" of literature. He knew well that written Ukrainian did not have the nuances of Russian, and that at most it could be used for minor topics, such as for example. folklore, songs, theatrical comedies. The Ukrainian language has always been considered by Russians to be a kind of dialect.

Gogol made a decisive contribution to the brotherhood of the two peoples, so much so that the Ukrainians (Little Russians) have never been considered an ethnic group like the Finns or the Balts. Like the Belarusians, the Ukrainians were recognized as having Russian nationality without question, also because they were of Orthodox religion and of Slavic origin. At most they were the Ukrainian intellectuals who resented the tsarist autocracy and who wanted to move from the concept of "people" to that of "nation" aware of their own specificity (which will happen towards the middle of the 19th century).

In concrete terms, Russian-Ukrainian relations have always been enormous. Indeed, it is precisely these relationships that explain why, in the current conflict, Putin's Russia is behaving so carefully. If the Kiev government were not completely manipulated by Western politics and NATO militarism, the special operation would have ended long ago.

Ukrainians and Belarusians have always been considered by the Russians as two children: they were not even obliged to have internal passports, imposed by tsarism in 1895. What is certain is that, having to choose who to give preference to, the Russians opted for the Ukrainians, but not because their lands produced the best wheat in the world. The real reason lay in the fact that Ukraine represented (especially for romantic Slavophiles) a more genuine rural past, with more authentic traditions, which in Russia, due to the Westernization desired by Peter the Great, were being lost.

The current government in Kiev does not realize that having exercised neo-Nazi authoritarianism, having imposed Russophobia on the whole of society, having adopted Western lifestyles (which greatly favored the excessive power of the oligarchs), the 'having spread the idea of being able to easily defeat a superpower like Russia... These are all aspects that over time will lead the population to prefer the stability guaranteed by Moscow.

When did Ukraine come under Russia?

Towards the middle of the 17th century, the Ukrainians had grown tired of Polish-Lithuanian domination, so they asked the Russians for help. Belarus also fell into Polish hands.

To tell the truth, the Ukrainians were divided into two large categories: on the one hand the feudal agrarians, who had completely accepted the Poles, including their religion; on the other, the great mass of peasants, hostile both to the servitude of the local Ukrainian magnates and to the forced conversion to Catholicism.

Only the Cossacks knew how to stand up to the Poles, also thanks to an alliance with the Tatars present in Crimea, dependent on the Ottoman Empire. In particular, the Cossack Bogdan Khmelnitsky stood out, receiving a congratulatory message from Oliver Cromwell for having "flagellated" the Polish nobility and "exterminated the Roman pretum".

However, it was now understood that without union with Russia, it would have been impossible to definitively get rid of the Polish-Lithuanians.

And so in 1653 Moscow approved the annexation of Ukraine to the Russian state and declared war on Poland. The Cossacks were granted extensive rights and privileges.

The war against Poland (which lasted until 1667) involved two other states that feared Russian expansionism: Sweden and the Ottoman Empire. Of the two, it was the first to engage the Russians more.

Sweden in fact took advantage of the moment to occupy a large part of Poland, greatly weakened by the ongoing war.

Moscow, having understood that Sweden was the new rising star, and intending to open access to the Baltic Sea, declared war on it (1656-58), after having signed an armistice with Poland, to which it granted only Ukraine. the territories of Galicia and Volhynia, with the important city of Lviv.

However, Poland quickly recovered: she drove the Swedes out of her territory and declared war on the Russians to gain possession of the whole of Ukraine.

In 1667 the two states concluded an armistice: Kiev and the eastern area of the Dnieper river passed to the Russians, while the western area and Belarus returned to the Poles.

Why did Moscow fail to deliver the definitive knockout to Poland? It was, as often happens with Russians, due to internal disputes. In fact, the government, trying to find financial means for the conduct of the war, had minted copper coins with a nominal value equal to those of silver, but in such quantities that they had greatly depreciated. Furthermore, he demanded that taxes be paid in silver, while salaries for officials and workers were given in copper.

Faced with unsustainable inflation, the peasants rose up, also because they could not stand the yoke of the feudal lords. However, in 1662 the revolt was bloodily repressed.

We had to wait until Tsar Peter I (1672-1725) to see the Swedes, after 21 years of war, reduced to nothing, and therefore no longer able to exclusively control the Baltic coast (Russia had also taken Estonia and Latvia).

And we had to wait for Tsarina Catherine II (1729-96) to see the Ottomans greatly reduced in size in southern Ukraine and above all to see Poland disappear from the geographical maps, being made the object of partition between Russia, Prussia and Austria (1796-1918).

However, precisely under both Russian emperors the serfdom of the peasants reached absolutely shameful heights.

May 30

The origin of Russian-Ukrainian hatred

One of the historical causes that triggered the enmity between Russians and Ukrainians was the tsarist elimination of the Cyril-Methodian Brotherhood, founded in Kiev in 1846, at the head of which the two most important intellectuals were Nikolai Kostomarov (1817-85), natural son of a politically moderate Russian landowner and a Ukrainian maid; and Taras Ševčenko (1814-61), a politically radical former serf.

It was the two of them who fully developed the idea of a "Ukrainian nationality", which the peasants, who were very poorly literate, only acquired at the turn of the 19th and 20th centuries.

As for Cyril and Methodius, Orthodox theologians of Thessalonica in the 9th century, it is known that they were the first evangelizers of the Slavs, as well as the creators of the Cyrillic alphabet still in use today in various Eastern European nations. What did the aforementioned Brotherhood say that was so shocking that it led to its immediate dissolution by Tsar Nicholas I in 1847?

Here are the highlights:

1- liberation of Slavic nationalities from foreign dominations (in reference to those subjected to the Ottoman and Austro-Hungarian empires);

2- organizations of the Slavs in independent "political societies", linked by a federal bond, within the context of a republican state, of which Kiev would be the capital (against autocratic tsarist centralism);

3- abolition of any type of serfdom (which in Russia only happened in 1861 and in a rather fraudulent manner);

4- suppression of all class privileges and prerogatives (i.e. the democratic ideals of the French Revolution had to outclass the aristocratic ones of the agro-feudal nobility);

5- full freedom and tolerance in the religious field;

6- use of a single Slavic language for the celebrations of all religious cults (Slavic, from all cultural points of view, was considered as a synthesis between Latin and Germanic, as well as a continuation of Greek);

7- absolute freedom of thought, education and press;

8- teaching of all dialects and all Slavic literatures.

Of all these programmatic points, the tsarist power, which had become increasingly conservative, already at the time of the Congress of Vienna (1814), did not accept even one.

It took the defeat of the Crimean War (1853-56), which Russia suffered due to the coalition of various European powers, to allow Ukrainophilism a new season, again thanks to Kostomarov, whose Slavophile and pan-Slavist thought, however, was not able to give itself any adequate tool to realize the ideals of the aforementioned Brotherhood.

The very fact that Ukrainian intellectuals considered themselves the link between the Great Russians and the Western Slavic populations was the most unrealistic thing one could think of. It cannot be ruled out that the Kiev junta's neo-Nazism today is also a form of reaction to the frustrations suffered in the past.

It is no coincidence that the extremist Ševčenko, in order to give vent to his Russophobia, sought the collaboration of Poland, the ancient ruler of the Ukrainians themselves. Paradoxically however, since he came from marginal backgrounds and had been persecuted by tsarism, Soviet historiography saw him as an internationalist ante-litteram, obviously not without first having completely belittled his patriotic-nationalistic side.

May 31

Who commands and who obeys

To justify the special military operation in Ukraine, Putin, in February 2022, took it out not only against NATO and the neo-Nazism of the Kiev coup plotters, but also against Lenin, for the fact - according to him - of having divided the territories of the USSR were wrong, having granted too much freedom and autonomy to ethnic groups.

It seemed like a statement close to Stalinist theses, even though Stalin himself wanted to incorporate two very un-"Ukrainian" territories into Ukraine: Galicia and Volhynia.

Then again, the Ukrainians are an ethnic group so to speak: they speak a language considered by Russians to be a dialect; professes the same Orthodox religion, although the Kiev patriarchate has been at odds with that of Moscow since 2018; furthermore, Ukrainians are Slavs like Russians and Belarusians.

In a certain sense there shouldn't even be a "Ukrainian state" or even a "nation". At most there can be a "people", which however is divided into various components or minorities, of which the Russian-speaking one is undoubtedly the most significant, even if the nationalists and neo-Nazis of Kiev refuse to recognize it. In the 19th century the Russians considered Ukraine as their own "backyard", a peripheral territory. Trying to differentiate oneself from these people, on a political or institutional level, would not have made sense.

If it depended on Putin and others like him, Ukraine would probably be dismembered among the various nations that claim its border territories, where the relevant ethnic minorities are present. For example, Hungary could incorporate the 156,000 Magyars of Transcarpathia; Poland could recover Galicia and Volhynia, where there are around 265,000 Poles; the over 150,000 Romanians and the over 250,000 Moldovans could obtain Bessarabia; the 276,000 Belarusians could also claim something. But there are other significant minorities that do not border their respective nations: for example. the 274,000 Bulgarians. Naturally, this is based on data from the last Ukrainian census of 2001.

As it stands now, Ukraine would cease to exist: there would be something left on the western bank of the Dnieper. In this sense, it must be excluded a priori that, during negotiations, Kiev will ever be able to claim to regain the territories acquired from the Russian Federation. It will already be a lot if it manages to preserve Odessa and prevent Transnistria from being reunited with Donbass.

It's good to look reality in the face. What did the Europeans do with Yugoslavia? Haven't they perhaps separated a whole into its individual elements, penalizing Serbia above all, from which Kosovo was taken away, by placing a powerful NATO base here? Why would we be shocked if Russia did the same thing to Ukraine?

The difference between Ukraine and Yugoslavia lies only in the fact that the former borders Russia, and the latter does not want military bases (potentially nuclear) that threaten it.

If in order to end this ongoing war, Russia will have to recognize territories foreign to the Slavic-Orthodox traditions of the nations bordering Ukraine, I don't think that any peremptory preliminary questions will be asked. But if NATO thinks of setting up its own bases in the territories that the Russians or Russian-speakers will not manage directly, then this war is destined to drag on for a long time, with very unpleasant consequences for everyone.

Finland itself, which has 1,300 km of border with Russia, should not be surprised, now that it has agreed to join NATO, if one day it discovers that it no longer exists either as a state or as a nation. When you live in an apartment building, you can't abuse the patience of your neighbors.

Be that as it may, this Russian-Ukrainian war has demonstrated one thing very clearly: the West cannot accept the principle of unity in diversity. Someone must always command and others must always obey.

June

June 1st

Antonov's use value

In 1988, a Russian professor of technical sciences and director of the Institute of World Economy and International Relations of the Academy of Sciences, Mikhail Antonov, criticized what for him was the fundamental flaw of Gorbachev's perestroika, economism, saying things that, due to their originality, left me amazed.

The Stalinists exploited him, but did not grasp the importance of his words, which had a very different meaning. In fact, he wondered whether economic science was really the most suitable tool for overcoming the limits in which Soviet society found itself at that time. Indeed, he believed that science in itself could do very little when faced with problems of a social, spiritual and moral nature.

This is because modern science, especially economic science, imposes a certain hierarchization of knowledge, between the upper layers that know and the lower layers that don't know. Those at the top give general orders, without worrying about the needs and actual capabilities of those at the bottom; and those at the bottom are absolutely unable to have an overall vision of the entire society.

The inevitable outcome of this discrepancy between theoretical directives and practical realizations was that, in state socialism, we deceived each other. The intelligentsia and the nomenklatura painted the so-called "real socialism" pink, in the belief that the distortions of the particular would be easily resolved over time. Instead, those distortions, adding one upon the other, had produced an unsustainable situation.

But why was the economic science of nationalized socialism unable to see the real problems of civil society? The main reason – according to Antonov – is that use value was never talked about. Something that the main economist of perestroika, Abel Aganbeghjan, did not do either.

Economic science, whether socialist or capitalist, limits itself to seeing the human being as a simple worker who produces and consumes. The difference between the two economic systems lies in the fact that in socialism the State is concerned with guaranteeing the citizen more social rights (education, healthcare, etc.).

The citizen is never seen in his entirety, that is, as a subject who needs things that no State can provide, and that any private enterprise (typical of capitalism) offers in the wrong way, simply to acquire a profit.

Use value instead implies the self-production and self-consumption of a society that has no need either of the paternalistic State (which becomes authoritarian when things do not proceed according to a preconceived pattern), nor of the bourgeois market, in which the producer imposes its arbitrary laws and its unquestionable products to the consumer.

Use value (typical of pre-slavery societies) implies a community of intent, a common feeling, which goes far beyond merely economic aspects. In fact it is a value decided by use not by exchange, that is, by traditions, by the actual needs of the collective that uses certain goods. The individual is not a number, a component without personality.

In the community there is an ethic that explains to the economy how and what it must produce. There is no need for five-year plans drawn from above. Nor do we have a duty to let ourselves be tossed around by the anarchic fluctuations of international markets. The only true property that one must take care of is, at the same time, the personal and social property of the collective to which it belongs, it is not the state property (in an abstract and impersonal sense), nor the private one (in the hedonistic and individualistic sense).

Men do not need an economy regulated by the State, nor an economy that, illusorily, regulates itself through the market, where crises, failures and unemployment are the order of the day. We need an economy regulated by the self-government of society, in which the reproductive needs of nature are the first aspect to be placed under observation with the utmost attention. The quality of life cannot be determined by the quantitative increase in goods that ensure a certain material well-being. Life must become an experience in which need is shared: a need that is both material and immaterial.

June 2

Is showing your teeth necessary?

I find it very difficult to accept the speeches of those who maintain that we have fallen into the current world chaos due to the implosion of the USSR, which would have further fueled the power projections of the USA and the West in general.

It is undoubtedly true that in the 1990s NATO was unleashed in its expansion towards Eastern Europe. It is also true that in that period the international dominance of the petrodollar reached its highest peaks; and that the Third World felt destabilized, after having trusted in the power of the USSR for the purposes of its own decolonization.

But we forgot that the Cold War was a kind of world war and that there were many cases in which it could have really broken out: the most serious was that of Cuba at the time of Kennedy and Khrushchev, but also that of the Cruise missiles and Pershing 2 in Europe was no different.

Can we perhaps say with certainty that a real world war did not happen just because the balance of terror dominated? What security can there be when you live in daily fear? And in any case, was it right for humanity to live in the anguish of thinking that the edge of the sword of Damocles could break at any moment?

Didn't we breathe a sigh of relief when Gorbachev induced the USA to sign treaties for world peace? Those treaties that the USA itself then reneged on one after the other?

Of course, Gorbachev made unilateral military concessions. He allowed the Berlin Wall to be torn down. He withdrew the armed contingent from Afghanistan, leaving the country in the hands of the Taliban... Perhaps these and other things could appear excessive, typical of a naive idealist, of a political visionary. But they gave hope. They made it clear that world peace was possible.

Now instead we have to hear someone who claims the times when the USSR scared the USA. Is this what we want? Illusion ourselves that we have more confidence by adopting bully attitudes?

The USSR did not implode due to a nuclear war against the West, but due to its own internal contradictions. It did not collapse because Gorbachev wanted to make socialism more democratic. This is a pro-Stalinist thesis.

With his all-out pacifism Gorbachev annoyed the war-mongering West. The USSR would have been attacked anyway, since it is the nature of capitalism to expand at the expense of others. And when it fails, it becomes extremely aggressive. Who do we want to blame for this aggression? Perhaps to those who fight for peace and democracy? That is, who doesn't show his teeth in a threatening manner?

We must not want more democracy to bring more capitalism, but to bring more socialism. State capitalism is not enough for us, nor even mercantile socialism. The State must be managed by the workers and the workers must become so democratic that they can do without any State.

June 3

A useful lesson for us too?

Sometimes I wonder what could happen to a gigantic country like Russia, whose existence is linked to an enormous availability of energy resources, if the rest of the world accepted a green transition, in which hydrocarbons were destined to progressively disappear.

Russia does not have a light industry (manufacturing) like China. If it were to ignore fossil exports, what would it have left? Timber from forests? The boundless expanses of land to be cultivated with cereals? Any metallurgical products? Don't the Russians know that those who produce raw materials are always weaker than those who transform them? Besides, who wants to endure freezing Siberian temperatures? If it were that easy, by now Russia, given the great resources it has, would be the most populous country in the world.

In any case, Russia must not delude itself into thinking it is a militarily invincible country. If anything, she must count on the fact that with every war defeat, she was able to recover magnificently. For example. the harsh Tatar-Mongol invasion (1237-1480) taught her that by remaining divided, one always loses.

The Northern War (1700-21) against Sweden marked Russia's rise as a great European power, but the Russians did not forget that a small country like that was capable of invading them.

Napoleon's invasion of Russia in 1812 led to the total destruction of Moscow, although the French retreat was absolutely disastrous for their army, so much so that it marked the end of the emperor himself.

During the Crimean War (1853-56) Russia was invaded by an alliance of European powers, including France, Great Britain, the Ottoman Empire and Sardinia. Access to the Mediterranean was denied. However, tsarism understood that it had to allow an end to serfdom.

The defeat with Japan in 1905 led the population, with the revolution of the same year, to give the first push against tsarism.

This could go on for a while. But here we want to limit ourselves to asking a simple question: are all Russia's defeats a sign of its intrinsic weakness? This is to say that, despite having recovered well after each defeat, there is nothing to suggest that she cannot be defeated again.

However, I ask myself: who are we Europeans to consider ourselves better than the Russians? By chance, don't we also need a great lesson to rethink the root of our existence, which is so miserable in terms of values?

June 4

An example of war madness

To demonstrate that the West is not as strong militarily as it seems, it will be enough to remember, by way of example, the defeat of Gallipoli from April 1915 to January 1916, in the midst of the world war.

The original plan was the one wanted by the First Lord of the British Admiralty, Winston Churchill: to strike the Central Powers (Germany, Austria-Hungary, Ottoman Empire) on a new front in south-eastern Europe, that is, to conquer the Gallipoli peninsula, in Dardanelles Strait, and pave the way for the Royal Navy to bring the Turkish capital Constantinople (now Istanbul) under attack, forcing the Ottomans to surrender. Furthermore, Churchill was convinced that in this way his country's oil interests in the Middle East would be guaranteed; and that the undecided Balkan states, including Bulgaria and Greece, would join the Allies. He had no doubts that the victory would be rapid, as he believed the Ottomans were very weak.

At the beginning of 1915 the Allies (British Empire, France, Russian Empire, later joined by Italy, Japan and the USA) were in a stalemate with Germany on the Western Front, while the Russian army was in difficulty on the Eastern Front, but they planned to take the Dardanelles Strait and Constantinople itself if the English helped them.

The Mediterranean Expeditionary Force included 16 warships with over 70,000 units of various nationalities: English, French, British India, Australia, Newfoundland and New Zealand.

The Dardanelles strategy began with an attempt to force the straits with naval power alone. But the first bombardments of the coastal forts failed: three Allied battleships were lost to Turkish sea mines and three others were seriously damaged. Senior Allied officers decided that success in the Dardanelles required an amphibious landing of 3 divisions on 6 different beaches on the small Ottoman peninsula of Gallipoli (unsuitable for a long campaign, as the terrain was rocky, with little vegetation and steep ravines). Then they sent 11 more.

After 8 months the disaster was total, due to the ineffective organization (poor information on the battlefield, out-of-date geographical maps, lack of coordination between all the troops); but above all due to the unexpected resistance of the Ottoman units, trained by German officers and placed in a higher position than that of the allies. In particular, the Australian and New Zealand Army Corps (ANZACs) suffered appalling losses, before all the soldiers were evacuated.

Of the estimated 213,000 British fatalities, 145,000 were due to disease. The surviving fighters remembered the terrible problems linked to the intense heat: unburied, rotting bodies (they could not be recovered without risking new victims), enormous swarms of flies, large infestations of lice, widespread dysentery (and the latrines were a prime target for snipers), serious lack of drinking water and insufficient and often inedible food rations. During the winter of 1915 they were freezing in the trenches due to the uniforms being too light. The total casualties of the campaign (including Ottoman ones) were more than half a million.

Of all the various parts of the world where British and Commonwealth forces were deployed during the First World War, Gallipoli was remembered by veterans as one of the worst ever.

On that occasion, the military value of the young Colonel Mustafa Kemal emerged, who after the end of the war would be the main architect of modern Turkey, which went down in history with the name of Atatürk.

Australia and New Zealand took advantage of that episode to claim greater independence from the British Empire.

Churchill had to resign and was replaced by the wretched Lord Balfour who allowed the Zionists to establish their "home" in Palestine, a source of serious misfortune for the native Islamic populations. The film that narrates the story in a fictionalized way is "The Broken Years", by Peter Weir, who wanted to make people understand the absurdity of war.

June 5

The use value between memory and desire

In 1975 the publisher Jaca Book published a debate, entitled Which 1984, which took place between the great Marxist economists of the Third World: Samir Amin, Hosea Jaffe and Gunder Frank.

That was a particular year, since for the first time, faced with the oil embargo of the Arab countries, the West realized that its wealth was based on fragile foundations. Today it seems that all the issues have come to a head.

Well, among the various topics discussed, one struck me in particular: the question of use value. It went so far as to say that, while all pre-capitalist social formations had a global method of organizing the use of use values, in that they had their own cultural identity, capitalism instead imposes exchange value precisely to destroy every culture, every civilization.

In feudal societies, peasants fought for an egalitarian participation in the consumption of use values. There existed in their memory a community tradition that the feudal income tried to diminish and weaken.

Today this memory no longer exists in the West. The commodity, the most typical element of exchange value, only expresses a generalized alienation: everything is divided, starting from work and the means of production. At most, when, throughout history, the industrial proletariat or the petty bourgeoisie fight for their survival or even to overthrow the system, we see the emergence of a desire for collectivism, a demand for social justice.

Today this desire also seems to have died out in the West. When we see it resurface, it is not in our home, but in Africa, in Asia, in Latin America, that is, in the places where the populations want to free themselves from us, from our globalist neoliberalism, from our imperialist hegemony.

We Westerners are on the defensive, because we don't want to lose the privileges we have acquired. In the rest of the world, an egalitarian instance seems to have remained, based on more or less collectivist traditions, those traditions that we, where we wanted to dominate, were unable to completely destroy.

However, we must stop thinking that democratic socialism must necessarily entail absolute domination over nature, in order to avoid the prospect of equality in material poverty.

In the 1970s, socialist theories absolutely did not want to give up the successes of the technical-scientific revolution. Today, however, we have to rethink everything. It is nature itself, which we have scourged like a Christ condemned to the cross, that imposes it on us.

June 6

The Orazi and the Curiazi will not be enough

Only statesmen and analysts tainted by Russophobic prejudices and warmongering interests are unable to accept the evidence that the Russian Federation is the largest European country.

In fact, not only is its most economically developed and densely inhabited part found in Europe, but it must also be admitted - if one does not want to appear completely ignorant of history - that in the last three centuries (i.e. starting from Tsar Peter I the Great) the politics, economy, science, culture and diplomacy of this enormous country have been connected above all with its European part.

From the Urals to the Pacific Ocean, that is, in Siberia, the Far East and Central Asia, European culture was spread. This process can be seen in a positive or negative way: in fact, no one can doubt it.

It would be enough to compare Russia with Turkey. In both cases the smallest part (in a geographical sense) of their territories is located in Europe, while the largest part is in Asia. However, while in the case of Russia it has always been a matter of a progressive enlargement of Europe from the West to the East; in the case of Turkey, however, the process was reversed: its European part, which appears more democratic to us Westerners, has been completely Islamized, so much so that the Turkish government does not even want to hear about the Orthodox Church, Byzantine culture or the influence of Greek world.

Turkey truly represents a singular case: practically nothing remains of the thousand-year-old and advanced Byzantine civilization that developed in its territory that has a significant impact on today's situation. Even today this country harbors expansionist delusions like when it was called the "Ottoman Empire".

On the other hand, Europe, the USA and Russia were not far behind. Undoubtedly the USA has dominated the world since the Second World War. But their projection of power comes from Western Europe, which has exercised it for an infinitely longer time (at least since the discovery/conquest of America). This influenced Russia itself in its attitude towards its Asian area.

The USA has always perceived the Europeans as rivals and the Russians as enemies: the former had to be dominated, the latter fought. Unfortunately, Western Europe allowed itself to be enormously influenced by the extremely aggressive posture of the USA, which did everything it could, taking advantage of the implosion of the USSR, to incorporate all the countries of Eastern Europe.

If we think about it, the imperialistic ambitions of the West have never ended. Only now are we beginning to see a significant shift or generalized downsizing due to two objective factors: Russia's military superiority and China's economic-productive superiority (which will probably be added, in the not too distant future, to that of India).

The idea of a multipolar world, whether Westerners share it or not, is an incontrovertible fact. It's just a matter of understanding whether we want to acknowledge it peacefully or whether we will try to hinder its realization by resorting to nuclear war.

In this second case it is useless to delude ourselves that in a bloody clash of an "existential" type we will limit ourselves to using merely conventional weapons, as if we were gentlemen. If we really want to hurt ourselves, we can't do it with white gloves.

We are not in the time of the Horatii and Curiatii. The war is destined to become "total", in which there will be no difference between civilians and soldiers, between men, women, children or the elderly. There will be no symbolic or exemplary clashes that can be used. The enemy will have to be defeated so heavily that he will have no way to recover for a very long time.

We are seeing it in recent months in the Gaza Strip: it is not just Israel that is fighting there, but the entire West. Indeed, let us prepare to see even greater brutality in the war against Russia waged in Ukraine.

Our economic hegemony of the world is supported not only by financial might, but also by military might. At this moment it is unthinkable for Western statesmen to enter into negotiations from a losing position. If NATO were to be defeated, whether in a proxy or direct war, the consequences for the collective West would be catastrophic.

June 7

Foucault's pendulum

Processes, especially economic ones, matter more than people. Once upon a time the enemy was easily identifiable; today he is invisible. He realizes the harm he does when it is too late to defend himself.

Throughout the West, and therefore also in Italy, the process began at the end of the 1970s, when the role of the State in the economic-productive field began to be dismantled.

Perhaps it is not so strange that today the collective West is suffering demolition blows from those states that prefer a mixed economy, avoiding giving in to the lure of neoliberalism.

The most singular thing was that after the Wall Street stock market crash of 1929, and after the West had understood that it was better to rely on Keynesian theories, in which the role of the State was central, in the 1970s once again to exalt liberalism, that is, the same disaster that had led to the failure of 1929. As if we were under Foucault's pendulum.

Even the Nobel Prizes in economics were given only to exponents of neoliberalism: Friedrich von Hayek, Milton Friedman, George Stigler, etc. The doctrines from the Chicago School were the gospel for all. We easily remember the world leaders of ad libitum deregulation: Margaret Thatcher (1979-90) and Ronald Reagan (1981-89).

When the USSR imploded, it seemed that Western neoliberalism had no more obstacles to overcome.

In Italy in the two-year period 1992-93 there was a real change of system. It began to be said that state enterprises (IRI, ENI, ENEL, INA,

IMI etc.) absolutely needed to be privatised, transformed into joint-stock companies.

The reasons for doing so were naturally false, but everyone believed them: the public sector is inefficient and too expensive, the services it offers are unsatisfactory, etc.

Instead, it was precisely that sector that corrected market failures, that guaranteed the most useful investments for the community, the containment of unemployment, the reduction of regional inequalities... And it kept the lobbying pressures that conditioned the formation of parliamentary laws under control.

Today another catastrophe inevitably looms over the West. Whether it is caused by a world war or another sensational financial crash makes little difference. It is important to know that the pendulum is swinging the other way. And this time it's the rest of humanity that wants it.

The collective West seems to have outgrown all its economic models. It seems that there is nothing else available after the years of privatizations and neoliberalism. State capitalism in China and Russia is outperforming market capitalism in most economic sectors, even under the pressures of war, as seen in the Russia-Ukraine conflict. The Global South, for very good reasons, no longer trusts Western imperialism and this is changing the overall geopolitical equation.

The world cannot be privatized. It is absurd that economic policy should be enslaved by political economy. Or that the precondition that states must accept, to be admitted to financial assistance from world banks, is the renunciation of their autonomy.

June 8

Challenge to the O.K. Corral

If we think about it, the 2014 neo-Nazi coup in Kiev resembles General Francisco Franco's attempt to overthrow the Spanish democratic-republican government in 1936. Everyone knew that if the fascists hadn't been helped from outside, they would never have made it. This is why Germany and Italy openly intervened in the civil war.

In Ukraine, however, it was the entire NATO that supported the coup plotters in various ways, as Russia had decided to intervene militarily in 2022 alongside the Russian speakers persecuted in Donbass. The difference lies in this: in 1936 all the governments of the Western powers did not lift a finger to stop the Italian-German aggression. Today, however, within the EU only Hungary has shown itself reluctant to declare itself hostile to Russia. Slovakia was added to it, but its prime minister Fico risked being killed.

In 1937 the USA showed itself to be particularly hypocritical, as by decreeing the embargo on arms exports, it put the legitimate Spanish government, which did not have sufficient weapons and ammunition, in great difficulty, while Germany and Italy had no such problems. Not only that, but the USA was able to supply the Nazi-fascist countries with all the strategic raw materials needed to bomb Spain.

But why did Western countries hate the Spanish republicans so much and protect the fascists following Franco? Simply because it was thought that this war would be the dress rehearsal for Germany before it declared war on Bolshevik Russia. That is, it would have been the last war in Europe, in such a way that the two major powers, the United Kingdom and France, would have kept their empires intact from the expansionist aims of the Germans.

Hitler himself said that his task at that moment was to make people believe that Germany would be the last bastion against the "red flood". He also invented the fake news according to which the help that Stalin's Russia was giving to the Spanish republicans would have been the antechamber to occupy France.

Also in 1937, no Western power said a single word when the Japanese began invading China. In fact, everyone was convinced that Japan was an excellent watchdog against the USSR. It defeated the Russians in the Battle of Mukden at the beginning of 1905 and participated in the war of intervention in Siberia in 1918-22 where, however, it lost.

It is no coincidence that the Rome-Berlin axis and the Rome-Berlin-Tokyo axis were formed in the two-year period 1936-37. Two alliances that were not only against world communism, but, in Europe, also against Austria, Czechoslovakia (for the Sudetenland question) and Poland (for the East Prussia question).

Western statesmen knew very well the intentions of the Nazis, and were careful not to hinder them, even if they feared that by occupying Poland Germany would become too powerful a country in Europe.

Today Russia is no longer communist, but its resources are still tempting; and since the colonial empires of the past no longer exist, it is the collective West that is moving towards a deadly challenge like the one at the O.K. Corral, which inspired numerous western films.

June 9

From state capitalism to socialism

Shortly before Lenin suffered a stroke, Arthur Ransome (1884-1967), journalist for the "Manchester Guardian", wanted to interview him. Ransome had married Trotsky's personal secretary and perhaps for this reason the British secret services never stopped suspecting that he was a Soviet spy.

In the interview all his questions were focused on a single, somewhat devious topic: "you communists have given yourself the opportunity to get rich with the NEP, but by doing so how will you keep your ideals standing?"

He was referring to the figure of the so-called "nepman", that is, someone who, taking advantage of the New Economic Policy, inaugurated by Lenin, felt free to trade as and when he pleased, albeit within certain limits. A situation very similar to what is occurring today in China's mercantile socialism.

Lenin, of course, was too smart to fall into the journalist's trap, and so he replied:

1- the lower middle class (in particular the farmers, who at that time were 80% of the workers) does not constitute a threat to the State, because, although they can buy or sell consumer goods, all the land belongs to the State, which it gives it in usufruct to cooperative companies that want to work on it and that do not exploit the work of others [note that these companies were also helped with machinery, seeds, etc.];

2- the NEP replaced the forced requisitions of the civil war period (war communism) with a tax in kind (generally wheat); once the tax has been paid, it is possible to sell your surplus on the free market;

3- the bulk of production, the industrial one, is divided between private contractors [state-owned but managed by a private tenant] and actual state officials;

4- Russia can also achieve socialism through state capitalism, given that the state is in the hands of the working class [naturally in that period there were also rich landowners, small industrialists and private traders who employed paid labor];

5- all foreign trade is in the hands of the State (as well as finances and transport), so the Nepman cannot interfere with prices, which are mainly based on wheat, a part of which is in the hands of the State in form of tax.

In essence, Lenin was in favor of a mixed economy, in which economic calculation had its importance. There was no hiding the risk that, by dint of getting rich, the producers might one day say enough to socialism. However, to avoid this eventuality, it had to be - according to him -

socialism that demonstrated that it was more efficient or convenient than private capitalism.

Stalin, on the other hand, did not like risks and did not want to know about this mixed economy, clearly preferring a completely nationalized socialism. Naturally in today's Russia, where state capitalism dominates, there is no talk of socialism at all, as the state does not belong to the working class.

June 10

Asia and Africa increasingly united

China is not the only Asian country to expand its trade with Africa. For example. there is also South Korea, which wants to imitate China, by far Africa's main trading partner in terms of total volume (we are almost at 300 billion dollars).

These Asian countries mainly import raw materials (especially fuels) and export manufactured goods. However, there is a substantial difference. Africa's trade deficit with China in 2022 was $47 billion, while its trade deficit with India was only $4.5 billion and its trade deficit with South Korea was even less: $1.7 billion. It should be noted that India has already surpassed the USA in the volume of bilateral trade with African countries. In any case, they are dangerous deficits for the African continent (typical of those who export raw materials and import finished products), which do not help it achieve its economic independence.

China is already tending to reduce development loans in a context of increasingly unsustainable debt for Africa. It also reduced them because the Chinese recovery following the pandemic was fragile (compared to their standards of course), and the problems related to the real estate sector were unexpectedly serious, to the point that the Chinese today prefer to turn to assets that are safer than bricks, such as, for example, gold. It is no coincidence that the Chinese government is scaling back its international "Belt and Road" infrastructure initiative, favoring smaller projects.

Such a situation can favor competition from India and South Korea, even if China is able to guarantee significant tariff relief to many African countries; indeed, duty-free access has recently been provided to six countries (Angola, Gambia, Congo, Madagascar, Mali and Mauritania) to promote their agricultural exports and rebalance trade. Something that no country in the collective West has ever dreamed of doing. We like to subjugate them, either with weapons or with technology or with capital. This was how we tried to impose our culture on the whole world.

It will be decided all the subcutaneous chip

Italy is like a prostitute who, as she gets older, lowers her rates. Actually worse. We are like those prostitutes who delude themselves, by selling their body, that they are not also selling their soul.

I am referring to the fact that we no longer have any decision-making autonomy: we have become a country with limited sovereignty, like those that for us were once the satellite countries of the USSR.

We are not only dominated by NATO, the US dollar, the ECB, the European Commission, but also by international credit institutions. We are increasingly dominated by world finance, which induces us to renounce the welfare state, to privatize public goods, to subordinate politics to the productive economy and the latter to finance.

We are naive people, who think we can resist these destructive blows thanks to private savings (which is in fact enormous), the spirit of sacrifice, the sense of human solidarity and other values that are progressively disappearing.

Powerful global financial corporations increasingly feel entitled to interfere in our domestic and foreign politics. For example. in 2013 the US investment bank, J.P. Morgan, proposed that EU states rewrite the "antifascist constitutions". This is because it saw them as too influenced by socialist ideas, which prevented the application of rigid austerity measures.

In 2016, the Fitch rating agency, with offices in New York and London, allowed itself to say that the economic and constitutional reforms wanted by the Renzi government were going in the right direction. Even today these agencies claim the right and duty to give scores on our ability to implement neoliberal directives.

Some time ago it was thought that this interference only concerned Third World countries, with their elites easily corrupted by Western capitalism. Today, however, they also turn to the most advanced democracies.

In 2015, the Renzi government, through a simple decree-law, forced cooperative banks, with assets above a certain threshold, to transform themselves into joint-stock companies, exposing the smaller banks to the greed of the large international banking lobbies. Italy is increasingly for sale to foreigners, who buy our goods for pennies.

The reckless management of the Covid pandemic, chronologically subsequent to the global stock market disaster of 2008, the effects of which are thought to have been resolved by printing banknotes as if central banks were printing presses; and now the clear cut in trade relations with Russia: these are all factors that are not only leading us to de-industrialization and a growing recession, but do not even offer us any alternative to the increasingly structural crisis of Western private capitalism. The economy is worsening inexorably and no one knows how to propose something alternative.

Does it make sense to stop having children or go and live abroad where taxation on pensions is minimal and the cost of living is acceptable? Does it make sense to ask young people to emigrate where they can make their fortune? Or think we can survive by focusing on services, we who are almost totally devoid of raw materials?

Italy is slowly dying: this can also be seen from a demographic point of view: we are a country of elderly people, without a real generational turnover. We are ready to be checked even in our private lives. We are waiting for them to put a chip under the skin, which will have the purpose of telling us how we should behave.

June 12

Franks and Lombards

The Hungarian uprising of 1956, the Prague Spring of 1968, the Polish strikes of 1980, the fall of the Berlin Wall and the coup in Romania in 1989 had a single factor that united them: anti-communism, in the version of socialism state made in the USSR.

We took it out on the Russians a lot, but ultimately they were the first to attempt a concrete and lasting experience of modern socialism. When criticizing the results of this unprecedented experiment we should have a minimum of indulgence.

Did those countries have the right to rebel? It is the people who decide when it is time to claim rights and when it is necessary to distinguish them from privileges, that is, when it is necessary to oppose false rights, wrong requests.

When a people claims certain political objectives they should avoid any external support, be it financial or military, unless their very existence is compromised. Or in any case foreign states should refrain from applying pressure that affects people's affairs, even if in an interconnected world like ours, this is practically impossible.

Among the nations mentioned above, have any managed to achieve truly democratic socialism? None. They all moved from state socialism to private capitalism, allowing themselves to be plundered by private capitalisms stronger than them, the Western ones.

The only country that managed to put a stop to the horrors of neoliberalism was Putin's Russia, which created state-controlled capitalism. It is this country that, alone, is opposing the private capitalisms of the collective West and the former Comecon countries. We should have a certain amount of gratitude, whatever our opinion on Putin and current Russia.

So, reasoning with the benefit of hindsight, let's ask ourselves: would it have been better to prevent this dramatic capitalist involution of half of Europe with the force of tanks, which certainly caused a lot of damage to countless people? Maybe, but it certainly wouldn't have been a democratic solution.

Peoples cannot be other-directed, as if they were subjects incapable of understanding and wanting. They must experience first-hand the consequences of freedom of choice. From 1956 to today they have understood one very clear thing: capitalism does not passively watch the processes that take place around it. Where tensions arise between populations and institutions, it immediately takes advantage of this to further destabilize the situation and overthrow the governments in office. It is enough for it to side with someone in the opposition, exploiting their claims.

Regardless of what science thinks, absolute vacuum does not exist. If you open the window to get rid of house dust, you have to expect something else to come in through the door.

This is why the people must be continually warned about the dangers they can run by misusing their free will. But for the people to be convinced that the institutions are right, they must be able to benefit from effective decision-making power. If it perceives the institutions as foreign, as distant from itself, it will do nothing to defend them, it will rely on foreign powers, in the illusion that they are better.

Manzoni had already said it: do you really think that Charlemagne's Franks are better than Desiderio's Lombards?

June 13

Three against two and two against three

Anyone who thinks that democratic socialism is something similar to the humanistic or ethical socialism of Alexander Dubček (1921-92) or the Charter 77 movement is misguided.

Czechoslovakian socialism has always had a fundamental limit:

subordinating politics to ethics. An armed socialism against Western capitalism would have been unthinkable, as non-violence was considered a dogma. Which, evidently, appeared revolutionary against Soviet-style state socialism. This is not to argue that ethics should be subordinated to politics, as Stalinism wanted, but also the founder of the science of politics: Niccolò Machiavelli.

It is sufficient to understand that when one wants to seek an alternative ethic to the bourgeois one, one must, at a certain point, take into account that the opposition must become political to be truly effective; and a political opposition that does not know how to defend itself militarily is worth nothing. Lenin *docet*.

Bourgeois ethics is not simply something "moral". Formally it appears democratic in all its aspects; similar, in some ways, to the ideas of Christianity; makes use of all the best expressions of the law; it is supported by mountains of religious, philosophical, psycho-pedagogical and sociological texts; It has a history spanning a millennium.

However, in reality, we are dealing with something violent, inhuman, something that, if it fails to obtain economic or financial supremacy, becomes ferocious, it has no qualms about anything. Those who fail to grasp this fundamental hypocrisy in bourgeois ethics or minimize it, and limit themselves to countering it with words alone or good example, the willingness to suffer any suffering, up to martyrdom, will always be defeated. The Roman Empire did not accept Christianity out of amazement at its resilience after three centuries of persecution, but because it understood that a social system based on slavery could no longer stand up.

Politics is the acquisition of a space in which to exercise ethics, but politics is not just ideas and diplomacy: it can also be armed revolution, civil war... The choice to arm oneself depends on the behavior of the enemy. If there is room for maneuver in which full freedom is ensured, there is no need to resort to force.

It is important to make your opponent understand that you do not want interference or unwanted interference in your home. A state cannot be dominated by another state, in any way. Political independence is a fundamental requirement to assert freedom of action.

However, if we think that political independence is enough to achieve democratic socialism, we do not leave the realm of illusions. In fact, social justice is also needed, that is, the overcoming of class and class conflicts. This is to say that even if a state were to win a war against another state, the next step would always remain to be taken, which could be even more painful.

Civil war means that those who oppose social justice, the common ownership of the fundamental means of production, the self-management of the common good, direct democracy, gender equality, the protection of the reproductive needs of nature, and all that it gives concreteness to a truly human and natural ethic, should be considered an "enemy at home".

Even the gospels were clear on this: "from now on, if there are five people in a house, they will be divided three against two and two against three" (Lk 12,52).

June 14

The better it will be for everyone

Étienne Balibar said that two great forms of racism have existed in modern Europe: one internal (anti-Semitism) and the other external (colonialism).

I, however, have the impression that forms of racism, instead of decreasing, are increasing. The very fact that there is no desire to negotiate in any way with Putin's Russia suggests that there is a high degree of Russophobia, therefore a certain form of racism. I say this regardless of economic or geopolitical issues.

In fact, it is not normal that when Putin proposes negotiations to resolve the Ukrainian conflict, we automatically think that he is lying or that he is making an admission of weakness, in the face of which we must feel authorized to take advantage.

Racism means that you don't want to have anything to do with a certain population. In this sense it becomes inevitable to use increasingly violent, discriminatory and offensive methods. And the use of war, not even nuclear war, is not ruled out.

Certainly we Westerners can ask Putin to make a difference between governments and peoples, but in contemporary states governments confront governments. If a Western population cannot make its own narrative prevail over that of its government, what should Putin's government think? Why should he make concessions to Western governments, showing that he is lenient towards their respective populations? That is, why would he be required to make a substantial difference between the Western government and population, when we are the first ones not to do so towards Russia? Do we want to understand that in a world war (even more so if it is nuclear) no one will be able to exhibit a particular title of merit to be spared? Haven't we already seen the carnage against civilians in the Second World War? And don't we continue to see them in what Israel does in Gaza?

Racism means that a specific population must either disappear or submit to the dominant population, which claims a superior culture or civilization, from all points of view. Racism means not recognizing any quality, any right, any prerogative of those who are different.

We Westerners have been displaying such behavior since the time of the Greco-Roman civilization, and since then we have only modified it in relation to the prevailing ideologies, to which we have given our assent: paganism, Christianity and secularism.

These days we see it in the violent relationship that the Israelis use towards the Palestinians. The Zionists seem to be a creature of Euro-American racism, to the point that those who equate them with Hitlerian Nazis are not wrong. They do not come from the same ideology, but want to impose their own using the same inhumane means and methods.

The Palestinians seem to have to suffer a fate not very different from that of the populations that the West wanted to colonize.

When, after the attack on the Twin Towers, the USA launched the idea of fighting international terrorism, the West became blatantly racist towards the Islamic world.

Today we are racist towards the Russians, since our limited and self-interested narrative sees them as "invaders" of a democratic, peaceful, pro-European country, under our protection.

Tomorrow we will be racist towards the Chinese, as we consider Taiwan our protectorate.

In short, we have an unconscious racism, which we let emerge when it suits us, when we consider it useful for the affirmation of our identity.

I don't know what civilization will emerge after ours: perhaps, in a multipolar world, there will be more than one. I only know that ours is a scourge for all humanity, and the sooner it disappears, the better it will be for everyone.[6]

---

[6] Racism is a form of fear expressed as prejudice. All racist attitudes are part and parcel of a concept that one individual or race is superior to another. It's as if the human brain is unable to deal with diversity in nature, be it racial, gender or sexual. Systemic racism encompasses both class and nationalistic hatred. It is used as a means to oppress one's own people or one race to oppress another. For me class hatred expressed as elitism is at the core of all forms of racism. The elitists in fear of losing their privileges prefer to instill racism in order to maintain their oppression on the exploited. The elitists use whatever means possible to infuse national pride amongst the masses to divert the working class away from class oppression. They thus use this method to redirect national hatred towards other countries when required. It is in the interests of the elitists to normalize racism in order for the

June 15

The end of Europe

A Europe that, after two devastating world wars, seeks a third, does not deserve to exist. Also because, if we exclude Japan, both were born on our continent.

A new conflict within the European perimeter, which will inevitably be nuclear, since the Russian Federation certainly cannot be compared to the former Yugoslavia, would spell the end of national representative democracy. In fact, it would be unleashed by governments without a popular mandate, as it is clear that at this moment no European people want a war, much less a nuclear one.

At the very least, the governments in office, if they really claim to call themselves democratic, should subject the decision to declare war on Russia to a referendum.

Western political democracy is revealing itself for what it is: the mask with which they want to exercise a dictatorship. It is the dictatorship of the strong powers, who live on the shoulders of others.

In the Middle Ages these powers were the owners of the land, who wanted to live off the income, exploiting the work of the peasants. Today they are the owners of industries and capital. They demand the maximum of freedom for themselves and the minimum of equality for others, as if there was an inversely proportional correlation between the two terms: the more true freedom concerns a very few privileged people, the more the real equality of all people is denied.

Not only has parliamentary democracy failed, which clearly made its debut in the European political lexicon during the bourgeois revolution in England, but constitutionalism has also ended. In fact, the need for war, and therefore the renunciation of any form of negotiation, nullifies in an instant all the principles of the Fundamental Law, all its values.

From this aspect it is absolutely senseless to think that the direct election of the head of state represents a greater level of democracy. For this reason, there was more democracy in the ancient Greek *póleis*, where laws and political decisions were approved directly by the citizens gathered in assembly, although women, slaves and foreigners were excluded.

The First World War was sought by late-feudal empires (Austro-

---

latter to expand their interests, be it national or international. (Added by the translator).

Hungarian, Prussian, Russian and Ottoman), which were unable to stand comparison with the advanced capitalism of centralized national states.

The second was desired by those dictatorial, Nazi-fascist nations (such as Germany, Italy and Japan...) who needed to make up for lost time on the road to colonization of the planet, already undertaken by other capitalist countries (Spain, Portugal, the United Kingdom, France, USA etc.).

The third is about to be unleashed by the collective West, which can no longer arbitrarily manage the entire world.

It will be the numbers that will crush us, the enormous numbers of the Asian populations, which, over time, have also grown on an economic-financial and military level. We wanted to exploit them by relocating our production activities, using their cheap labor and their cheap raw materials, and their large markets. Today they are making us understand that they learned quickly and no longer harbor any inferiority complex.[7]

---

[7] If the geopolitical position of the European continent is in difficulty it is purely due to the poor leadership of the European Union, a sign that democracy, as the West has been experiencing for little more than a century, is failing on all fronts. The crisis the EU finds itself in is purely self-produced. Although Russia provided the old continent with the cheapest energy possible, which allowed it to be competitive on the global market, it immediately decided to go to war against the latter to the point of causing the most serious escalation we have witnessed since times of the Cuban missile crisis, from which there may perhaps be no return. The EU leaders failed to show any form of moderation and balanced thinking and immediately aligned themselves with their US masters without thinking about any of the consequences. Now, their economic weakness leads them to the conclusion that Russia cannot be allowed to win a conventional war despite having lost. Not only has it blindly relied on the colonialism of the Global South and the Asian continent, but for some delusional reason it now believes it can carry on in the same way simply because it sees itself as a superior and exceptional race, the dictator of history. They fail to see the obvious, that the world is changing and that the decline of the West has begun and instead of accepting this change they opt for war in the same way they have produced two of the most devastating world wars humanity has ever seen. (Added by the translator).

Conclusion

I

Sometimes I think that writing books like this, which are clearly anti-system, is useless. In fact, even as I do it, I need elements that pollute nature: electricity, plastic and other non-recyclable components that make the computer work, destined, sooner or later, for a landfill. But then to which landfill? Local, regional, national, international? Much of our waste ends up in Germany, France, Austria and Hungary.

Not only that, but there is always someone who, with tools much more powerful than mine, checks what I write, so that every word complies with Facebook policy, and in doing so does not realize that he is causing serious damage to the environment, without then considering that his own psychology is irreparably damaged by dint of enjoying the pleasure of censoring the literary production of others.

But it's not over. This book, when someone buys it in paper format, contributes to killing some trees. Afterwards the book will be sent by one or more couriers who will surely, with their means of transport, contribute to polluting the air we breathe, increasing the probability of some serious illness of ours. And so on.

We are immersed in a paradoxical situation, from which it seems impossible to escape. We are born naked from our mother's womb, but we are absolutely unable to return naked to the earth. When we take our last breath, we will have brought with us many of those superfluous things that will certainly have damaged the health of someone or something, and which will continue to do so for who knows how long.

We like to admire the remains of the civilizations that preceded us and we fail to see that the best, from the point of view of nature, were precisely those that left no traces of their permanence. This book talks about the collapse of Western civilization, but with a modicum of wisdom one can easily understand that here it is the very term "civilization" that needs to be totally rethought.

II

If the possibility of a cultural, scientific, commercial exchange is missing..., it's over. People close in on themselves, and so do peoples and states. We all become autistic, we impoverish ourselves ethically, spiritually, intellectually. Even technical-scientific innovation suffers damage, as when the Wright brothers argued all their lives with Glenn Curtiss over the issue of the patent on their newly invented aircraft.

If we do not accept dissent, divergent opinions, "heresies", we will kill democracy and pluralism. We begin to live in mutual suspicion, in fear of losing something.

More than war, this is the true tragedy of humanity in our damned present. After every war, in fact, comes peace: the dead are commemorated, the wounded and maimed are cared for, destroyed buildings are rebuilt. But after hatred for those who are not like us, what comes next? What do we need to change our mentality, if not even a war is enough? With how much commiseration will future generations think of us?

I can already hear them saying: "They had everything, the best of technological progress, but it was of no use. They were slaves to their prejudices and died in desperate solitude."

Here, I would like to be able to say with Andrej Sinjavskij (1925-97) that "the word is not an act, but only a word and that the author does not identify with the protagonist". But he was just a great deluded person. In fact, the reality is precisely this, that our words are stones that condemn us, and that behind the protagonists of our narrative there are only faceless authors.

III

We still have not understood that, if we want to survive, and if we want to do it in a human and natural way, we must give up everything that characterizes modernity.

Not only the State (centralized or federated) must be abolished, but also the market, and not only the market (free or controlled), but also technical-scientific progress. We must rethink everything, because everything we have created since we emerged from the Middle Ages has not convincingly resolved the two fundamental problems of feudalism: the income demanded by landowners and the clericalism demanded by intellectuals.

These two serious problems have simply been transformed into other problems, no less serious, indeed, considering our level of technology, infinitely more serious. We deluded ourselves that technical-scientific progress was sufficient to overcome the harmful consequences of social antagonism. We deluded ourselves that by being a merchant, a banker, an entrepreneur, an investor, a usurer, a money changer... we would be freer than the landowner, more emancipated than the farmer.

If in the Middle Ages the antagonism was due to the substantial difference between feudal lord and serf; in the modern era it is due to the difference between entrepreneur and worker, between the owner of capital and the have-nots, between the owner of productive and financial means and the owner of physical and intellectual labor power, between professionals with specialized knowledge and the naive.

We thought that the city made us freer than the countryside, but that was a mistake. We believed that national representative democracy was better than feudal empires, secular and ecclesiastical aristocracies. As if formal democracy was in itself better than real dictatorship.

We thought it was right to dominate nature with technology, but it was another mistake.

We have given ourselves institutional structures (political, bureaucratic, military, espionage, media...) which instead of increasing freedom, have decreased it. They are all superfetations that do not guarantee equality at all, but only population control, mass conformism, the narrative of the dominant powers.

Since the so-called "civilizations" were born, we have gone from one form of slavery to another. There has been no real progress, but only a diversification of forms. And these forms have become increasingly difficult to manage, increasingly dangerous, for our existence and for that of nature. And in any case, even when we had the perception of a positive change in reality, the price of this change was paid by populations weaker than us on a military level.

We have not yet understood something of fundamental importance: the human being is a natural entity. That is, it must live in accordance with the reproductive needs of nature. It is a huge mistake not to feel obliged to respect these needs. We must live within the limits that nature imposes on us. Our "humanity" cannot define itself independently from "naturalness".

We will pay harshly for the consequences of our ignorance and our arrogance. As has already happened in the past. The desertified areas of the planet will increase dramatically, not only because we continue to exploit natural resources as if there were no tomorrow; not only because, on the basis of this savage exploitation, the climate is dangerously changing, but also because the use of nuclear power, the use of chemical, biological and bacteriological substances have uncontrollable, absolutely devastating effects.

The meaning of history lies solely in this, in trying to understand all forms incompatible with human nature.

IV

One day we will have to ask ourselves why the expectations of a better world are far superior to the concrete achievements. And the answer certainly cannot be limited to a simple observation. In fact, after having criticized the means and methods used to tackle the problems, we will have to indicate to ourselves immediately practicable alternatives. This is because when we say that praxis is the criterion of truth, we cannot console ourselves behind a mere theoretical statement. We must take this discrepancy between theory and practice seriously, putting ourselves out there personally.

It is absolutely necessary to take risks, which can even be very high, since here the clash is between opposing, objectively irreconcilable forces, of which the hegemonic one wants the death of the other or in any case its subjection, its silence.

However, to be at least sure that you are not raving, that you are not fighting a battle against windmills, at least two fundamental conditions are needed: 1) joining with someone who feels the same demands for liberation, discussing as much as possible the means and methods to achieve them; 2) start from local needs, trying to solve concrete problems and offering one's action a broader scope only as time passes.

We can start from the local level and then progressively reach the national level. But, once the conditions have been created to resolve the problem of antagonism on a national level in an effective, realistic manner, we must return to the local level, since this is the only one that guarantees true social concreteness to our daily actions. The local area always remains our litmus test, our thermometer.

Politics must be conceived, ultimately, as a tool at the service of natural liveability at a local level. We can have a battle and even a war (civil or interstate) at a national level, but then the seed that nourishes us (materially and spiritually) must be planted on the ground under our house.

Anyone who thinks that such a solution is parochial, provincial, or corporate has understood nothing about life, precisely because it places politics (and therefore the State, with all its coercive institutions) above everything.

Of course, it is important to overcome irreducible antagonisms, but even more so is the need to live a human social relationship within the reproductive limits that nature imposes on us.

Index